Stanley Cavell and Literary Studies

Stanley Cavell and Literary Studies

Consequences of Skepticism

Edited by
Richard Eldridge and Bernard Rhie

continuum

Continuum International Publishing Group
80 Maiden Lane, New York, NY 10038
The Tower Building, 11 York Road, London SE1 7NX

www.continuumbooks.com

ISBN: 978-1-4411-6495-7 (hardcover)
       978-1-4411-2945-1 (paperback)
       978-1-4411-2986-4 (PDF)
       978-0-8264-2615-4 (ePub)

Library of Congress Cataloging-in-Publication Data

Stanley Cavell and literary studies : consequences of skepticism / edited
by Richard Eldridge and Bernie Rhie.
     p. cm.
   Summary: "A groundbreaking and timely collection that draws out the
full implications of Stanley Cavell's writings and ideas for literary
studies"-- Provided by publisher.
   Includes bibliographical references and index.
ISBN-13: 978-1-4411-2945-1 (pbk.)
ISBN-10: 1-4411-2945-6 (paperback)
ISBN-13: 978-1-4411-6495-7 (hardback)
   1. Literature--History and criticism--Theory, etc. 2. Cavell, Stanley, 1926-
3. Criticism. 4. Philosophy. I. Eldridge, Richard Thomas, 1953- II. Rhie,
Bernard. III. Title.

   PN441.S73 2011
   801'.95--dc23

                              2011029168

Typeset by Saxon Graphics Ltd, Derby DE21 4SZ
Printed in the United States of America

Contents

PN
441
.S73
2011

Notes on Contributors

Charles Altieri is Professor of English at the University of California, Berkeley. He is the author of numerous articles and books on literary criticism, literary theory, and philosophy and literature. His many influential books include: *Painterly Abstraction in Modernist American Poetry* (Cambridge 1989), *The Particulars of Rapture: An Aesthetics of the Affects* (Cornell 2003), and *The Art of Twentieth-Century American Poetry: Modernism and After* (Blackwell 2006).

Sarah Beckwith is Professor of English and Theater Studies at Duke University and Chair of the Theater Studies Department. She is a former editor of the *Journal of Medieval and Early Modern Studies*, co-founder of the new book series *Re-Formations*, and the author of *Christ's Body: Identity, Culture and Society in Late Medieval Writings* (Routledge, 1993), *Signifying God: Social Relation and Symbolic Act in York Corpus Christi Plays*, (University of Chicago Press, 2001), and *Shakespeare and the Grammar of Forgiveness* (Cornell University Press, 2011). She is currently at work on a book on Shakespearean tragedy.

R. M. Berry is Professor and Chair of the Department of English at Florida State University. Berry is author, most recently, of the novel *Frank* (Chiasmus 2005), an "unwriting" of Mary Shelley's *Frankenstein* and the story collections *Dictionary of Modern Anguish* (FC2 2000) and *Plane Geometry and Other Affairs of the Heart* (Fiction Collective 1985). His novel about the last day in Leonardo Da Vinci's life, *Leonardo's Horse*, was a *N.Y. Times* "notable book" of 1998, and his literary criticism has appeared in *Soundings, Symploke, Philosophy and Literature, Narrative, Rain Taxi, American Book Review,* and numerous anthologies. He is editor with Jeffrey Di Leo of *Fiction's Present: Situating Contemporary Narrative Innovation* (SUNY 2007) and of the FC2 anthology, *Forms at War: FC2 1999–2009* (University of Alabama 2009).

Simona Bertacco is an assistant professor of Humanities at the University of Louisville and was previously a ricercatrice at the University of

Milan, Italy. Her research focuses on issues in postcolonialism, women's and gender studies and translation studies. Her most recent publications include: "Postcolonialism", in *The Oxford Companion of Philosophy and Literature* edited by Richard Eldridge (2009) and "Death and its rites in contemporary art and culture," Simona Bertacco and Nicoletta Vallorani (eds.), *Other Modernities* (Issue 4: October 2010).

Anthony J. Cascardi is director of the Townsend Center for the Humanities and Ancker Professor in the Departments of Comparative Literature, Rhetoric, and Spanish at the University of California, Berkeley. He is the author of numerous essays and books, including *The Subject of Modernity* (Cambridge 1992) and *Consequences of Enlightenment* (Cambridge 1999), and is editor of *Literature and the Question of Philosophy* (Johns Hopkins 1989). He serves on numerous boards and as the general academic editor of the Penn State series of books in Literature and Philosophy.

Robert Chodat is Associate Professor of English at Boston University, where he specializes in post-WWII American fiction. He is the author of *Worldly Acts and Sentient Things: The Persistence of Agency from Stein to DeLillo* (Cornell 2008), and has published essays in *New Literary History*, *Modernism/Modernity*, and *Contemporary Pragmatism*.

Richard Eldridge is the Charles and Harriett Cox McDowell Professor of Philosophy at Swarthmore College. He specializes in philosophy and literature, Wittgenstein, and aesthetics, and has published and edited a number of books on these topics, including: *On Moral Personhood: Philosophy, Literature, Criticism, and Self-Understanding* (1989), *Leading a Human Life: Wittgenstein, Intentionality, and Romanticism* (1997), *The Persistence of Romanticism* (2001), *Stanley Cavell* (ed.), (2003), *Literature, Life, and Modernity* (2008), and *The Oxford Handbook of Philosophy and Literature* (ed.) (2009).

John Gibson is Associate Professor of Philosophy at the University of Louisville. He is the author of *Fiction and the Weave of Life* (Oxford 2007) and coeditor of *A Sense of the World: Essays on Fiction, Narrative and Knowledge* (Routledge 2007) and *The Literary Wittgenstein* (Routledge 2004).

Paul Grimstad is Assistant Professor of English at Yale University, where he specializes in nineteenth and early twentieth-century American literature. He is at work on a book entitled *Experience and*

Experimental Writing from Emerson to the Jameses, which explores the links between philosophies of experience and literary innovation in Emerson, Poe, Melville, Charles Peirce, William and Henry James, and John Dewey. His publications include: "Is 'against theory' a pragmatism?" in *The Minnesota Review*, "Pym, Poe, and the 'Golden Bowl'," in *The Henry James Review*, "Emerson's adjacencies," in *The Other Emerson* (Minnesota University Press, 2010); and "Antebellum AI," in *Poetics Today* (Winter 2010).

Andrew Miller is Professor of English at Indiana University at Bloomington. He is the author of two books: *Novels Behind Plate-Glass: Commodity Culture and Victorian Narrative* (Cambridge 1995) and *The Burdens of Perfection: On Ethics and Reading Nineteenth Century Literature* (Cornell 2008). He also serves as Editor of the journal *Victorian Studies*.

Toril Moi is the James B. Duke Professor of Literature and Romance Studies and Professor of English and Professor of Theater Studies at Duke University. Her books include *Sexual/Textual Politics: Feminist Literary Theory* (Routledge 1985), *Simone de Beauvoir: The Making of an Intellectual Woman* (Oxford 1994; 2nd edn 2008); and *What Is a Woman? And Other Essays* (Oxford 1999), republished in a shorter version as *Sex, Gender and the Body* (Oxford 2005). She is the editor of *The Kristeva Reader* (Columbia 1986), and of *French Feminist Thought* (Blackwell 1987). She is also the author of *Henrik Ibsen and the Birth of Modernism: Art, Theater, Philosophy*, which was published in 2006 by Oxford University Press. The book won the MLA's Aldo and Jeanne Scaglione Prize for the best book in Comparative Literary Studies in 2007.

Elisa New is Professor of English at Harvard University. She writes on subjects including the American Puritans, nineteenth-century American literature, American poetry 1630s to the present day, and the literature of American Jews. The author of *The Regenerate Lyric: Theology and Innovation in American Poetry* (Cambridge 1993) and *The Line's Eye: Poetic Experience, American Sight* (Harvard 1999). More recent projects include *Jacob's Cane: A Memoir of Jewish Civilization* (Basic Books 2009) and *Where the Meanings Are: The Literature of New England Reappraised* (forthcoming from Harvard University Press).

Bernard Rhie is Associate Professor of English at Williams College, where he teaches courses on modern literature and on the connections between philosophy and literature. He is at work on a study of the significance of faces, face perception, and physiognomy in twentieth-century philosophy and critical theory, entitled *The Philosophy of the Face in the 20th Century.*

Lawrence Rhu holds the William Joseph Todd Chair in the Italian Renaissance at the University of South Carolina, where he is a Professor of English and Comparative Literature. He has written two books, *The Genesis of Tasso's Narrative Theory* (Wayne State 1993) and *Stanley Cavell's American Dream* (Fordham 2006), and published numerous articles on Renaissance literature. He is currently translating *The Book of the Courtier* by Baldassar Castiglione for Hackett Publishing. His edition of *The Winter's Tale* in the Evans Shakespeare series is forthcoming from Cengage in April 2011.

Naomi Scheman is Professor of Philosophy and Gender, Women, and Sexuality Studies at the University of Minnesota, and from 2009 to 2013 a guest researcher at the Umeå Centre for Gender Studies in Sweden. Her articles on re-envisioning epistemology through the lenses of Wittgenstein and feminist theory are collected in *Engenderings: Constructions of Knowledge, Authority, and Privilege* (Routledge 1993) and in *Shifting Ground: Knowledge and Reality, Transgression and Trustworthiness* (Oxford 2011). She has also co-edited *Is Academic Feminism Dead?: Theory in Practice* (NYU 2000) and *Feminist Interpretations of Wittgenstein* (Penn State 2002).

Garrett Stewart is the James O. Freedman Professor of Letters in the Department of English at the University of Iowa. He is the author of numerous books, most recently: *Between Film and Screen: Modernism's Photo Synthesis* (Chicago 1999); *The Look of Reading: Book, Painting, Text* (Chicago 2006); *Framed Time: Toward a Postfilmic Cinema* (Chicago 2007); *Novel Violence: A Narratography of Victorian Fiction* (Chicago 2009), which was awarded the Perkins Prize from the International Society for the Study of Narrative; and *Bookwork: Medium to Object to Concept to Art* (Chicago 2011). He was elected in 2010 to the American Academy of Arts and Sciences.

Joshua Wilner is Professor of English and Comparative Literature at City College and the Graduate Center, The City University of New York. He is the author of the book *Feeding on Infinity: Readings in the Romantic Rhetoric of Internalization* (Johns Hopkins 2000), as well as essays in collections and various journals, including *Diacritics, Modern Language Notes, Genre, Romantic Circles Praxis,* and *The Wordsworth Circle.*

Abbreviations of Works by Stanley Cavell

CHU	*Conditions Handsome and Unhandsome: The Constitution of Emersonian Perfectionism* (Chicago, IL: University of Chicago Press, 1990)
CR	*The Claim of Reason: Wittgenstein, Skepticism, Morality, and Tragedy* (Oxford: Clarendon Press, 1979; Oxford: Oxford University Press, 1982)
CT	*Contesting Tears: The Hollywood Melodrama of the Unknown Woman* (Chicago, IL: University of Chicago Press, 1996)
CW	*Cities of Words: Pedagogical Letters on a Register of the Moral Life* (Cambridge, MA: Harvard University Press, 2004)
DK	*Disowning Knowledge: In Six Plays of Shakespeare* (Cambridge: Cambridge University Press, 1987; updated 2003 to *Disowning Knowledge: In Seven Plays of Shakespeare*)
ETE	*Emerson's Transcendental Etudes* (Stanford, CA: Stanford University Press, 2003)
IQO	*In Quest of the Ordinary: Lines of Skepticism and Romanticism* (Chicago, IL: Chicago University Press, 1988)
LDIK	*Little Did I Know: Excerpts from Memory* (Stanford, CA: Stanford University Press, 2010)
MWM	*Must We Mean What We Say? A Book of Essays* (New York: Charles Scribner's Sons, 1969; Cambridge: Cambridge University Press, 1977; updated version, 2002)
NYUA	*This New Yet Unapproachable America: Lectures after Emerson after Wittgenstein* (Chicago, IL: University of Chicago Press, 1989)
PDAT	*Philosophy The Day After Tomorrow* (Cambridge, MA: Harvard University Press, 2006)
PH	*Pursuits of Happiness: The Hollywood Comedy of Remarriage* (Cambridge, MA: Harvard University Press, 1981)
PoP	*A Pitch of Philosophy: Autobiographical Exercises* (Cambridge, MA: Harvard University Press, 1994)

PP   *Philosophical Passages: Wittgenstein, Emerson, Austin, Derrida*
          (Oxford: Blackwell, 1995)
SW   *The Senses of Walden: An Expanded Edition*, including new:
          "Thinking of Emerson" and "An Emerson mood" (San
          Francisco, CA: North Point Press, 1981; Chicago, IL:
          University of Chicago Press, 1992)
TOS   *Themes Out of School: Effects and Causes* (San Francisco, CA:
          North Point Press, 1984; Chicago, IL: University of Chicago
          Press, 1988)
WV   *The World Viewed: Reflections on the Ontology of Film*
          (enlarged edition), including new: "Foreword to the
          enlarged edition" and "More of The World Viewed"
          (Cambridge, MA: Harvard University Press, 1979)

1 Introduction

Cavell, Literary Studies, and the Human Subject: Consequences of Skepticism

Richard Eldridge and Bernard Rhie

For over fifty years, Stanley Cavell has been giving voice to some of the most innovative and independent-minded philosophical ideas of the late modern era. By synthesizing lessons about ordinary language he first learned from J. L. Austin with the teachings of the later Wittgenstein, Cavell early on developed a radically original interpretation of skepticism that would go on to inform all his subsequent philosophical investigations. For Cavell, skeptical doubt about the external world or other minds is neither an intellectual error in need of logical refutation (as philosophy has traditionally assumed), nor an ill-formed worry that we might readily put behind us, but a reflection of the inescapable finitude that characterizes every human life. Skepticism is thus an existential condition that is inevitably lived, whether destructively or productively. Finite human beings are bereft of knowledge of metaphysical absolutes and given over always to the active claiming of reason, fruitfully or tyrannically, as may be. Tracing out the myriad manifestations and sometimes tragic, sometimes comic consequences of the truth of skepticism in various regions of human life and culture, Cavell has throughout his long career produced a remarkable series of adventurous and wide-ranging reflections on philosophy, literature, film, and music.

Nowhere is the revolutionary promise of Cavell's novel approach to philosophy more evident than in his numerous, and justly famous, interpretations of literary texts, from Shakespeare's *King Lear* to Thoreau's *Walden*, and from Emerson's "Experience" to Beckett's *Endgame*. The art of attentive, careful reading lies at the very heart of Cavell's conception of philosophical method; reason can be claimed productively only through patient attention to, and apt modification of, past efforts at such claiming. The philosopher's activity therefore resembles the compositional activity of the modernist writer, seeking to make new sense through situated engagements with, and departures from, precursors. Hence it is natural that Cavell would devote so much time and energy to the study of literary texts, where efforts to find and make sense are foregrounded over proofs and fixed results. And given his philosophical attention to questions of method (in literary study as well as elsewhere), it is also unsurprising that Cavell has often written about conceptual issues of interest to literary theorists, such as meaning, interpretation, metaphor, genre, and so on. Arguably no other living philosopher has done as much as Cavell to show the common cause shared by literature and philosophy, where both only stand to lose by failing to acknowledge and embrace the claims of the other.

It would seem, therefore, that literary critics, in particular, would have much to gain by engaging seriously with Cavell's work. Yet widespread admiration for Cavell by literary critics has only infrequently resulted in anything discernable as real intellectual influence. Indeed, the ambivalent reception of Cavell in literary studies (an odd mixture of admiration and apathy, which seems to treat him as worthy of praise yet somehow safe to ignore) is a vexing curiosity: obviously held in high esteem, he is rarely cited, and more rarely yet do his insights and ideas establish the terms of professional debate within literary studies about a given intellectual issue, whether theoretical or interpretive. Compared to the palpable influence upon literary studies of others of Cavell's philosophical contemporaries (Derrida, Foucault, and Lacan, or now Levinas and Deleuze, to name only the most obvious) the extent to which Cavell has been overlooked, even avoided, by literary critics is striking indeed.

It is a methodological principle of Wittgenstein's (and thus Cavell's) therapeutic and conversational approach to philosophy that no philosophical account or therapy can be accepted as correct if the person to whom it is offered cannot recognize him- or herself in its terms. (Freudian psychoanalysis is also an important influence on Cavell's commitment to this thought.) Indeed, such recognition is criterial of an account's truth: for Wittgenstein and Cavell, there is no philosophical knowledge that is not first validated as self-knowledge, as new knowledge about one's own commitments, longings, wishes, needs, and fantasies, where that knowledge is found at least good enough by (some) others and by oneself over (some) time.

If we take Cavell's project seriously, no one can compel another (even by means of logic) to accept the truth of a particular philosophical account, such as about the privacy (or publicity, for that matter) of mental states: each participant in the philosophical conversation must recognize and authenticate the truth of a particular account for herself. Since philosophical accounts or accountings aim at (new) self-knowledge, the demand to arrive at recognition and authentication puts pressure on the subject and its commitments as they stand. This pressure is likely to prove, at various times, off-putting, outrageous, entrancing, and risky. There is, moreover, no fixed, rule-circumscribed method for relieving this pressure, nor any possibility of getting free of it once and for all.

In the absence of freely given agreement, then, there is no alternative to further philosophical conversation. It follows, therefore, that if most literary critics have to date been unable to recognize themselves and their professional concerns in Cavell's work, then this cannot (in good faith) simply be blamed on them (say, for not being able to grasp its logical truth). The true student of Cavell or Wittgenstein can, in the face of such disagreement or indifference, do nothing other than attempt once again—with as much grace, tact, and sympathy as possible—to continue and deepen the critical conversation, acknowledging the misunderstandings and sincere differences of opinion that have brought that conversation, in the past, to the awkward silence that, in most quarters, characterizes its present condition.

We believe that there can be no reframing of Cavell that will make him newly interesting to literary scholars in the present that is not, at the same time, a therapeutic uncovering of the resistances that have led to the repression of his voice and work in the past. The two tasks—taking up the critical past so as to engage productively with interests and work that lie, so far, aslant Cavell's, and reanimating his work for the future—must go hand in hand. What, then, might be the nature of the intellectual resistance that has led literary critics, as it were, to avoid Cavell? Why might Cavell's voice and thought have failed to influence the literary critical community? Addressing these questions is a principal task and accomplishment of the essays that follow, and we cannot nor would we wish to preempt their detailed work. But it may nonetheless be helpful to have on hand our articulation of some very general suspicions about sources of resistance to Cavell within great stretches of literary studies, suspicions that we initially articulated in this way to our contributors, as we invited them then to go further.

We begin with the observation that ordinary language philosophy (so crucial to Cavell's work) is often, in its appeals to "what we say when," taken to be a form of "commons-room" authoritarianism that is both class-biased and inattentive to the varieties of demotic speech. This widely held view has certainly been one stumbling block to the general acceptance of ordinary language procedures in literary studies. In our view, however, this understanding of ordinary language philosophy is badly mistaken. There is, to be sure, a normativity to ordinary language: Cavell has always emphasized the "simultaneous tolerance and intolerance of words" (CR 186) and has made clear that words cannot be given just any meaning or reach. But the normativity of ordinary language appeals to "what we say" is not ideological in nature, arbitrarily invoking some imagined community's customs as a fixed standard (as a skeptical cultural studies critic might think). Nor do such appeals work by invoking a set system or framework of linguistic rules (as more traditionally minded analytic philosophers might believe). Instead, for Cavell, the appeal to ordinary language is entered precisely when the very existence of any "we" is in doubt, and claims to "what we say" are by their very nature vulnerable, naked, and exposed (subject to rebuke, indifference, or any other number of ways such claims might misfire). Therefore, appeals to ordinary language work, when they work at all, by effecting a liberating transformation—a sense of arrival at felt rightness—in the ear both of the one entering the claim and the ear of anyone who follows its rightness. When this happens, a new or transformed "we" is composed or revealed, consisting of new or transformed subjects, who have entered into this new we from the resources of their own subjectivities. This is as much true of the one entering the claim to what we say, from within a situation of crisis, as of the ones, if any, who respond. Consolidation of one's subjectivity in possession of an articulated sense of what we say is a new achievement for any human subject, and the pursuit of this begins in doubt and remains fraught with risk. We think this is an important (and hardly conservative) image of what a "we" can be, with profound implications not only for aesthetics but for ethics and political theory as well.

Having addressed the stumbling block of misconceptions about "ordinary language," however, we are now ready to suggest another—and perhaps even deeper—reason that literary studies has found so little use for Cavell's ideas: his humanism. The literary critic Garrett Stewart has, in fact, suggested that it is precisely Cavell's affirmation of the concept of "the human" that has put him at odds with so much literary theory which, at the very historical moment Cavell was emerging on the philosophical scene, believed it was putting "the human" behind it, to be discarded in the dustbin of the metaphysical past, in favor of more objective and less human-subject-centered study of the linguistic and material-cultural conditions of the production and reception of texts. The concept of the human is quite obviously at the very heart of Cavell's project, and its fundamental importance is evident in Cavell's reliance on, and frequent invocation of, a series of related concepts that, in our current critical environment, must seem woefully outdated to many: in particular, concepts like "voice," "self," and "subject." Cavell employs these terms freely, and without irony; in fact he declared in *The Claim of*

Reason that he practiced ordinary language philosophy in order "to reclaim the human self from its denial and neglect by modern philosophy" (CR 154). Sentiments and intellectual commitments like these, we suggest, have a great deal to do with why (however much Cavell's creativity, style, and specific critical insights may occasionally be admired by literary critics) his work has resisted ready assimilation to literary criticism under a dominant anti- or post-humanist dispensation.

We believe Stewart has identified something very important here, and indeed recent literary theoretical work that engages with Cavell confirms Stewart's suggestion about the importance of the idea of "the human" to the allergic reaction literary theory has had to Cavell. Consider, for instance, the recently published volume, *Philosophy and Animal Life* (Columbia 2008), which collects an essay by Cora Diamond on J. M. Coetzee's *The Lives of Animals*, along with responses to Diamond by Cavell, John McDowell, and Ian Hacking, all introduced by the deconstructive literary critic Cary Wolfe. In his introduction, Wolfe argues that the "fundamental difference" between Derrida and thinkers like Cavell (and Diamond) is that the latter hold on (nostalgically, mistakenly) to the importance of the concept of "the human" for philosophical (especially moral) thought, while Derrida, on the other hand, has shown us how to overcome that outmoded metaphysical category. Reading Wolfe's stimulating and provocative introduction, we could not help but recall Cavell's oft-repeated point that there is in fact nothing more human than the desire to transcend the human (to become, even, somehow inhuman or post-human). Far from actually succeeding in leaving behind (by deconstructing) the category of the human, we believe that poststructuralist antihumanism is itself but another (very sophisticated) expression of one of the deepest and most characteristic of human impulses—the wish humans have always had to transcend their own finitude. This is obviously a contentious claim, one which needs to be handled with care, and this is certainly not the place to settle responsibly such a complex and consequential issue. All we wish to suggest is the centrality of the concept of the human both to Cavell's project and to literary theoretical resistance to it. Therefore, any attempt to make Cavell speak to contemporary literary studies must directly address (indeed defend) his interest in, and allegiance to, the human (the human voice, the human self). If, as we believe, theoretical antihumanism (or more recently, posthumanism) is indeed one of the key reasons Cavell's work continues to suffer from a strange aura of untimeliness—of a curious "lack of fit" with contemporary critical concerns—then a fresh consideration of the Cavellian understanding of the human must play a central role in any reframing of that work for a literary critical audience.

When Cavell wrote that he hoped to reclaim the human self from its neglect by modern thought, he was, in fact, not simply summarizing one goal of *The Claim of Reason* alone, but succinctly characterizing the ambit of his entire intellectual career. What it means to be a human being, to lead a (truly) human life, is exactly what Cavell has always been asking after. That he finds it necessary to continue to ask should immediately suggest how complex and sophisticated is his (still unfolding) account, and it should give us pause before we too quickly identify Cavell's vision of humanity with the metaphysical "universal human substance" that is generally the target of suspicious antihumanists. Indeed, for Cavell, there is nothing more uncanny than the human, just as there is, in a way, nothing more extraordinary than the ordinary. Or as Cavell himself put it in characterizing the sense of the uncanniness of the ordinary—and of the human—that lies at the heart of his work: "I might describe my philosophical task as one of outlining the necessity, and the lack of necessity, in the sense of the human as inherently strange, say unstable, its quotidian as forever fantastic" (IQO 154).

Human beings are then always (at least potentially) haunted by experiences of the strangeness of themselves to themselves and to others: human selfhood is a fragile achievement to be sought (to be claimed and then re-claimed) and never simply some stable psychic state or metaphysical substance to be complacently stood upon. Indeed, one can be summoned or called, surprisingly, by things, events, and persons that one does not anticipate or expect, to a sense of one's non-self-present-ness, one's radical otherness to oneself, and then (sometimes, but then again sometimes not) to a further sense of reintegration of the self in the recovery or establishment of one's human voice. These claims apply equally to a human community's possibilities of a sense of strangeness to itself and of reconsolidation. Both ordinary language philosophy as Cavell sees it and Cavellian reading (of writers like Emerson and Thoreau) track what might be called *essentially finite* pursuits of selfhood and community under conditions of uncanny loss and fallenness. To attempt in these conditions to stand on what is said, where that is taken to be fixed as a matter of linguistic or social fact, is to follow Torvald in *A Doll's House* in taking himself to be "above reproach" and thus to refuse the passionate utterance of another from within a moment of crisis. To attempt to control the terms of judgment absolutely, say by insisting on proofs one can hold within one's own consciousness apart from any conversation, is to follow Othello in his desperate impulse toward intactness. Nothing is more human than such efforts. But they are efforts of situated, finite selves, driven by anxieties and wishes they have taken on via their particular routes of fragile entry into language and human community. Cavellian ordinary language philosophy and Cavellian criticism undertake to describe, understand, assess, enact, and improve upon such finite pursuits of selfhood and community from within a sense of shared situations and complexities of impulse, rather than from a self-certain and all-knowing place apart, from which the human could be taken as already specified, factually or ideally. Such, at least, is our sense of the complexity and dynamism of Cavell's multilayered account of the human, and we think the reclamation of the human self against its neglect by modern thought is as necessary and urgent today as it was when Cavell first began his long career.

Roughly thirty pages from the end of *The Claim of Reason*, there is a section entitled, somewhat cryptically, "proving the existence of the human" (CR 465–68). Prior to that, the bulk of Parts I, II, and III of *The Claim of Reason* is devoted to close analysis of the roles of criteria and of claims about criteria in philosophy and in human life. Some principal results that emerge are that criteria function as standards for reasonable judgment and that claims about what our criteria are are properly entered when those criteria have somehow fallen into doubt (perhaps someone is ignoring them), so that we need, or someone needs, reminding of them. When it comes, however, to criteria for knowledge of the presence of a generic object—that is, an ordinary object of common experience such as a tomato or an envelope or a human hand; cases in which there could be no issue of distinguishing a specially tricky or difficult object (say, a pi-meson trace in a cloud chamber) from others, where expertise may be required—then the *only* thing that a request to know one's criteria for saying "I know" *could* mean is that the very existence before one of the generic object, and so of the world as a whole, is somehow called into question. Once it has been thus called into question, then there is no way back to establishing contact with, let alone intimacy with, objects in the world in general via contact with something else (sense-data, ideas, impressions). Appeals to what our criteria are are impotent to establish the existence of generic objects. The skeptic already knows everything there is to know about when we *ordinarily* say "I know" (that there's cheese in the cupboard or a goldfinch in the garden), and for him that is not enough. The criteria for ordinary knowing have lost their grip on him, and no reminder of the availability of criteria in ordinary cases, for good enough practical purposes, will help. Hence, Cavell asks, "Shall we say that we have *faith* that the things of our world exist? But how is that faith achieved, how expressed, how maintained, how deepened, how lost?" (CR 243).

The theme that thus arises of faithfulness vs. faithlessness, or of intimacy vs. alienation with the things and persons of a world, is then

woven through detailed accounts of language-learning and the formation of the human subject as a subject capable of judgment and of moral
conversation. There is, we think, little if anything in the philosophical
literature that is better than these pages—that is more perceptive, intimately accurate, or phenomenologically acute in tracing the formation
and vicissitudes of lives of human subjects who have emerged,
somehow, without absolute ground in cognitive contact with an absolute given, into a world of socially existent, contested, and sometimes
resolvable, but sometimes irreparably divided, judgment-making. What
it is to judge anything at all to be thus and so, exactly how others are
present, always, within the practices of judgment and moral conversation (as, among other things, introjected images of power or cold
provokers of anxiety), but also how withdrawal and alienation from
these practices can be possible and deeply tempting—all this is as good
as it gets.

But there is also some danger that all of Parts I and II will be read,
first, as intended to be foundational for the somewhat freer Part III,
about morality, and Part IV about "the problem of others." After all,
Parts I and II are about the concepts and phenomena of knowledge and
judgment, and surely (it will be thought) the task of the philosopher,
and a task Cavell seems to be undertaking, is to get those concepts and
phenomena *right*, before turning to the consequences of correct vs.
incorrect understandings of these concepts and phenomena for other
regions of human life. And, second, once so read, there is a danger that
the enterprise will be assessed as a failure in being, let us say, too phe-
nomenological-descriptive and not systematic-theoretical enough. If we
want to know what knowledge and judgment really are, would we not
do much better (it may be argued) to look to empirical cognitive psychology or, more recently, to talk of neural connections, MRI images,
and brain regions, or perhaps to evolutionary psychology and biology?
These styles of inquiry have, after all, begun even to invade literary
studies. And the reason for this assessment is all too natural. If we want
to know what knowing and judging are, shouldn't we turn to a systematic, scientific account of what the evolved, biological-material, human
organism is, at bottom, doing? Or, in a different idiom, why not pay
attention to the social-material conditioning of human subjects, along
the lines of Althusserian interpellation? Why not a material politics
instead of and beneath descriptive-critical phenomenology?

In contrast, Cavell's remarks about moments of hesitation, imitation,
and intimacy felt and then ruptured within the scene of language-learning, and within the formation and continuing life of a human subject of
judgment, can seem merely phenomenological, too surfacy. Sure, that's

the way it looks to him, as a casual, non-scientific and not immediately political outsider, but why should we trust his impressions? Why should we worry so much about a liability or tendency to skeptical anxieties taken as "a natural expression of a creature complicated or burdened enough to possess language at all" (CR 140)? One way or another, let's get serious about what's really going on.

It is against this background of worry that it is particularly useful to turn to the section "proving the existence of the human." Here in particular we can see a *history* of the phenomena of knowing and judging, a history that situates and deepens the earlier phenomenology, just as the phenomenology informs the history. The resulting combination of phenomenology and history into a philosophical anthropology should be read as a unified whole, and it should be understood as a *reading* of our history, a claim—tentative, defeasible, and yet potentially illuminating—about central *topoi* of that history and about how human nature is made manifest within it, both variously and recognizably.

So how does the history go? And what could a history of phenomena of knowing and judging have to do with the topic of proving the existence of the human? The topic itself is initially unclear. Surely I am a human being in virtue of my biological constitution, a fact that needs no proof, let alone one by me. So what is the task at issue, and how does it have a history?

Descartes and Rousseau are crucial figures. Cavell cites with approval Anthony Kenny's observation that "Descartes's innovation in the philosophy of mind" is "the substitution of privacy for rationality as the mark of the mental" (CR 470). But we already know three things from the earlier remarks on criteria about Cavell's views about the nature of this achievement:

(1) it cannot consist in the discovery that judgment begins in a private encounter with a purely internal mental object of judgment, for judgment as an activity begins only in and through initiation by others into the life of language;
(2) instead, a sense of one's essential privacy is an expression of alienation from common life; and
(3) there is no simple, straightforward route back from alienation to reintegration with the ordinary.

Because, we conjecture, of the development of increasingly specialized and skill-based modern labor, human beings in growing up must now pass through longer periods of training, including internal reflection on how complex tasks are best done in varying circumstances. Because, further, of the development of market economies, social stations are less fixed than they once were, and it is less clear what is wanted or expected of anyone entering into grown-up life. The development of suitable skills and of broader modes of public comportment within a diverse society, for the sakes of both a wage and recognition as an accomplished grown-up, is now in principle open to everyone (even if for many still blocked in fact), but exactly how to take up this possibility is less specified than it was in a culture of direct apprenticeship within the way of life of one's parents and clan. Descartes' initial sense of privacy expresses this sense of a power to develop worthwhile skills coupled with uncertainty about how to do so in detail, in ways that may generally be ratified by others.

This sense of privacy is then even more marked in Rousseau. Rousseau's sense of privacy verges on the paranoid, but also records a common-enough sense among modern human subjects. As Cavell describes it, Rousseau

> has the sense [first] that he has become unknowable—private—because to know him would be to know the sentiments of his heart—in particular, his pity for others and his fears of them—and the sentiments of his heart have become unintelligible to (inexpressible by) other human beings (as a result of what they perceive as human progress); second, that our social bonds are not the realization but the betrayal of the social contract, in a word conspiracies, so that there is among us no public thing at all.
>
> (CR 469)

As though literalizing and hyperbolizing Descartes' sense of privacy as alienation, it is for Rousseau as if others were zombies and he were mad. Caught up in their routines of exercising skills and responding to the demands of others, but without any expressions of interest, feeling, and commitment in relation to their activities that are legible to him, Rousseau finds himself cast upon himself, "maddened through an isolation" (CR 469), as Cavell puts it. Perhaps many or most of us, much of the time, are lucky enough not to feel this sense of isolation. Work and family and participation in public institutions may be good enough. But then for some—perhaps for many, at least sometimes—perhaps not.

And then, for Cavell, following Rousseau, one is first of all thrown back upon oneself. "To possess my existence" (as a being capable of feeling, interest, animation, and commitment) "I must declare it" (CR 462). Rather than denying one's condition in coldness, dullness, or a reversion to routine that foregoes hope, one must face "the apprehension that human subjectivity, the concept of human selfhood, is threatened, that it must be found and may be lost; that if one's existence is to be proven it can be proven only from oneself" (CR 465). But here simple assertion of one's own interest as idiosyncratically one's own will not do either. I might declare my interest in playing fifteenth century viola da gamba music or in the history of cricket or, say, in philosophy. But if no or very few others find sense and worth in what I then declare and do, then recognition will not be forthcoming, and the sense of moving as a ghost through a world of zombies will not cease. Instead, my declaration and enactment of my interests may and must be in "faithfulness to [the] desire [for] union or reunion, call it community" (CR 463). Somehow, the task of "the acknowledgment of the existence of finite others" (CR 463), with passions and interests different from one's own, must be managed, but in such a way that some form of mutual sense is achieved and enacted, so that we are, or are no longer, for one another mere satellites around one another's isolated egos or mere objects of instrumental use.

The good news is that Cavell holds out and declares hope that this can still be done, even if the work of acknowledgment and of the enactment of interest is also never finished, but remains always to be redone. Drawing always on both ordinary language philosophy in its declaration and discovery of what we really want to say, and also on the criticism of modern works of art that aims at declaring what we feel in an encounter with the difficult and new, Cavell turns to literary texts and films—to Shakespeare, Coleridge, Thoreau, Hawks, and Capra, among many others—in order to track declarations and denials of interest, skeins of acknowledgment and avoidance. This mode of attention to the literary or filmic text is different from focusing on texts in a detached, positivistic spirit as mere shapes of black ink on white pages, and it is different, too, from focusing on ink-on-pages as produced and consumed by impersonal social forces or movements of power. Those ways of proceeding have their points: deconstruction in directing our attentions to textual ambiguities and ambivalences, to failures of control of the text by a single-presiding, self-present voice; various forms of New Historicism or Cultural Studies in directing our attention to the situation of the production and reception of texts within contested social and political life. There are insights to be won here, and Cavell does not deny them. Yet woven throughout and legible within both textual indeterminacies and plays of social contestation there remains too, for Cavell, an agon of human subjectivity, poised between acknowledgment and avoidance, and seeking further and fuller accounts and enactments of interest. Hence Cavell's criticism is all at once characterological (oriented toward texts and lines within texts as voiced by a subject), allegorical (in finding, always, partial successes and failures of contextual enactments of interest), deconstructionist (in seeing language and culture as always inherited and to be inherited, in ways that outrun full control), and political (in seeing agons of the human played out in specific sociopolitical settings). The range, complexity, and intimacy of the form of attention that inhabits Cavell's criticism are, in short, remarkable.

The epigraph to Part I of *The Claim of Reason* is a line from Ludwig Feuerbach's *The Essence of Christianity*: "This philosophy does not rest on an Understanding *per se*, on an absolute, nameless understanding, belonging one knows not to whom, but on the understanding of man; —though not, I grant, on that of man enervated by speculation and dogma; —and it speaks the language of men, not an empty, unknown tongue" (cited CR 1). This implies that we can ask about any piece of this philosophy—or criticism or literature or film, in their affinities to philosophy—: who is speaking or writing, here and now, in light of what occasions, and more specifically in light of exactly what kind of prompted alienation, what kind of occasioned failure of joint sense-making? And it implies, second, that *philosophy* (or literature or criticism) can still be written or spoken, that is, that what is then said or written need not be, always, merely personal or idiosyncratic, though that is always a risk when mutual isolation and alienation are the points of departure. It is possible that what reveal themselves as *our* interests in *our* lives will be declared, revealed, and enacted, that *our* sense, including our differing contributions to it, will be found and made. A claim of reason—a claim about what we do or say, made in the interest of self-knowledge, community, and the life of reason—can be entered and can, sometimes, be redeemed. Acknowledgment, an active responsiveness to others, can overcome avoidance; expressiveness can overcome dullness and repression. But either way, we are fated to move in the space between acknowledgment and avoidance (see CR 451), bereft of absolute solutions, but with—at least it may be hoped—some possibilities of mutual, sense-making life, woven through continuing difference. One might hope to come productively, at least for a time, to "confront the culture with itself, along the lines in which it meets in me" (CR 125).

Without fixed ground, without assurance of success, this is, Cavell argues, a task and a possibility that is allotted simultaneously to philosophy, literature, and critical study. Whatever their relative differences from one another—philosophy's turns to abstraction and impersonality, literature's emphases on figuration and particular emplotment, and criticism's mediating engagements involving all of theory, close reading, history, and comparison—this is an image that can be, and in Cavell's hands has been, immensely fruitful for understanding both human life and some central literary texts of that life. In the spirit of this thought, we hope for, urge, and prophetically expect a creative, open, renewed critical reception of Cavell within contemporary literary studies, in a way that accepts, but also deepens, literary studies' current self-understandings and critical achievements. But of course only time will tell.

One major consequence of Cavell's interest in the human subject in language and culture and of his ways of doing both criticism and philosophy is that there is rarely a sharp division between theoretical reflection and critical reading. Nor is any such sharp division evident among the essays that compose this volume. Nonetheless it seemed helpful enough to divide the essays provisionally into those that are concerned primarily with canonical philosophical texts (Kant and Wittgenstein in particular) and with questions of aesthetic and critical theory and those that are concerned primarily with developing (and of course commenting on) practices of reading. We mention here the presence of this rough organizational division that we have introduced in order to remind readers not to take it too seriously.

We are happy to conclude these introductory remarks by adding that it has been a continuous pleasure for us to work with our contributors to this volume. Not all editors of collections are in a position to say what we are able to say wholeheartedly: that our contributors produced their essays on time and were always graciously and imaginatively responsive to comments and suggestions from us. We have the greatest confidence in their powers and insights, both in general and as they are embodied in these essays, and we are grateful to them for their work.

I Principles

2 The Adventure of Reading
Literature and Philosophy, Cavell and Beauvoir[1]

Toril Moi

The Question of Literature and Philosophy

"The clash between literature and philosophy does not need to be resolved. On the contrary, only if we think of it as permanent but ever new does it guarantee us that the sclerosis of words will not close over us like a sheet of ice," Italo Calvino writes.[2] He was right: the relationship between philosophy and literature is not a thing to be discovered and described once and for all, but rather a question constantly recreated by writers, critics, and philosophers responding to new situations. People become interested in the relationship between philosophy and literature for different reasons at different times, and different reasons for raising the question will require different answers.[3]

Attempts to define the relationship between philosophy and literature have often been formalistic in the sense that they set out a list of binary oppositions (universal vs. particular, reason vs. imagination, insight vs. emotion, argument vs. form) intended to settle the question once and for all. Such lists often disappoint.[4] It is easy to find exceptions on both sides of the divide, and it is only too clear that they flatter the self-image of philosophers more than the self-image of writers. To cast philosophers as the guardians of universality, reason, insight, and argument is to strip literature of its ambition to provide knowledge, thought, and truth. It is also to ban passion and beauty from philosophy, although I haven't seen too many philosophers complain about that. Such lists also have an unfortunate tendency to reproduce a stereotypical gender hierarchy, in which the terms on the left get coded as masculine and superior, and those on the right as feminine and inferior. Men think, women feel; men do philosophy, women write romantic novels.

Lists of features assume that the answer to the question of the relationship between literature and philosophy must take the form of a definition of the two terms. Given that philosophers have never agreed on what philosophy is, and given that even the most agile minds have failed to produce a convincing definition of literature, this is not a promising path. Moreover, most of us don't wonder about the relationship between philosophy and literature because we have trouble telling them apart. (If we did, a checklist of features that could help us decide whether we were dealing with an instance of philosophy or literature would be quite useful.) Rather, we raise the question for other reasons, reasons we often fail to make completely clear even to ourselves. No wonder we often feel that the answers we get don't address what we really want to know.

The challenge for someone who wants to think about literature and philosophy, then, is to figure out what her question actually is. Usually the question is triggered by a sense of irritation, a conviction that someone is failing to do justice to something we care about. In the postwar era, for example, the question of the relationship between literature and philosophy often took the form of complaints about the "novel of ideas" (the *roman à thèse*) or novels with a "message." This reaction was triggered by the popularity of existentialism, its faith in the philosophical novel, and its call for committed literature. Fundamentally, the debate turned on aesthetic norms: adherents of the aesthetic values of late modernism rejected what they took to be the message-oriented realism of the existentialists. In this case, then, the answer to the question of literature and philosophy would have to be something like a theory of the novel.

My own interest in the relationship between literature and philosophy has to do with the question of philosophical reading. I have long been frustrated with criticism that reduces the literary text to an example of a pre-existing theory or philosophy, whether this means looking for convincing illustrations of existing positions in moral philosophy in Dickens or Woolf, or tracking down Foucault in Jane Austen, Derrida in George Eliot, or Deleuze in Ibsen. What is the point of reading literature if all we manage to see in it is a theory we already know? Why not simply stick to reading theory and philosophy if that's what we really want to do? At the same time, I don't want to separate my interest in literature from my interest in philosophy and theory. I share the conviction that literary criticism would be the poorer without them. In the hands of the best practitioners, to read literature with philosophy is to enrich both. The question is how to achieve this.

I would like to find ways to read philosophically without falling into the trap of casting the critic, the theorist or the philosopher as necessarily wiser, deeper, more intelligent, more politically correct than the writer. The tendency to turn the critic into a champion of critique has been a common failing of the hermeneutics of suspicion, which has dominated literary criticism for a long time. The spirit of the hermeneutics of suspicion has made us believe that to read critically is necessarily to debunk, deconstruct, take apart, and tear down, not to praise and admire. On this view, it is easier to justify the role of critics (they defend us against the ideological machinations of the text) than the works they labor so mightily to take apart.

For me, then, the question of literature and philosophy really is a question of reading, or, more broadly, of criticism. How can we read philosophically without reducing the text to a witting or unwitting illustration of a pre-existing theory? How can we read literature with philosophy in ways that suggest that the writer may actually have something to tell the philosopher? And more radically: Is there a way to read philosophically without having recourse to a given philosophy at all? Can criticism itself be philosophy?

As I formulate these questions, I realize that I probably would not have expressed them in just this way if I had never read anything by Stanley Cavell. (Even the most deeply felt ideas are inspired by others.) To deepen my sense of what it might mean to read philosophically, therefore, I shall turn to Cavell's own reflections on literature and philosophy. How does he conceive of the question? What can someone interested in reading literature learn from the way he connects the two fields?

Criticism as Philosophy: Cavell on Literature and Philosophy
Cavell ends his reading of *Othello*, which itself ends *The Claim of Reason*, by raising a version of the question of the relationship between literature and philosophy:

> Can philosophy accept them [Othello and Desdemona] back at the hands of poetry? Certainly not so long as philosophy continues, as it has from the first, to demand the banishment of poetry from its republic. Perhaps it could if it could itself become literature. But can philosophy become literature and still know itself?
>
> (CR 496)

By "still know itself" I think Cavell means still recognize itself as philosophy, still be philosophy.

One way to take this question is to say that Cavell wonders whether Shakespeare, and Othello, and Desdemona could ever be recognized as philosophers by other philosophers. For someone who believes that a work of art can have philosophical insights this is a natural question. After all, if philosophy is taking place in works of art, philosophers ought to be able to recognize it as philosophy. This raises the question of what Cavell thinks philosophy is:

> [P]hilosophy, as I understand it, is indeed outrageous, inherently so. It seeks to disquiet the foundations of our lives and to offer us in recompense nothing better than itself—and this on the basis of no expert knowledge, of nothing closed to the ordinary human being, once, that is to say, that being lets himself or herself be informed by the process and the ambition of philosophy.
>
> (PH 8–9)

To do philosophy we have to be willing to have philosophy unsettle the "foundations of our lives." Philosophy will ask awkward questions about why we do what we do, and why we think what we think. (There is more than a shade of Socrates here.) Since the activity requires no expert knowledge, we should expect to come across it outside academia, and in texts not traditionally marked as philosophy. So why not in plays and films? For Cavell, it is quite natural to claim that the film director Frank Capra can enter into a productive philosophical conversation with the philosopher Immanuel Kant.[5] (This may be the moment to stress that in so far as they turn on the question of aesthetic judgment, most of the questions raised in this paper are equally pertinent to literature, theater, and film.)

At the end of *The Claim of Reason* Cavell does not just offer Shakespeare but specifically his own attentive elucidation of Desdemona's love and Othello's plight of mind back to philosophy. The question, therefore, is not just whether philosophy can acknowledge literature, but whether it can acknowledge that *criticism*—the work of reading, thinking, and writing about literature and other art forms—can be a part of philosophy. Cavell's own work—his many books on film and theater—shows that for him criticism is a privileged site for philosophy. Criticism is an activity in which the philosopher, encountering the work of art, can attempt to get clear on questions he couldn't get clear on in any other way. Thinking about *Othello*, Cavell pushes his own understanding of skepticism further than he could have done otherwise.

In a dense passage from 2002, written in a moment when he looked back on his work, Cavell connects self-expression and self-exploration to the question of literature (and film) and philosophy:

> Only in stages have I come to see that each of my ventures in and from philosophy bears on ways of understanding the extent to which my relation to myself is figured in my relation to my words. This establishes from the beginning my sense that in appealing from philosophy to, for example, literature, I am not seeking illustrations for truths philosophy already knows, but illumination of

philosophical pertinence that philosophy alone has not surely grasped—as though an essential part of its task must work behind its back. I do not understand such appeals as "going outside" philosophy.[6]

Literature works "behind philosophy's back." Yet its work is not "outside" philosophy, but "essential" to it, as if philosophy has to turn around, to look behind itself to find fundamental "illuminations" it can't find in any other way. By neglecting the turn, or return to literature, philosophy will overlook fundamental insights available only to the philosopher willing to stop, pause, turn back, and pick up the pearls strewn on a path he thought he had already explored. Criticism—the work of reading—is here connected to the idea of stopping, pausing, paying attention, and looking more closely.

But what has all this to do with the "extent to which my relation to myself is figured in my relation to my words"? I think this phrase gestures towards Cavell's larger philosophical project: to work out a vision of language in which words and world are intertwined, to understand language as something we do (rather than, say, as a purely formal structure), so that our words reveal us, our values and commitments, and what we take ourselves to be responsible for. What I say or write will reveal my blindness and my callousness, my insights and my generosity, my failures and my achievements. The enduring themes in Cavell's criticism—marriage and remarriage, skepticism, acknowledgment, loneliness and madness, voice, melodrama and opera—show what he takes himself to be responsible for.

Cavell wants to make a place for literature within philosophy, both because he thinks literature contains illuminations of value to philosophy, and because he thinks that the questions of expression and experience lie at the very heart of philosophy. On this view, criticism—the act of accounting for one's experience of a work of art—can be philosophy.

Criticism and Experience

Good criticism requires a wide range of skills and knowledge. But whatever else it takes, criticism is always based on the critic's judgment. To make an aesthetic judgment, Kant claims, is to be willing to stake one's authority on nothing but one's own experience: when we declare that something is beautiful we have nothing but our own subjectivity to go on. While we feel, spontaneously, that others simply *must* see what we see, we can't ground the claim in anything more tangible than our own judgment that this is beautiful.[7] This feels risky. It exposes our judgment to the potential ridicule of the world. (Surely this is another reason why we are so quick to hide behind the authority of acknowledged master thinkers in our readings and viewings.)

To account for one's experience of a work of art requires a willingness to pay close attention to that experience. It also requires us to trust it, and to find it worth expressing: "Without this trust in one's experience, expressed as a willingness to find words for it, without thus taking an interest in it, one is without authority in one's experience" (PH 12). There are four tasks here: to be willing to have the experience (in the sense of paying attention to it), to judge it important enough to be expressed, to find words for it, and to claim authority for it.

I am struck by the parallels between this view and the work going on in feminist consciousness-raising groups in the 1960s and 1970s. The purpose of these groups was to encourage women to take an interest in their own experiences, to be willing to voice them, and to claim authority for them. The result was revolutionary. The women's understanding of themselves and their experiences was transformed. This goes to show that the difficulties involved in "taking an interest in one's experience" are the same in life and in art, as Cavell points out: "The difficulty of assessing [one's experience of a film] is the same as the difficulty of assessing everyday experience, the difficulty of expressing oneself satisfactorily, of making oneself find words for what one is specifically interested to say, which comes to the difficulty, as I put it, of finding the right to be thus interested" (PH 41–42). For Cavell, aesthetic experience is not divorced from ordinary experience: to find out what it means entails the same difficulties and joys as the investigations of ordinary experiences.[8]

In the 1970s, many feminists made the mistake of considering experience to be infallible. To them, the "authority of experience" meant that a woman could never be wrong about the nature of her own experience, once she had found the words to express it. This is not Cavell's view. It "needs constant admission," he writes, "that one's experience may be wrong, or misformed or inattentive and inconstant."[9] Cavell's sense of the fallibility of experience coalesces around the idea of "checking one's experience" against the work of art. He uses the term "checking" to:

> capture the sense at the same time of consulting one's experience and of subjecting it to examination, and beyond these, of momentarily stopping, turning yourself away from whatever your preoccupations and turning your experience away from its expected, habitual track, to find itself, its own track: coming to attention. The moral of this practice is to educate your experience sufficiently so that it is worthy of trust.
>
> (PH 12)

The education of one's experience by paying careful attention to it: what a hopeful idea! Experience is not fixed; previous experience does not doom me forever to repeat the same mistakes. (This is like psychoanalysis: There is a way to break the old patterns! Experience can be trained!) I must be prepared to discover that my sense of the work was profoundly mistaken, but that discovery will itself be part of my further education as a critic. Here too there is no difference between aesthetic experience (our experience of the work of art), and ordinary experience (what we experience in life).

Sometimes a book will completely transform our understanding of a phenomenon or a problem. Reading *Ulysses* changed many readers' understanding of the novel, and of literature too. Films and plays and books can help us overcome, or undo, our existing beliefs. Just like other experiences, the experience of film, theater, literature has the power to change us. This means that we won't regularly be transformed by reading (we aren't regularly transformed by ordinary experiences either), but it also means that reading (and viewing) can expand our understanding of the world, and ourselves, if we let it.

My original question was how to read philosophically in a way that avoids imposing my pre-existing theory on the work of art. While Cavell's insistence that I must be willing to let the work of art—my experience of the work of art—change my previous beliefs or perceptions is helpful in this respect, it doesn't provide a method for how to do this. Cavell is not interested in laying down requirements for how to read. The nearest I can get to some kind of Cavellian guideline for how to read philosophically is an appeal "to let the object or the work of your interest teach you how to consider it" (PH 10). But how are we to do that? The only hint Cavell provides is to say that we usually have no trouble letting a work of theory or philosophy teach us how to read it. I think this means that the right sort of reading would emerge if we simply read literature or watch films in much the same way as we read philosophy.

What does this sort of reading look like? Well, we often begin by trying to get at least a general idea of what the work is about, what its major concerns and concepts are. At first, we may only form a hazy idea of the whole. To get a clearer view, we zoom in on key concepts, study the examples, circle back to passages that illuminate them, look for the arguments, the contradictions, and the exceptions. In the end we come out with a workable understanding of the book's concerns. If it really fascinates us, we may engage with it again, maybe revise some of our initial impressions, try to get clear on why it strikes us as important, reflect on what we can use it for in our own work.

Why do we imagine that it is always much harder to let a novel or a play teach us how to read it than it is for a theoretical essay to do so? Why do we so quickly reach for the philosophy or theory and try to make the work fit its concepts, rather than trying to figure out what the work's own concepts and preoccupations might be? Maybe because we lack practice. We are not used to looking for the work's own concepts when that work is a novel or a play. Also, we may fear that a reading emerging from such a process might not look all that impressive. After all, it would have to be built on concepts supplied by the work itself, rather than concepts supplied by a specific philosophy.[10] When the critic "checks her experience" against the work, however, she will draw on her full knowledge of those concepts. This may (or may not) give rise to philosophically interesting readings. A critic who proceeds in this manner may easily come to look guileless, as if she hadn't heard of the sophisticated concepts on display in the work of the masters of suspicious critique. To be willing to learn from the work requires a critic capable of a certain degree of humility.

The Writer's Point of View: Simone de Beauvoir's Understanding of Reading

Cavell raises the question of literature and philosophy from the point of view of the philosopher, in the sense that he begins by wondering whether a philosopher can find philosophy in literature and other arts. I have shown that his answer makes criticism a potential place for philosophy, and also addresses the literary critic's question about how to read philosophically. Missing so far is the writer's perspective. To ensure that I don't unwittingly give priority to philosophy's notion of what it is to read, it seems useful to check the philosopher's point of view against the view of a writer with a strong passion for philosophy. At this point, Simone de Beauvoir's reflections on philosophy and literature strike me as particularly relevant.

All her life, Beauvoir was passionately engaged in both philosophy and literature. In the mid-1940s Beauvoir's interests were strikingly similar to Cavell's. She was obsessed with the question of the Other and, like Cavell, thought of writing as an act implicating the Other.[11] "Any speech, any expression is an appeal," she notes in *Pyrrhus and Cinéas*, an essay written immediately after the publication of her first novel, *L'Invitée* (*She Came to Stay*, 1943).[12] Like Cavell, Beauvoir also took for granted that literature and philosophy work on the same kinds of problems, and that these problems are relevant to ordinary life. "In truth, there is no divorce between philosophy and life," she declared in 1948.[13]

Nevertheless, in her first attempt to investigate the problem of the Other, Beauvoir did not hesitate to write a novel rather than a philosophical essay. In *L'Invitée* Beauvoir studies the situation of a woman, Françoise, who suffers from a severe case of solipsism: she has trouble understanding that others exist.[14] When another woman, Xavière, begins truly to exist for her, Françoise constructs her as a hostile presence, as a threat to her own existence. At the end of the novel, she kills Xavière because she cannot live in the presence of her alien consciousness.

To understand Beauvoir's conception of the relationship between literature and philosophy in *L'Invitée*, it would be necessary to read it in detail, and situate it against the background of the French preoccupation with the "metaphysical novel" in the 1940s. But this is not the place to do this.[15] Let me just say that there is no doubt that both Beauvoir and her old friend Maurice Merleau-Ponty considered *L'Invitée* to be a significant "metaphysical novel," by which they meant a novel setting out to convey the attitude a human being takes up in relation to a fundamental aspect of human existence: being, time, consciousness, the Other, freedom, separation, finitude, and so on.[16]

Why did Beauvoir prefer to write a novel rather than a philosophical essay about Otherness? In her 1946 essay "Literature and metaphysics," she claims that only the novel enables the writer to convey "an aspect of metaphysical experience that cannot otherwise be manifested: its subjective, singular and dramatic character, as well as its ambiguity."[17] She also stresses that the novel alone conveys the temporal nature of existence.[18] Interestingly, however, much of her essay on the novel focuses on the reader's experience. Here, as everywhere else in her writings on literature, Beauvoir writes as the passionate and voracious reader she was. (Her memoirs and diaries are full of examples of her passion for reading.) Unlike the philosophical essay, Beauvoir writes, a good novel "imitates the opacity, ambiguity, impartiality of life; spellbound by the story he is told, the reader responds as he would to events he had experienced."[19] To read is to have experiences one would otherwise not have. Readers of fiction have a larger world than non-readers of fiction. For Beauvoir, a philosophical essay doesn't draw in the reader in the same way, doesn't produce the sense of experience that literature offers.

A good novel, for Beauvoir, is an invitation to the reader to share the author's sense of exploration [*recherche*] and discovery, to join her on an "authentic adventure of the mind."[20] Beauvoir's reader has to be open-minded. She has to be willing to take up the writer's invitation to join her on an adventure. If the experience of reading disappoints, the responsibility for the result does not rest with the writer alone. The reader can fail the book by refusing to "participate sincerely in the experience the author is trying to involve him in; he does not read as he demands that one writes, he is afraid of risks, of adventure."[21] When both parties participate in equal measure, however, nothing, not even pure philosophy, is more powerful than a novel: "A metaphysical novel that is honestly read, and honestly written, provides a disclosure of existence in a way unequaled by any other mode of expression."[22]

A reader who willingly participates in the adventure of the novel lets herself be absorbed by it. All her life, Beauvoir praised novels that allowed her to feel immersed, absorbed, spellbound. A novel had to "take" [*prendre*]: take her in (make her believe in it) and take her over (spellbind her).[23] She read novels not just to learn, but to feel, and to identify with the author, or the characters, or both. For Beauvoir, then, a good novel had to have the power to absorb, to hold and bewitch, to transport the reader into its world, to make him or her not so much take the fiction for reality, as to be able to experience the fiction as deeply as reality, while full well knowing that it is fiction.[24]

The power to absorb and transport distinguishes literature from philosophy, according to Beauvoir. In an essay on literature from 1964 she notes that however artful, and however full of information it may be, an essay or a scholarly book fails to transport the reader out of herself ("I don't change universe").[25] Only literature has the power to let the reader see the world from the Other's point of view.[26] Reading a novel enables Beauvoir to feel that she, for a moment, genuinely becomes the Other without ceasing to be herself. This is surely why Beauvoir quotes fiction and autobiographical writing so copiously in *The Second Sex*: such works provide windows on to the world from the perspective of another person, and thus give access to insights and experiences we would never otherwise have:

> Kafka, Balzac, Robbe-Grillet seek me out, convince me to move, at least for a moment, to the heart of another world. And this is the miracle of literature, which distinguishes it from information: that an *other* truth becomes mine without ceasing to be other. I renounce my own 'I' in favor of the speaker; and yet I remain myself.
>
>   It is an intermingling ceaselessly begun and ceaselessly undone, and it is the only kind of communication capable of giving me that which cannot be communicated, capable of giving me the taste of another life.[27]

Literature is privileged over non-fiction or academic writing (what she calls "information") because it allows us to see the world from the point of view of the Other without ceasing to be ourselves.

Here Beauvoir has reached Cavell's neighborhood: Writing and the Other are intrinsically connected. But rather than asking whether philosophy can accept Desdemona and Othello back at the hands of poetry, Beauvoir inspires us to reflect on the reader's experience of the "miracle of literature." However passionately we may feel about it, philosophy does not offer the reader the same degree of absorption, loss of self, as literature, nor the same possibilities for identification.[28] This is a major reason why Beauvoir chose to write fiction and memoirs: she wanted to write works that would give readers a chance to identify with her, and her characters, in the same way she identified with George Eliot and Maggie Tulliver. After reading *The Mill on the Floss* the fourteen-year-old Simone cried for hours over Maggie's death, and vowed to become a writer herself: "one day another adolescent girl would bathe with her tears a novel in which I would tell my own story."[29] Although the adult Beauvoir no longer cried for hours over a novel, she continued to think that only literature could provide this kind of experience.

We don't have to choose between Cavell's and Beauvoir's way of raising the question about literature and philosophy. Beauvoir's emphasis on the experience of reading fiction, on the reader's willingness to respond to the author's invitation to set out on an adventure, and Cavell's conviction that literature can offer illumination to philosophy are not incompatible. Both Beauvoir and Cavell agree that writing and the question of the Other are intertwined, that literature offers the reader new and potentially transformative experiences, and that these experiences can be relevant to philosophy as well as life.

Tales of Adventure: On Reading in a Certain Spirit

What kind of philosophical reading emerges from these considerations? Is there a case for calling it "ordinary language criticism"?[30] The latter has the advantage of economically signaling the connection to Cavell's "ordinary language philosophy." But there are significant drawbacks. As far as I know, Cavell never uses the term.[31] I think this is because he rightly thinks that his responses to Shakespeare, Hollywood remarriage comedies and Hollywood melodrama may just as well be called philosophy. The term "ordinary language criticism" risks turning Cavell, Wittgenstein, and Austin into a new set of master thinkers whose characteristic preoccupations are now to be imposed on the literary text. While I want to acknowledge that many texts (and films and plays) are preoccupied by the same concerns as Cavell (expression, language, human embodiment, knowledge, acknowledgment, and skepticism, for example), a criticism frantically searching for "Cavellian" themes is not an answer to my question of how to read philosophically without reducing the text to a reflection of a pre-existing theory. It would also flatly contradict Cavell's own advice to let the work teach us how to read it.

Cavell neither proposes a specific method for literary criticism, nor lays down requirements for what a criticism inspired by his work, or by ordinary language philosophy more generally, must be about. That is not surprising, since he stresses that ordinary language philosophy itself has no specific thematic limits: "Ordinary language philosophy is about whatever ordinary language is about" (MWM 95). Similarly, ordinary language criticism, if the word is to be used, would have to be about whatever works of literature or films or plays are about. ("Let the work teach you how to read it," is a different way of saying the same thing.) A critic inspired by ordinary language philosophy claims her identity not by invoking a set of pre-existing philosophical themes, and certainly not by making a show of her knowledge of Wittgenstein or Cavell, but by approaching the work, and the task of the critic, in a certain way, and in a certain spirit, a spirit that may be exemplified and defined by, but certainly not limited to, ordinary language philosophers. For this reason, I feel that "ordinary language criticism" may actually be too constraining a term for the kind of criticism that comes to mind after reading Cavell. For now, I'll leave open the question of what to call this kind of practice, and turn instead to the mysterious "spirit" I just mentioned.

To describe that spirit is no easy task. It does value a certain kind of attention, one that understands itself as being a response to a work. Moreover, the kind of attention valued by Cavell and Beauvoir is not the sort of attention that arises from a spirit of suspicion. The Wittgensteinian philosopher Cora Diamond, who called her own collection of essays *The Realistic Spirit*, offers a thought-provoking alternative, by suggesting that to read well is to bring to the text a certain quality of attention which she characterizes as a willingness to participate in the "adventure" offered by the text. As we have seen, fifty years earlier, Simone de Beauvoir used the very same term to describe what she expected from a reader.

Diamond introduces the idea of reading as an adventure by quoting the British mountaineer George Mallory, who disappeared on Mount Everest in 1924. Asked why mountaineers climb mountains, he answered: "Our case […] is not unlike that of one who has, for instance, a gift for music. There may be inconvenience, and even damage, to be sustained in devoting time to music; but the greatest danger is in not devoting enough, for music is this man's adventure. … To refuse the adventure is to run the risk of drying up like a pea in its shell."[32]

Diamond finds in Henry James a very similar understanding of what the reader's adventure may be: "[F]or James, the adventurous reader is one who delights in there being more in things than meets the eye, who delights in the invitation the tale offers to find, to make, adventure in reading."[33] Adventure and attention are intrinsically linked. The bad reader is the inattentive reader, the reader who "misses the adventure." Such readers miss the characters' adventures, miss "[their] own possible adventure in reading," and, finally, miss the chance to emerge from their shell, to open themselves to the new, the different, the challenging: "The greater danger is inattention, the refusal of adventure," Diamond writes. "The risk there, as Mallory puts it, is of drying up like a pea in its shell."[34] To be open to adventure is to be ready to be illuminated by the text, to assume that it can work the "miracle of literature" and show us things we had never suspected, show us "another world," as Beauvoir puts it.

There is self-exposure in aesthetic judgment. It makes us vulnerable. The critic reveals how she sees the work, and the world, and what matters to her, existentially, intellectually, politically, morally. She reveals, too, the quality of her attention, the depth of her imagination, her capacity for philosophy. Aesthetic judgment, moreover, is an appeal to the Other: the critic's characteristic gesture is to say "This is what I see. Can you see it too?"[35] The appeal may go unanswered. We may discover, painfully, that we are alone in our perceptions of what matters in the world.[36] Nevertheless, to retreat from the challenges of honest judgment is to choose to "[dry] up like a pea in its shell." To give an account of one's reading is to tell the tale of an adventure. The best criticism is at once an account of an adventure and an invitation to new adventures.

3   "Is 'Us' Me?"

Cultural Studies and the Universality of Aesthetic Judgments[1]

R. M. Berry

The Aesthetics of Cultural Studies

In his introduction to the 2005 volume *The Aesthetics of Cultural Studies* Michael Bérubé professes "incredulity" at a 1998 quote by Marjorie Perloff in *The Chronicle of Higher Education* in which she pits aesthetics and cultural studies against each other.[2] Bérubé's contention is that cultural studies has always been engaged with aesthetics, and he sets out to elaborate the aesthetic theory underlying their engagement. I do not find Bérubé's aesthetic theory satisfying, and one reason will motivate my discussion here. For me, the aesthetics of cultural studies unwittingly legitimates the dominant discursive regime of contemporary poetry and fiction—by which I mean the mutually supporting system of university creative writing programs, literary reviews, cultural support foundations, trade publishers, bookstore chains, mass-circulation reviews, national book prizes, subsidiary and foreign rights agents, and the global marketing apparatus with which this regime is continuous. In short, I consider Bérubé's aesthetic theory ideological, where I use the word "ideology" to refer to the misrepresentation of a contested position as the natural or obvious one, that is, as what goes without saying. Since Bérubé's ambition is precisely to dislodge hegemony of this kind, my claim that he has done the opposite demands elaboration. I cannot satisfy that demand at the outset, but I can state the source of my dissatisfaction succinctly: it is that, while Bérubé questions the stability of our aesthetic concepts, he goes right on using the word "aesthetic" as though his questioning requires no answer.

Bérubé's proposed reconciliation of evaluative criticism with social critique involves a model of aesthetics drawn from Jan Mukarovsky's 1936 work *Aesthetic Function, Norm, and Value as Social Facts*. In this model, according to Bérubé, the meaning of aesthetics varies with "the social and historical circumstances in which cultural works are produced and perceived" (ACS 12). As Mukarovsky says, "The limits of the province of aesthetics ... are not provided by reality itself and are exceedingly changeable" (quoted ACS 12). It does not trouble Bérubé that Mukarovsky's observation would apply to virtually *every* English noun, including "power," "rape," "poverty," and "genocide," or that all concepts depend for their intelligibility on particular historical and social circumstances, and the reason for his equanimity appears to be that Bérubé does not regard the exceeding changeableness of the word "aesthetic" as any obstacle to its present use. On the contrary, in the very next sentence Bérubé remarks: "Mukarovsky points out that *what we now call the aesthetic function* is not a transhistorical category" (ACS 12; italics mine). I feel like asking: just what do we now call the aesthetic function?

A close reading of Bérubé's essay will show, I believe, that whenever Bérubé does give a concrete meaning to such words as "aesthetic" or "literary," he assumes a conventional, uncritical, or commonsensical understanding of these concepts. That is, his use confirms Simon Frith's premise about how "all cultural judgments work," specifically, that "people bring similar questions to high and low art, that their pleasures and satisfaction are rooted in similar analytic issues," a premise that Frith elaborates by listing the topics of middle-brow aesthetic discourse: "believability," "coherence," "familiarity," "usefulness," etc.[3] Contrary to what some imagine, it is not obvious that this middle-brow program represents "what we now call the aesthetic function." To explain how Bérubé's attempt to reconcile our aesthetic and social criticism could so utterly backfire, however, I need to go back to his 1996 review of George Levine's *Aesthetics and Ideology*. In the introduction to this volume Levine expresses a hope of preserving literature's distinctiveness and poses the question of what knowledge a novel or poem might provide that is not equally available from non-literary texts. Why, he asks, "should we read literature at all if what we want to know can be discovered through other materials?"[4] Bérubé, in his review, understands Levine here to be demanding "a unique kind of informational content that can be found nowhere else in the world."[5] That is, Bérubé assumes, as Raymond Williams famously does in *Marxism and Literature*, that a unique informational content of literature, or in Mukarovsky's formulation, a real basis of aesthetics in the material properties of objects, would necessitate a historically invariable meaning of the words "literature" and "aesthetics." And is that true?

In his 1969 work on modernism and philosophy, *Must We Mean What We Say?*, Stanley Cavell has described a problem within contemporary aesthetics that may be the source of Bérubé's defensiveness. Cavell has claimed that a suspicion of art's fraudulence—that is, of the possibility that art works might not actually *be* art—is not merely our lingering response to Duchamp's having placed a urinal in an art exhibition, but has always been constitutive of the aesthetic. What someone like John Cage has revealed, Cavell explains,

> is that the possibility of fraudulence, and the experience of fraudulence, is endemic in the experience of contemporary music; that its full impact, even its immediate relevance, depends upon a willingness to trust the object, knowing that the time spent with its difficulties may be betrayed. I do not see how anyone who has experienced modern art can have avoided such experiences, and not just in the case of music. Is Pop Art art? Are canvases with a few stripes or chevrons on them art? Are the novels of Raymond Roussel or Alain Robbe-Grillet? Are art movies? A familiar answer is that time will tell. But my question is: *What* will time tell? That certain departures in art-like pursuits have become established (among certain audiences, in textbooks, on walls, in college courses); that *someone* is treating them with the respect due, we feel, to art; that one no longer has the right to question their status? But in waiting for time to tell that, we miss what the present tells— that the dangers of fraudulence, and of trust, are essential to the experience of art … Contemporary music is only the clearest case of something common to modernism as a whole, and modernism only makes explicit and bare what has always been true of art.[6]

The consequences of this rich passage are far-reaching, but its underlying point is that modernist art brings us up against the limit of knowledge itself. Recognizing this limit is what Cavell calls "the truth of skepticism"—not that we can never know reality as such, but rather that the existence of our world rests, finally, not upon knowledge, but upon acknowledgment. Bérubé's conviction that, in reality, literary works possess no distinctive qualities does not result from any lack of knowledge of what literature is. His distinction between aesthetic concepts and reality expresses, on the contrary, a desire that some threat posed by literary works be closed off. If the question I ask of a novel is, "What is a novel?" then I am seeking an informational content that can be found nowhere in the world more primitively than in novels themselves. Having spent years reading novels, Bérubé is hardly unfamiliar with it. What isn't he acknowledging?

What initially interested me about Bérubé's project was both its continuity with and striking differences from Philippe Lacoue-Labarthe and Jean-Luc Nancy's 1978 account of the romantic origins of modern literature, *The Literary Absolute*.[7] For both Bérubé and the French philosophers, doing justice to the aesthetic requires that we theorize, an activity simultaneously historical and speculative, and also for both, the ambition of theorizing is to account for "what we now call the aesthetic function." However, Lacoue-Labarthe and Nancy differ sharply from Bérubé on who the "we" of contemporary aesthetics is—by which I mean that social group that persists, in spite of exceeding changeableness, in calling something literature or art. Here's how Lacoue-Labarthe and Nancy describe us:

> For insofar as we are, we are all preoccupied with fragmentation, the absolute novel, anonymity, collective practice, the journal, and the manifesto; as a necessary corollary, we are all threatened by indisputable authorities, petty dictatorships, and the simplistic and brutal discussions that are capable of interrupting questioning for decades; we are all, still and always, aware of the Crisis [of Kant's philosophy], convinced that 'interventions' are necessary and that the least of texts is immediately 'effective;' we all think, as if it went without saying, that politics passes through the literary …
>
> (LA 16–17)

Needless to say, we may not recognize contemporary America in this description, since several of the terms (e.g., "the absolute novel") are unfamiliar, while others rarely occur outside an academic setting, suggesting that, in Lacoue-Labarthe and Nancy's account, a tiny group of intellectuals is trying to pass itself off as everybody. And Lacoue-Labarthe and Nancy appear sensitive to this suspicion, since they begin with a reservation: "For insofar as we are …" But this reservation only discloses a deeper problem, namely that the accuracy of their account cannot be confirmed in the way Simon Frith's can, that is through a poll of contemporary audiences.[8] For, even if we were able to decide that Frith is correct, that those of us who go to movies and buy books are more concerned with familiarity and believability than with, say, *ostranenie* or remediation, would that prove Lacoue-Labarthe and Nancy were wrong, that we are not inhabiting the crisis of Kant's philosophy? Or would it just instance their reservation, specifically, that we are not us, that, insofar as we do not recognize ourselves in their description, we are alienated, living in avoidance of our own historical circumstances? In short, our responses to contemporary literature and art could be displacing our aesthetic values as readily as instancing them. To become ourselves, then, we would need to confront what they call our "repetitive compulsion," that is, would need to understand why, despite wanting to destabilize our concepts of aesthetics, cultural studies continues to rely on them anyway.

In contrast to Bérubé's and Frith's alignment of contemporary aesthetics with the categories of popular reception, Lacoue-Labarthe and Nancy's work radicalizes the problem of knowing what we now call the aesthetic function. When Cavell says that he does not see how anyone who has experienced modern art can have avoided a suspicion of fraudulence, he gives voice to that radicalization, implying that no value judgment, regardless how sociologically documentable, will comprise unimpeachable evidence. Only an uncritical conformity would be scandalized at his suggestion that, for determining our aesthetics, some popular enthusiasms are simply irrelevant. If I want to know what a novel is, it matters hugely that the objects from which I seek this information *really are* novels, that the qualities I find significant about them are qualities of novels, not of something else in novelistic drag.

Therefore Bérubé and Williams are hardly wrong to draw attention to the way historically specific groups have advanced different aesthetic programs. Such attentiveness opens up two questions. First, it forces us to ask how aesthetic discourse has functioned to legitimate values that are not specifically artistic. Placing a soup can on a pedestal not only mocks the fashionable credulousness of New York cognoscenti; it also asks, "What is an art institution?" Whether asked about MOMA, an academic discipline, or a literary device, this question focuses criticism on that nexus of intellectual, social, political, and economic interests that can magically transform household garbage into cultural capital. Understood empirically, it sets a task for cultural history and the sociology of art, and understood theoretically, it sets the task for critique, for a Foucauldian account of the relationship of aesthetic concepts to discursive regimes. By exposing such interdependencies, Cultural Studies can show that a particular construction of aesthetics or literature is not identical with aesthetics or literature and may be something else entirely.

What turns answers to this first question, "What is an art institution?" into a fruitless skepticism, however, is our confusing them with answers to the second question, "What is art?" This confusion reduces art to its institutionalization and denies that *any* construction of aesthetics or literature could be, in reality, aesthetics and literature. The threat of fraudulence now vanishes, since fraudulence no longer distinguishes one version of aesthetics from others, having merged with the aesthetic as such. *This* threat, that my historically particular concept of a novel might expose me, is the threat that Bérubé's insistence on the instability of aesthetic concepts hopes to close off. And it traps him in ideology. Bérubé's reluctance to give his aesthetic concepts any specific informational content requires that his aesthetic concepts go without saying, pass silently as "ours." And this is not just false; it is hegemonic. One aim of twentieth century philosophy, from Heidegger and Adorno through Cavell, has also been to disclose the history on which our aesthetic concepts depend, but the effect of *their* work has been to radicalize the stakes of such a disclosure. What a work like *The Literary Absolute* shows is not merely that apart from Kant's philosophy our aesthetic concepts would be different, but that apart from the crisis that Kant's philosophy articulated we really have no aesthetic concepts. Fraudulence is one of Cavell's names for this crisis, and the originality of his interpretation is not that we can never know for sure whether our particular construction of aesthetics is the real one, but rather that overcoming the suspicion of fraudulence is now part of what comprises the aesthetic function. Failing to acknowledge this suspicion means failing to inhabit our historical situation. If our taste in books and movies shows little concern for it, then that counts as evidence that we are not us.

The Aesthetics of Modernism

One version of the Kantian crisis can be found in the opening sections of *Critique of Judgment*, where Kant argues that while personal preferences can be idiosyncratic and still genuine, aesthetic judgments are necessarily spoken in "a universal voice."[9] Kant seems a little astonished by his own claim, since it implies something like a logical necessity in conflict with present facts. That is, our expectation that others will share our aesthetic experiences not only lacks a solid basis in others' past behavior but can persist even when others do not, in fact, share them. Kant leads up to this point by giving wide latitude to our individual enjoyments: "With regard to the agreeable," he explains, "everyone is content that his judgment, which he grounds on a private feeling, and in which he says of an object that it pleases him, be restricted merely to his own person" (CJ §7, p. 97). The ordinary expression for such pleasure is, "It's agreeable *to me*." In other words, if I prefer strawberry yogurt and you prefer vanilla, our tastes certainly don't agree, but we'll have a hard time getting into an argument over them. The reason is that my delight in strawberry, even if combined with my bullying insistence that vanilla tastes insipid, can be perfectly genuine without conflicting in any way with your conviction that vanilla tastes divine. In fact, the validity of my experience isn't even grounds for questioning yours, for suspecting that you're inexperienced in fruit flavors or repressing your true appetites. If I say otherwise, you won't just think I'm dogmatic; you'll think I'm crazy. That is, I won't be demanding that you agree with my opinion; I'll be acting like we inhabit the same body, that I can actually have your sensations, taste your tastes. Normally, I just won't try to provide a justification for my saying the taste of strawberry is superior to that of vanilla, or cite evidence why you ought to like it, too. The phrase "to me" doesn't seem merely *added* to statements of preference, say, to protect them from criticism; its implication of privacy, of a strictly individual validity, seems already there, even if my form of expression leaves it out.[10]

By contrast, what Kant finds striking about aesthetic experiences is that arguments over them *can* occur, that people often will, when challenged, try to offer reasons for their judgments. In examining these arguments, Cavell has shown that their reasonableness is not just illusory, that it makes good sense, assuming we are both experienced in art, to expect you to recognize which facts are at least relevant to judgment. Knowing such things is part of knowing what art is. However, it is exactly here that the universal voice of aesthetics looks so perverse, for even if you do recognize my judgment's reasonableness, we are no closer to agreement than before. If you see no reason for calling Gertrude Stein's *The Making of Americans* a novel, then the most my reasons can do is get you to open up, to give Stein's writing a closer look, but the whole point of arguing is for you to see *for yourself* why it is a novel. Kant's discovery, on Cavell's interpretation, is that aesthetic experiences are just as subjective as personal preferences in that no one else can have yours for you, but unlike the latter, their genuineness can be and often is threatened by others' disagreement. When Kant remarks that "he must not call it beautiful if it pleases merely him," he does not mean, when others disagree, we should concede our mistake. Quite the contrary, Kant means we are likely to engage in what, for all the world, looks like an *ad hominem* attack. We will "rebuke" the other, "demand" that she see what we see, and insist that, if she does not see it, well, she "ought" to. It is as though, not just the work's genuineness, but *my* genuineness were at issue. In short, Kant's discovery is that, if you do not see in *The Making of Americans* what I see, then a problem not merely of reasons and facts but of character, of my motives for projecting value onto reality or yours for repressing it, is apt to arise.

In Kant's *Critique of Judgment* there is no simple solution to this problem of practical aesthetics. Although acknowledging that doubts inevitably arise when others disagree (CJ §33, p. 165), Kant mentions only two ways of overcoming them. Either we need to take a broader-minded, less parochial and sensually immediate, view of our own aesthetic experience (§40), or we need to acquire more aesthetic experience (§32–§33). Kant conceives the first solution privatively, as an act of self-alienation in which we put ourselves "into the position of everyone else, merely by abstracting from the limitations that contingently attach to our own judging" (§40, p. 174), while the second appears simply to be the first put into practice. After all, acquiring more experience of what others have called art is what overcoming one's aesthetic limitations means (§32, pp. 163–64). In recommending that the doubtful judge abstract from "the subjective private conditions of the judgment" in this way (§40, p. 175), Kant does not appear to worry, as does Cultural Studies, that overcoming my parochialism might actually be manifesting it, projecting onto the art of other peoples and times, not the contentless form of human subjectivity, but the historically relative content of my own. Quite the contrary, Kant seems confident that the more rigorously we alienate ourselves from our immediate experience, the more empirically universal our aesthetic experiences will become. Nowhere in *Critique of Judgment* does Kant mention his theory's equally plausible but opposite potential, that acquiring more aesthetic experience could isolate me, disclosing aesthetic satisfactions that no one else acknowledges.

In his early writings on modernism, Cavell does not differ from Kant over the big themes of Kantian aesthetics: the centrality of form, its homology with representational conditions, art's historical autonomy, or the insufficiency of rules. On each of these issues, Cavell leaves Kantian aesthetic theory fundamentally intact. Where Cavell differs from Kant is over his examples. Instead of disagreements resulting from insufficient aesthetic experience or a lack of critical distance, Cavell's examples involve aesthetic objects about which even the most experienced and cosmopolitan critics will disagree: unparaphrasable metaphors, atonal music, experimental theater, abstract paintings, non-narrative fiction. One significance of this difference is that, unlike Kant and Bérubé, Cavell cannot assume his audience knows what he is talking about. For Cavell, aesthetic discussion is meaningful only if something goes without saying, but how far aesthetic discussion is still meaningful, does not, for Cavell, go without saying. On the contrary, it is what his writing tests, and if, despite such fundamental disagreements, some readers see what he means, then that is not because Cavell resolves these disagreements. It is because fundamental, irresolvable disagreement is internal to the present experience of art. Although agreements in taste of the kind documented by Pierre Bourdieu or Simon Frith might, for Kant, confirm that human subjectivity is more than private, the meaning of Cavell's writing is that, for the us we now are, empirical universality is simply irrelevant. If Taliban operatives in Afghanistan watch American television, does that count as evidence of our shared humanity? Or is it evidence of an alienation from which no one today is insulated? Aesthetic discussion is still meaningful only if what goes without saying is still art, a peculiar form of life with objects and others, and for anyone participating in it, what art is, even if institutionally unrecognized, is nothing that cannot be said.

In his commentary (MWM 74–82) on literature's canonical version of Kantian aesthetics, Cleanth Brooks's "The heresy of paraphrase," Cavell makes clear that the limit on the meaningfulness of aesthetic discussion today is not due to any lack of unique informational content in art works. Although Brooks's explicit disagreement with Yvor Winters is over the relationship of criticism to its object, motivating it is a more concrete disagreement over experimental uses of language in modernist poetry, uses exemplified by Wallace Stevens's line "as a calm darkens among water-lights." According to Cavell, the problem such lines pose is that, unlike other figurative expressions, knowing what they mean does not necessarily imply knowing how to say what they mean. For Brooks, this problem merely results from confusing poetry with what critics have said about it, and his solution is a theory of poetry in which all poems, not merely modernist ones, are strictly formal unities without determinate meaning. For Winters, by contrast, the problem is our mistaking these experimental uses of language for poetry. The only reason saying what they mean is difficult is that they mean almost nothing. Although Cavell does not share Winters's doubts about Stevens's line, he also has little faith that Brooks's theory overcomes these doubts. For Cavell, the problem of modernist poetry is practical, a problem of how anyone who sees the point of using words in these ways can get others to see it, too. In his aesthetics, the whole purpose of critical discussion is to solve problems of this kind, and the reason solving them has become so difficult is not that we cannot say what the lines in question mean. The difficulty is that the only way of overcoming a disagreement as fundamental as that between Brooks and Winters is to change one's life.

When in writing on modernism Cavell insists that "the dangers of fraudulence … are essential to the experience of art" (MWM 188–89), he is acknowledging this life-changing potential of modernist art. His parenthetical afterthought that making these dangers explicit is "almost a definition of modernism" (p. 189) suggests that as long as we find it unimaginable that creative writing programs, literary reviews, cultural support foundations, trade publishers, bookstore chains, mass-circulation reviews, national book prizes, subsidiary and foreign rights agents, and our current apparatus of global marketing could be displacing literature with its institutionalized imitation, no work of contemporary writing will do for us what Cavell claims Anthony Caro's sculpture did for him: namely, reveal that nothing that went without saying about art was true (MWM 216–17). Only so long as the very existence of art remains at issue in this way, can a single work acquire such revelatory force. In this sense, the threat of fraudulence is simply the verso of the logical universality of aesthetic judgments, and to acknowledge it is to accept, not that we can never say what literature is, but that seeing for oneself has become constitutive of the aesthetic.[11] When Cavell describes the lines at issue for Brooks and Winters as "touchstones of intimacy" (MWM 81) he makes clear that, in modernism's radical departures, what one is trying to see is the basis of one's life. That is, at issue is a connection so fundamental that, in Cavell's words, "[I]f someone does not get it he is not in one's world, or not of one's flesh." And if everyone's need to see them for him or herself represents the crisis of Kant's philosophy, then Kant's aesthetic theory, assuming it means anything anymore, means the universal voice of aesthetics will inevitably raise the question: Just who in the world do you think you are?

What is Literature?

Saying what art or poetry or sculpture or music is is meaningful only for participants, those speaking from within the experience of art, who see its connection to their lives. Seeing this connection, however, or enabling others to see it, seems an achievement of a different order. It is, after all, what the work of art itself must achieve. But it is also what the work of aesthetic judgment, of the criticism of art must achieve, and in modernism all such work takes a radical turn, attempting to know painting, poetry, music, and sculpture from their origin or basis. Although confusing art with what is said about it is an especially old form of aesthetic fraudulence, the academic one, Cavell's claim is that with modernism its risks prove unavoidable. Partly, this is because the subject matter of the work and of the criticism of the work is the same— "modernist painting is about *painting*" (MWM 207)—but more significantly, it is because the risks arise from modernism's success, from its depriving us, when it is genuine, of so much that has been said about art up to now. Because "the task of the modernist artist, as of the contemporary critic, is to find what it is his art finally depends upon" (MWM 219), criticism becomes "internal to the experience of art" (MWM 207), necessitating aesthetic judgments continually (MWM 191). In such circumstances the roles of artist and critic merge. Everybody becomes a discoverer of art.

And so, everybody gets lost. Among the arts, literature is particularly susceptible to confusion with what is said about it, superficially because, being verbal, literature and its criticism look so much alike, but more fundamentally, because both develop from a single potentiality, that of speaking representatively. In calling *The Making of Americans* a novel, I do not say that it is a novel only for me. I say that it represents what the

English word "novel" means, including what the non-English words translated by the word "novel" mean, thus replicating the novelist's prior audacity, her claim to speak for or in the voice of indefinite others. How is it possible to discover in a single work what others in my group call a novel, even if I have never polled the others to see whether they really do call *The Making of Americans* a novel? *Philosophical Investigations*[12] raises questions of just this kind, and three of its themes can help explicate Cavell's aesthetics. First, where a gap between what my group calls literature and what Mukarovsky calls "reality itself" results from no information about literary works available only to a few, then closing that gap requires acknowledging something obvious to everyone. When Wittgenstein says, "The aspects of things that are most important for us are hidden because of their simplicity and familiarity" (PI §129) he means what Cavell means in saying of Jackson Pollock that he "discovers, by painting, something ... that everybody has always known is true of paintings generally" (WV 109). In the modernist environment, knowing what a novel is means seeing a connection between something obvious about novels and what I do in reading *this* one.

Second, where the gap between our literary concepts and reality has been opened by our overlooking these connections, what we have ignored are not norms or conventions. We have ignored ourselves. When Wittgenstein remarks that "It can't be said of me at all (except perhaps as a joke) that I *know* I am in pain" (PI §246), he is not laughing at our grammar. His punchline is that, in trying to know, I've forgotten that *I'm in pain*. In characterizing modernist art as a return of the repressed (WV 113–14), Cavell recognizes this inseparability of aesthetic discoveries from our feelings and behavior, but his remark that what returns is hidden in consciousness rather than the unconscious (WV 109) suggests that art's need for discovery results from our alienation (MWM 172–73), not from any libidinal constraint. The difficulty of knowing what a novel is is not that real ones look so much like frauds. It is that, like King Lear, we *prefer* frauds (MWM 285–94.).

Third and last, where a gap between literature and reality has been opened by someone's speaking (possibly merely as though) in a universal voice, then what we need is not a theory of literature. We need literature. As Cavell recognizes, the mode of modernist art is "revelation" (WV 109; MWM 163–79); the feeling of artificiality about our aesthetic concepts results from confusion, not from parochialism or inexperience (MWM 164–66). In such circumstances, it must be overcome aesthetically; that is, literature's discovery must occur through the senses, where what is discovered will have the force of a clarification. Cavell's examples are Pollock's revelation that paintings are wholly manifest (WV

109) and Beckett's revelation that audiences are continuously present (MWM 157–58). What a novel is can be a revelation only because a novel is what reveals it.

My candidate for such revelation is Michael Martone's *The Blue Guide to Indiana*,[13] a work of American experimental fiction without claim, not just to empirical universality, but even to popularity. I choose it, in part, because even a superficial description of its contents raises questions about my calling it a novel, questions similar to those raised by Cavell's calling a canvas with a few chevrons on it a painting. *The Blue Guide to Indiana* is a book-length fiction composed to resemble, both in appearance and content, a publication in the Blue Guides international travel guide series. It begins with a section of practical information for travelers and then follows with proposed tours ("The death tour," "The sports tour"), sites of interest ("Eli Lilly Land"), and discussions of cuisine, roads, local history, and art. Among the featured attractions are the Trans-Indiana Mayonnaise Pipeline, the Hoosier Infidelity Resort Area, and the World's First Parking Lot. The front matter includes an acknowledgment of newspapers in which sections of the guide previously appeared and a list of Martone's other books, including *Let's Go: Terre Haute* and *Gary on $5 a Day*, which cannot be located on Amazon.com, as well as *Pensees: The Thoughts of Dan Quayle*, which can.

The obvious objection to calling *The Blue Guide to Indiana* a novel is that it has no story. Although names appear, most are references to local history ("Elwood Haynes demonstrated, in a Kokomo test run, the first mechanically successful, self-propelled, clutch driven automobile…" (p. 47)), and few references are sufficiently developed for even minimal characterization. The work's closest approach to literary narrative is its one-page account of the 1919 founding of Indiana's "Littlest Little Italy" by Antonio Martone (pp. 69–70), but no further mention of the character is made. *The Blue Guide*'s narrator maintains the flat neutrality of a textual function throughout the text, never using the first person pronoun, even in the concluding "Author's note," despite frequent direct addresses to the reader ("Also be on the lookout for the colorful tungsten pickers" (p. 78)). Narration in the literal sense of recounting an action is restricted to descriptions of scenery and customs, brief summaries of past occurrences of local significance ("the Tincture Boom of 1869" (p. 28)), and miscellaneous practical advice.

Since so much we normally associate with literary fiction is absent, it is tempting to classify *The Blue Guide to Indiana* as a parody, making it parasitical of the travel-guide genre and eliminating altogether the question of its relationship to novels. There are, however, two problems with this accommodation. The first is that while parodies take as their target the object they mimic, nowhere does *The Blue Guide to Indiana* ridicule travel guides. On the contrary, the form of *The Blue Guide* appears inseparable from its content, and nowhere are its conventions treated as artificial. Its relation to the conventions of travel guides more closely resembles an OULIPO novelist's respect for his or her arbitrary constraint, the only difference being that Martone's form is not arbitrary. On the contrary, the conventions of the travel guide are its conditions of existence. That is, they do not inflect the work so much as comprise it. Although there can be no debate about whether or not *The Blue Guide* imitates a travel guide, mimicry seems its way of becoming what it is, not a distancing of itself from anything it simply ridicules as other.

The second, more serious problem is that narrative's absence is fully accounted for by *The Blue Guide* itself. Even before reading the table of contents, we encounter a "Warning" that relating what happens in Indiana to us could prove impossible. The guide's announced function is to mediate between the reader and "the local population" (p. 17), making the latter's world accessible. Because the time of *The Blue Guide*'s writing and the time of our reading are not the same (p. 9), however, the guide cannot predict when the attractions it describes will open for us. Superficially, the difficulty is that the state we are trying to enter is surrounded by walls, barricades, fences, moats (p. 27), and the times we can get inside are subject to "constant alterations and exceptions" (p. 9), but more fundamentally, "time has always been problematic here" (p. 19). Not only does Indiana not participate in Daylight Savings Times, having fought two civil wars over it (pp. 104–05), but the present is everywhere determined locally, both by the sun's zenith relative to each town and by a location's historical, economic, or geographical peculiarities. In the southern counties all official clocks are set to the time of Lincoln's assassination (p. 20), and in Bristol past events appear to anticipate future ones (pp. 31–32). The town of Rising Sun manufactures its own days (p. 30), and in New Harmony a belief in the multiplicity of times results in everyone's spending theirs keeping track of others' (p. 29). In short, time is not itself universal in *The Blue Guide*, posing a question of whether the historical events shaping our world—including those contemporaneous with *The Blue Guide*'s publication in September, 2001—have occurred here.

This emphasis on history's historical relativity seems to replicate a hackneyed postmodern critique of representation, a form of skepticism in which reality perpetually defers to its imitations, and it is true that in Martone's Indiana the present appears everywhere preoccupied with reenactments, replicas, and memorializations. In South Bend (p. 30) *The Philadelphia Story* replays every midnight, and in Fort Wayne (pp. 40–41) the American invention of baking powder is allegorically reenacted every spring. The danger posed by these repetitions seems, however, much more existential than epistemological. Martone often warns readers of a potential for "disorientation" (p. 31), especially in localities where "a visitor quickly senses an uncanny pattern of sameness to the days here" (p. 32), and he recalls the Sturgis affair, in which tourists passing through the state started driving in circles, "once their confidence as to their direction and the distance toward their destination gave out" (p. 52). The idea seems to be, not that one can never tell when and where one is, but that one easily forgets, especially in the rituals of trying to. This peril is allegorized in the amusement ride at Eli Lilly Land called "The Gelatin Capsule House of Horrors" (p. 73), a "highly detailed and thoroughly accurate recreation of the alimentary canal" in which the transparent container protecting the visitor gradually dissolves during the course of the ride: "You race against time and the prospect of untimely elimination." In other words, the danger is more distraction than misrepresentation, as if what seems hardest to keep in mind is simply our bodies, circumstances, lives. In *The Blue Guide*'s terminal sentence Martone recalls the hospital waiting room where in 1979 he learned of his mother's failed hysterectomy. "The television was on, of course, an RCA model made in Bloomington, Indiana, and Martone remembers how hard it was not to watch it while, in a strange way, he also felt he was watching himself listening to Dr. Burns rehearse the final few minutes of his, Martone's, mother's life" (p. 120).

If representation itself contributes to this alienation, how could a novel overcome it? That is, how could any literary fiction orient me, if the source of my disorientation, of my failure to acknowledge the present of my own historicizing, is just my continuous effort to tell when and where I am? In a sense the question is as old as novels, having been raised by *Don Quixote* and *Northanger Abbey*, if not by *The Odyssey*, but unlike these classics, Martone's guide does not raise it by narrating about narrating. That is, *The Blue Guide* lacks the self-consciousness typical of metafictions. If its literariness depends on its revealing what a novel is, then as Wittgenstein has said, we should expect this informational content to be hidden only by its simplicity and familiarity. I will call it the fact of Martone's book. Seeing this fact's connection to what my group calls a novel means seeing *The Blue Guide*, not as a fiction about Indiana, but as a fictional object, a Borgesean *hrönir*,[14] brought into material existence by our conceptions of it. In other words, Martone's *Blue Guide* is a real travel guide, but to an Indiana not at present accessible. This potential Indiana, which seems at times a caricature of one we may have visited, can be mapped. If or when its borders open, Martone's guide will guide readers there. We will find directions, places to stay, information about currency and tipping, and numerous illuminating anecdotes. In short, *The Blue Guide* lacks no feature necessary to a thing of its kind, and it cannot, or not very satisfyingly, be read as anything else. It is composed for tourists, for those away from home who need orienting. But if I read *The Blue Guide* in this way, or find myself tempted to, where does that mean I am now?

The difficulty of answering this question accounts for the disorientation I sometimes feel when holding *The Blue Guide to Indiana* in my hand. There is something inconceivable, not about its fictional subject, but about its reality as an object. I want to say that it and I simply cannot occupy the same space and time. Normally, literary fictions are distinguishable from books. We assume, for example, that a book's cover exists independently of its content, so that when two editions of *Middlemarch* look different, we do not consider them different novels. Likewise, the acknowledgments or copyright page or biographical note can be changed without our feeling that George Eliot's fiction is affected, and when textual scholars reconstruct her text from variants, they will differentiate features of *Middlemarch* as a book from features of the work. In this sense, a book seems merely one vehicle, platform, or material support for a novel, which itself might just as well exist on a Kindle, or as a film, or in the reader's memory. In *The Blue Guide to Indiana*, however, such distinctions make little sense. The cover, jacket blurbs, publisher's notice, dedication, acknowledgments, and other front matters are all internal to its literariness. Its fictionality suffuses the book, conflating matter as subject with matter as object, and transforming its support into its value and meaning. In other words, I experience Martone's *Blue Guide* as the materialization of my dream. I want to say that it feels nearer to me than other books, as though it could not be at all without my acknowledging something about myself, about my being located here now. If I could believe that, in the absence of its represented state, *The Blue Guide to Indiana* were representing itself, I could substitute a meaning for my fix, defer it indefinitely, but *The Blue Guide* manifestly does not represent itself; it *is* itself. I have no concept of it independent of it, no meaning apart from what's in my hand. It is difficult to say in what sense this *hrönir* is still a fiction.

To know where I am, it helps to stop comparing *The Blue Guide to Indiana* with fiction and compare it with fraud. In saying this, I am less interested in the lawsuit threatened by W. W. Norton and A&C Black, the publishers of Blue Guides at the time of Martone's book's appearance in 2001, than in the formal agreement by which that lawsuit was avoided. All books in the initial print run of *The Blue Guide to Indiana* bore a label reading:

NOTICE! *The Blue Guide to Indiana* is in no way affiliated with, endorsed by, or in association with the series of travel books titled *Blue Guide* … *The Blue Guide to Indiana* in no way factually depicts or accurately represents the State of Indiana … This is a work of fiction.

That the work of Martone's guide is revelation seems attested, not so much by this notice, as by the need for it. Unlike conventional disclaimers, *The Blue Guide*'s acknowledgment is not needed to prevent anyone's taking it for a representation of Indiana. On the contrary, it is needed to reinstate our confusion about novels, specifically, that our relation to them is our relation to the events, societies, and locales they represent. Absent this latter relation, *The Blue Guide to Indiana* no longer seems to be what it pretends, as though engaged in some kind of hoax or deception. That our relation to a novel could be a relation to a material object, something so familiar that its significance remains largely hidden, means that what Martone unrepresses, the fact of his book, lies right on the surface of consciousness. Although saying what a novel is can be meaningful only to those who can see for themselves, I think there are at least two ways of saying what Martone's novel reveals about novels.

The first is that novels are portable. Even when translated from their place of reference, novels travel with us, making reading and writing a never-ending work of acculturation, of alienated and recovered perspective. In other words, the guiding function of *The Blue Guide to Indiana* is not a historically contingent feature of it, or if so, then it is a feature so inseparable from our present historical circumstances that I could represent it as contingent only if my life underwent fundamental change. For the us we now are, its guiding function remains indistinguishable from the aesthetic itself, from Kant's discovery that art is how modern subjects orient themselves. And, second, *The Blue Guide to Indiana* reveals that novels exist independently of us, as independently as facts. The genuineness of *The Blue Guide to Indiana* does not depend on its likeness to our world. It depends on the presentness of our world, of that form of life to which novels are connected. The reason this world's passing can seem like a threat is that, for fraudulence to be overcome, I must *make* connection, where that means living in relation to the fact of Martone's book such that its materiality ceases to be a joke. The threat, experienced most palpably today in experimental writing, is that we might all *prefer* fakes.

Making art's connection to life perspicuous is what we call the aesthetic function. When Cavell calls these points of connection "touchstones of intimacy," he means that your and my location in time can be identical, our cultural context the same, and still my words strike you as meaningless. There are no metaphysical limits to what can be said, but there are practical limits. To see what connection I am trying to make, you must eventually see for yourself, and "if someone does not get it he is not in one's world, or not of one's flesh."

4 Cavell and Kant
The Work of Criticism and the Work of Art

Anthony J. Cascardi

"Why do precisely these objects which we behold make a world?"
Henry David Thoreau, *Walden*,
Ch. 12 ("Brute Neighbors"); epigraph to Cavell, WV

The raw ingredients from which Stanley Cavell began to assemble his singularly rich and influential intellectual career, with its deep soundings of the relations among literature, philosophy, film, psychoanalysis, and opera, to name just a few, might not on the face of things have seemed very promising. On the contrary, consider the kinds of examples that were matters of considerable concern among many English and American philosophers when Cavell came on the scene. These included phrases like "There is a goldfinch at the bottom of the garden"; "Canary wine is pleasant"; "Here are two hands" (G. E. Moore[1]); "Excalibur has a sharp blade";[2] "How do I know that the arrow ➔ points this way?" (PI 454); "Did you ever think of one thing?" (Hamm in *Endgame*). This seemed not merely an implausible beginning, but beginning from an impoverished language, and in turn from an impoverished imagination.

By Cavell's own account it was his encounter with J. L. Austin's work, particularly on excuses and more generally on speech-acts, that knocked him off his intellectual horse in the early years of his philosophical career, and I imagine that it was Austin's opening up of questions about the forces and effects associated with various types of utterances that gripped his imagination and in some regards never let go. After all, so much of what he went on to do involved an exploration of the questions of the *forces* embedded in language rather than of its routes of reference. Those questions from the start reached beyond an analytic interest in the categories of utterances and their more or less predictable effects (even to the point of defending Austin against misinterpretations of him as a mere taxonomist) so as to embrace the far more nuanced and sometimes unchartable terrain of the speaker's relationship to his or her own words, or to language as such. Indeed, it was precisely this dimension of Austin's work that Cavell sought to draw out in his early essay "Austin at criticism." I quote a passage of that essay that seems to encapsulate some of these issues especially well:

> In proceeding from ordinary language, so far as that is philosophically pertinent, one is in a frame of mind in which it seems (1) that one can as appropriately or truly be said to be looking at the world as looking at language [and] 2) that one is seeking necessary truths "about" the world (or "about") language, and therefore cannot be satisfied with anything I, at least, would recognize as a description of how people in fact talk, and ... (3) that one is not finally interested *at all* in how "other" people talk, but in determining where and why one wishes, or hesitates, to use a particular expression oneself.[3]

I note that Cavell entitled this essay "Austin at *criticism*" and not, for instance, "Austin at *philosophy*." That detail in turn influenced my own intuition that Cavell's interests pointed in the direction of a philosophical work that would have to realize itself as a form of criticism—hardly a form of criticism *opposed* to philosophy, but rather as a kind of criticism that is an *expression* of philosophy—the realization of some possibility that philosophy seemed continuously to be promising and yet missing. To put this in the language of Cavell's early essays, at least through *The Claim of Reason* and indeed beyond, criticism is a way of engaging those things that philosophy—whether as epistemology or as metaphysics— had learned to avoid.

One must understand that "philosophy" in this context meant largely *modern* philosophy, whose anchor points lay in Descartes and Kant, and which had devoted its major efforts to the project of epistemology—i.e. to the defeat of skepticism by fortifying the foundations of knowledge. But in order to flesh out the importance of this understanding of *criticism* in relation to modern philosophy—hence in relation to the culture of Western modernity writ large—and thereby to inform our assessment of its possibilities at a time when we can look back with a critical eye towards modernity and modernism both, two allied factors need to be entered into the accounts. The first is the challenge posed by Wittgenstein's *Philosophical Investigations*, which some thinkers took as just another version of ordinary-language philosophy, but which, as demonstrated by Wittgenstein's preoccupation with signs, numbers, counting, and games, clearly wasn't just that, and whose inconclusiveness left ample room to wonder whether Wittgenstein was in fact sharing in the modern foundational philosophical project or undoing it. Needless to say, without Wittgenstein, Cavell's career might well have traveled along very different routes toward its destinations. One of the sources of the importance of the *Investigations* for Cavell—if one could attempt to say such a thing briefly at all—was methodological. From the very first paragraph on Augustine, the *Investigations* recognized that with respect to language and world one was always *in medias res* and without recourse to any beginning that we might ourselves initiate. Wittgenstein offered what seemed to be an informal set of philosophical procedures that, like Austin's work, stood at an oblique angle toward philosophy's "foundational" questions. The places where Wittgenstein was closest to Austin were just the places where the question of anyone's relationship to their particular, personal words (and to their meaning) could be brought into relief in relation to those words spoken impersonally within various language practices or "games," which nonetheless provide the condition of possibility of any words having any meaning at all.

The second factor that shaped Cavell's turn to criticism was his turn to contexts in which the language in question was extra-ordinary and embedded in complex works of art: in Shakespeare's or Beckett's plays, for example, and spoken by Hamm and Clov, Othello, Desdemona, Cordelia, Lear, the Fool, and other characters. The investigation of such literary words, themselves arguably *extra*ordinary, and the significance one might attribute to them, demanded an account of matters that neither ordinary language philosophy, nor Austin's speech-act theory, and not even Wittgenstein's later work, could readily provide. What drew Cavell was not the familiar question of the difference between literary language and ordinary speech but the relationship between works of art and whatever we might construe as "the world," and this as a means of exploring the various forms that our relationship to the world might take. His effort in response to the New Criticism in reading *King Lear*, for instance, was to bring the characters of the play and their words back together so that we could once again see their dilemmas of denial and avoidance, acknowledgment and refusal, as making claims on us. His engagement with such questions was not limited to literature in the narrow sense or to instances that might be regarded as "great works." At stake were a series of overarching questions about aesthetics. For Cavell, the question of how and why works of art could matter to anyone was equally resonant for the movies, in which the most common examples are as significant as the extraordinary cases. Indeed, something Cavell says in the course of *The World Viewed* is especially relevant to his development of some of the questions of aesthetics raised earlier in *Must We Mean What We Say?* One of the characteristics of the movies, attributable to their particular medium, he argued, is that they give us the *world viewed*, and not just *world views*. To recognize this requires resisting the common idea—common in many circles of criticism, at least—that a work comes from, or emerges out of, a world. To be sure, the movies reveal something unique about one's relationship to the world, something not revealed by paintings or plays. In movies, Cavell, says, our relationship to the world is *screened* ("What does the silver screen screen? It screens me from the world it holds," (WV 24)). But the larger point is that *any* work of art can show something particular about our relationship to the world.

As a way of following up some of what Cavell suggests about the relationship between work and world, I wish to explore the idea that a work, whether in the medium of words or in pictures or in sound, *(re) makes a world as a semblance*, makes *the semblance of a world*. Just how and why it is that any particular arrangement of words (or images) may go to make what seems to be a world will hardly be an unfamiliar question insofar as Cavell re-asked Thoreau's version of this question as the epigraph to WV cited above. And why, as he asked in the essays on romanticism (IQO), do they make a world that seems to be made *for us*? In order to say how, I will follow some of the leads that Cavell gives back to the two parts of Kant's third *Critique*—the "Critique of aesthetic judgement" and to the less-often read "Critique of teleological judgement." I do so in acknowledgment of the importance in MWM of various arts and of aesthetics generally: of music (specifically, in "Music discomposed"), of literature, and of drama (in the memorable essays "Ending the waiting game" and "The avoidance of love," on Beckett and Shakespeare, respectively), and of aesthetic theory (in "A matter of meaning it" and "Aesthetic problems of modern philosophy"). I am not the first to remark that the task of philosophy, as Cavell understood it, bore a surprising resemblance to the work of aesthetic reflective judgment in Kant's aesthetics. (Stephen Mulhall's 1994 book does an excellent job of exploring some of these connections.[4]) While the front-line philosophical engagements of MWM were with Austin and Wittgenstein, it would be almost impossible to draw out the importance of Cavell's particular angle of inflection vis-à-vis their work without some account of his encounter with Kant's third *Critique*, principally in the essay "Aesthetic problems of modern philosophy." It was surprising for Cavell to have placed Kant in relation to ordinary language philosophy for at least two reasons. First, the invocation of Kant in aesthetics at that moment implied things quite different from what Cavell had in mind: it implied a focus on aesthetic pleasure as "pure"; it suggested the banishment of everything that was inner-worldly, cultural, contingent, and material about art; and it suggested the association of art with a formalism that seemed to repudiate the very sensuousness and particularity that marked aesthetic judgments as distinct from other kinds of claims in the first place. Second, it seemed that the aims of ordinary language philosophy, particularly in its British version, lay in finding alternate routes toward certainties about fundamentally empirical matters—or, perhaps better put, in finding through non-technical methods a better way of satisfying the same desire for certainty that empiricism had pursued over the long course of its love–hate affair with rationalism and skepticism. Ordinary language philosophy offered a new and more pragmatic approach to such questions; its frame of reference and its evidentiary resources were one with its procedures in appealing to what "we" ordinarily say. As such, it often bore a heavily normativizing force, frequently closing off the question of just what sort of community this "we" was, how it was constructed, and what "my" relation to it might imply.

But Cavell could clearly see that Wittgenstein and Austin were after something else, something that was neither empiricist nor rationalist at heart. What they were after was never explicitly identified as "aesthetic," although my own sense, heavily influenced by Cavell's early essays, was that the field of their activity lay in a philosophical version of what we then called, and may still wish to call, "criticism." The work of criticism, I would suggest, recalls one way of enacting the broadest task that Kant ascribed to aesthetic reflective judgment, not just, as is often said, by offering insight into the constructedness of communities of judgment, or by demonstrating the limits of epistemic reasons when it comes to matters aesthetic, but by attempting to bridge the two domains of what Kant called "experience": the one which pertains to nature, and the other which pertains to human freedom. What does this imply for our notion of works of art as the domain over which aesthetic judgment is characteristically exercised? The issue is how we stand with respect to the possibility of capturing something that is lost in the division of experience into the domains of cognition and morality, namely the sense of experience as a whole.

One place to anchor this line of thought is in an explicit reference to Kant's theory of aesthetic judgment in "Aesthetic problems": "aesthetic judgment models the sort of claim entered by these [ordinary language] philosophers … the familiar lack of conclusiveness in aesthetic argument, rather than showing up as irrationality, shows the kind of rationality it has, and needs" (MWM 86). But what specifically is this form of rationality, and where does it abide? One of the gambits of Cavell's work was to proceed as if the words spoken by characters in literary works could and ought to be interrogated as if they were ordinary utterances; the expectation brought to both is that they are, or ought to be taken as, fully and completely *meant* (MWM 78–79). But this procedure also amounted to a defamiliarizing of literary texts by opening them to a set of philosophical questions that most literary critics at the time had learned to shun. The effect of Cavell's early essays about *King Lear* and Beckett, and later on about film, was to bring us near to questions of avoidance, shame, recognition, the failures of acknowledgment, and the like, because the characters in Shakespeare's plays, or in the movies, were deeply enmeshed in them. To see these characters so enmeshed implied a larger aesthetic theory, indeed an aesthetic theory about the nature of works of art, that was broader than the ideas about ordinary language philosophy articulated in MWM. Among other things, that aesthetic theory had to develop a robust sense of criticism as the *practice* that Kant's theory of aesthetic judgment was calling for.

How so? Without yet turning to a detailed engagement with the two parts of the *Critique of Judgement*, the beginning of an answer lies in the passage where Kant speaks of the claims that aesthetic judgments make, with particular regard to our demands of others, as universal demands. Kant proposes the following:

> The judgment of taste exacts agreement from everyone; and a person who describes something as beautiful insists that every one *ought* to give the object in question his approval and follow suit in describing it as beautiful … We are suitors for agreement from every one else [*Man wirbt um jedes andern Bestimmung*], because we are fortified with a ground common to all [*weil man dazu einen Grund hat, der allen gemein ist*].[5]

Cavell says that "Kant's 'universal voice' is, with perhaps a shift of accent, what we hear recorded in the philosopher's claim about what we say" (MWM 94). This solidifies the relationship between the methods of ordinary language philosophy and the kinds of judgments Kant labeled "aesthetic" and "reflective," but it leaves wide open the question of how and why this relationship may exist. Kant was clear to distinguish between aesthetic reflective judgments and "determinant" (also "subsumptive") judgments—to distinguish, that is, between claims in which one has to seek out universal categories beginning only with the particular, and the more familiar instances of cognition in which a general concept is available in advance of any particular instance. The claim "X is beautiful" only appears to be of the same form as "X is red." Indeed, Kant insists that in the former case we get no knowledge of a *thing* at all.

But what then does it mean to assimilate the procedures of ordinary language philosophy *überhaupt*, or of Wittgenstein's *Philosophical Investigations*, to those of aesthetic reflective judgments? Does it mean that *all* knowledge claims are essentially aesthetic judgments, subjective and reflective in the basis of their universality? The Wittgensteinian notion of seeing something "under an aspect" might well appear to make knowing *anything* dependent upon something like judgment; I will point below to instances in Kant's aesthetics that would seem to lend support to this same idea. Likewise, the appeal to what "we" ordinarily say in Cavell's interpretation seems to align itself with the solicitation of agreement in the first half of Kant's third *Critique*. But isn't there an important difference between an effort to probe the meaning of words by inquiring about "what *we* say when," and an effort to probe words spoken by, say, Lear?[6] Isn't there a difference between "ordinary" utterances and the more complex structures of discourse we find in works of literature, in film, in opera, and the other arts? And isn't that difference part of the very reason we appeal to such texts rather than to what *we* "ordinarily" say?

In response to the question of whether the literary work is ordinary or extraordinary in relation to "ordinary language" I want to answer both yes and no—that to deny the difference between them would be sheer madness, but that to insist upon it categorically would be to deny something we know deeply to be true, but may need help articulating: that the words literary characters are given to speak, and the works in which their speech is given to them to be spoken, do indeed have philosophical relevance for us as (ordinary) subjects. The wonder of the critic in the face of an extraordinary work lies in finding there something that may go unnoticed in ordinary language, namely "that just these orders of words can have been found, that these things can be said at all" (PDAT 36). Indeed, only a part of that relevance can be understood by aligning literary texts with the *thematic* set of questions, of which Cavell gives a nonetheless remarkable formulation as the vocation of philosophy in the "The Thought of Movies."

> I understand [philosophy] as a willingness to think not about something other than what ordinary human beings think about, but rather to learn to think undistractedly about things that ordinary human beings cannot help thinking about, or anyway cannot help having occur to them, sometimes in fantasy, sometimes as a flash across a landscape; such things, for example, as whether we can know the world as it is in itself, or whether others really know the nature of one's own experiences, or whether good and bad are

relative ... Such thoughts are instances of that characteristic human willingness to allow questions for itself which it cannot answer with satisfaction.[7]

The clear echo of the first paragraph of Kant's first *Critique* in this passage also points to a difference: to the fact that Cavell has consistently been interested in finding ways to give these questions their widest possible range, and even to marvel at their unanswerability, or interminability, rather than, as in Kant, in shoring up the abilities of reason by marking its boundaries. One account of this difference, which points in the direction of a theory of the artwork, would say that works of art are the very places where the practice of posing questions in the absence of answers is at once opened up to endless possibility and afforded some containment. Cavell approaches this issue in *The Senses of Walden* when he writes that "Human forms of feeling, objects of human attraction, our reactions constituted in art, are as universal and objective, as revelatory of the world, as the forms of the laws of physics" (SW 104).

But what exactly is left out of the standard philosophical account of the kinds of things ordinary human beings cannot sometimes help thinking about, and what can be gleaned from the fact that their unanswerability is given particular shape in literary and related works of art? Why indeed is it that apparently interminable questions can be satisfactorily and satisfyingly pursued through artworks, and why does that attach to their status as *works*? How do such works stand in relation to the world, and how do they stand in relation to us and to our relation to the world? It seems right but not enough to say that artworks raise unanswerable questions or, as Cavell suggests for Kant, that "apart from a certain spirit in which we make judgments we could have no concepts of the sort we think of as aesthetic" (MWM 89). This is true enough, as far as it goes. But it fails to recognize why Kant himself was interested in the question of aesthetic judgment, and fails likewise to explain why we might privilege artworks as the place where those judgments could best be exercised. That these are not *obviously* related matters may be suggested by the fact that Kant initially takes up the question of aesthetic judgment in relation to a field that does not distinguish between nature and art. Claims of taste matter "in those estimates that are called aesthetic, and which relate to the beautiful and the sublime, *whether of nature or of art*" (CJ Preface, p. 5, italics mine). Here, perhaps, is the place to turn to Kant and to make more explicit the basis of his interest in aesthetics, hoping also to draw out the implications for the work of art that are latent in Cavell's engagement with the work of criticism.

Kant's interest in aesthetic reflective judgment, and I am suggesting ours as well, tracks his interest in preserving something like the quality of experience as a whole at the very time when it seemed necessary to divide experience into separate domains, so as to sustain the difference between cognition and morality. That division can be marked as *modern* on the historical level. The so-called "separation of the value-spheres" in the modern age corresponds roughly to the separation of the world of "is" (as governed by science) from the world of "ought" (as governed by law, religion, and politics). The division of Kant's first two *Critiques* tracks this historical unfolding with substantial accuracy. The first, which is a critique of pure reason, addresses itself to the realm of "nature" as it gives itself to the understanding; its aim is to outline, among other things, the conditions for any *possible* experience. It gives us a picture of the human as it stands in relation to necessity, which is the principle, not to say the force, by which nature is determined according to laws. The second *Critique* gives us a picture of the human as it stands in relation to a realm quite distinct from nature—the realm of freedom. There is lawfulness here as well, but it is of a very different sort. Here, in the realm of freedom, lawfulness comes from the human ability to say categorically what *ought* to be done in view of the fact that human beings have the freedom to act as they wish.

It would be tedious to rehearse the importance of the difference between these two realms for Kant. Suffice it to say that he *insists* upon it, as for instance where he reminds us that "the concept of freedom just as little disturbs the legislation of nature as the concept of nature influences legislation through the concept of freedom" (CJ Introduction, p. 13). And yet, at the beginning of the third *Critique*, Kant also insists that to believe entirely in this distinction—and to believe that we cannot somehow construct a bridge between the two domains of experience—is equally mistaken. Experience must also be thought of as a whole. Understanding and reason have "jurisdiction" over one and the same territory (CJ Introduction, p. 13). The domain of the aesthetic, I would suggest, is the place where this problematic is disclosed as the experience of the human, both in its wholeness and in its contingency. The unity of experience itself, and the possibility of the human itself, is placed at risk if we think about human beings in relation to only one of the domains outlined by the first two *Critiques*, or as divisible along these lines without remainder. The question is how to imagine putting back in relation to one another the parts of experience that being human seems to requires us to hold apart. As human beings we are indeed divided creatures, and yet as humans we also strive to overcome the particular divisions that mark us.

Aesthetic judgment is called upon to perform the work of bridging these divisions. For Kant this means showing that it is possible to begin from the *this*, from the "free particular" that makes an incursion into cognition in the form of pleasure or un-pleasure, and to move from there to call for general agreement about what is beautiful or sublime, to assert what everyone *ought* to say about just this particular instance. In relation to representations of things that are in one respect no different from others within the field of cognition—a pattern of leaves, say, or the image of a field of flowers, or a structure of sounds and rhythm that we call a symphony—to have feelings and to make claims that have the force of an *ought*. To be able to do so, and to feel ourselves *compelled* to do so, is, for Kant, evidence of the fact that we are not merely creatures of nature who approach the world cognitively, or beings who enjoy freedoms and construct obligations for ourselves not dictated by nature's necessities, but are citizens of both worlds—citizens, better put, of one world, which we tend to think of as cleaved into two separate halves. Cavell's version of this problem is stated in a not altogether parenthetical passage on Emerson in *The Senses of Walden*: " 'The first class [materialists] founding on experience, the second [idealists] on consciousness; the first class beginning to think from the data of the senses, the second class perceive that the senses are not final, and say, The senses give us representations of things, but what are the things themselves, they cannot tell … [The idealist] concedes all that the other affirms, admits the impressions of sense, admits their coherency, their use and beauty, and then asks the materialist for his grounds of assurance that things are as his senses represent them. But I, he says, affirm facts not affected by the illusions of sense.' "[8] That we are drawn to make aesthetic judgments at all proves the inadequacy of the division of experience along the very lines that Kant insists upon in the first two *Critiques*; that we feel *compelled* to make such judgments testifies to a desire to recover the unity of experience—testifies, that is, to some of the very things that would be left out when human beings are conceived as strictly natural or as strictly moral beings.[9]

Whether this unity can in fact be recalled or recaptured, and if so how, constitutes one of the pivot points between romanticism and modernism. The modernist inflection of the desire for the wholeness of human experience uncovers the contingency of experience, a contingency that is located in the precarious enterprise of making aesthetic judgments and that extends to the objects of which those judgments are characteristically predicated, i.e. to works of art.[10] That aesthetics lies in the domain of the contingent is implicit in Kant's third *Critique*, though often suppressed, including sometimes by Kant himself, who remained desirous of a more rigorous derivation of the transcendental basis of taste than he was able to provide (CJ Preface, pp. 6–7). The "contingency" reflects the fact that the universality of agreement depends upon the construction of a community, hence risks the possibility that it may also fail. "The *ought* in aesthetic judgments … is only pronounced conditionally" (CJ §19, p. 82). As Stephen Mulhall put it in his book on Cavell,

> the possibility that we may find limits to that community is the price to be paid for the possibility of creating that community without sacrificing subjectivity. The fact that such a community of response and thought is not guaranteed shows something about the sort of community it is—one in which membership is freely willed, elicited rather than compelled from each individual. If this sort of community can result only from abandoning the guarantee of agreement, then it is hardly surprising that we sometimes choose abandonment; and with such a vision to prompt us, the risks involved in attempting to achieve it (humility, rebuff, the discovery of isolation) may seem well worth running.
>
> (*Stanley Cavell*, p. 29)

Criticism works in part, I have suggested following Kant, as a way to disclose and to articulate, to test and to sustain, the contingency of the human that subtends the unity of experience, which in Kant's language takes the form of (aesthetic) "common sense" (CJ § 20). What needs further acknowledgment is the fact that criticism addresses itself to *works*, and in the case of *works of art* that the logic of criticism reflects the place of feeling in the whole of experience. Wittgenstein's philosophy can be aligned with this project by recognizing the ways in which he sounds out the measure of sense or non-sense, of familiarity or strangeness, in what language tells us about the world we fashion in what we say and mean. There is a sensuousness in this sounding, an intelligent sensing, that retains something of the sensuousness that keeps human nature tethered to nature.[11] This sensuousness is precisely what cognitive and moral judgments do not have a complete way of accounting for, even while it is something they cannot entirely disown.

Here Wittgenstein's work resonates with Kant's commitment to the unity of experience in the third *Critique*. That Kant does not wish to think of the domain of aesthetic judgment as separate and distinct from understanding and reason, but rather as the arena in which nature and freedom might enter into dialogue with one another, may be gleaned from the fact he also postulates a moment of pleasure, albeit mostly forgotten or largely suppressed, that once characterized the human response to the unity of laws in nature. His speculation seems to be that the pleasure we take in beauty preserves a trace of some lost, archaic form of pleasure that we once took in the apprehension of something that was itself always beyond us, namely, the unity of nature as a whole:

> we do not, and cannot, find in ourselves the slightest effect on the feeling of pleasure from the coincidence of perceptions with the laws in accordance with the universal concepts of nature (the Categories) … But, while this is so, the discovery … that two or more empirical heterogeneous laws of nature are allied under one principle that embraces them both, is the ground of a very appreciable pleasure, often even of admiration, and such, too, as does not wear off even though we are already familiar with its object. It is true that we no longer notice any decided pleasure in the comprehensibility of nature, or in the unity of its divisions into general and species, without which the empirical concepts, that afford us our knowledge of nature in its particular ways, would not be possible. Still it is certain that the pleasure appeared in its due course, and only by reason of the most ordinary experience being impossible without it, has it become gradually fused with simple cognition, and no longer arrests particular attention.
>
> (CJ Introduction, pp. 27–28)

The unity of nature—the disclosure of nature *as a whole*—is something that we have no ability to experience directly. It is a source of pleasure when we do glimpse it, but for Kant that unity must itself be "presupposed and assumed … as otherwise we should not have a thoroughgoing connexion of empirical cognition in a whole of experience" (CJ Introduction, p. 23). The fact that we take, or once took, pleasure in the unity of nature, stands alongside the issue that is the principal concern of the second half of the *Critique of Judgement*—the *finality* of nature.[12] The task here is to discern whether nature may have a subjective finality, given the fact—which Kant readily accepts—that it has no objective finality. The question offers two ways of sorting nature in its relation to us (and our relation to it). In what might be called the Enlightenment account, nature is and ought to be defined as something wholly independent of human consciousness; the price of that independence, however, is the loss of any sense of the finality of nature whatsoever, whether objective or subjective. I understand this loss as one of the more powerful sources of what is sometimes called the "disenchantment" of the world, a consequence of which Heidegger called the transformation of the world into a picture.[13] In Cavell's writing, it derives from twin roots: as a consequence of skepticism, epitomized in Descartes' *Meditations*, and with particular importance for the development of romanticism, in the sense of world-loss that accompanied the Kantian "settlement" of the question about our ability to know things as they are in themselves. ("Thanks for nothing," IQO 53). On the romantic account, nature appears as an alienated part of human subjectivity, and we of it, such that the task ahead would be to place these alienated portions in relation to one another again. The desire to do so virtually follows from a passage from Coleridge's *Biographia Literaria* that Cavell cites in his essay "Emerson, Coleridge, Kant" in *The Senses of Walden*:

> all these Theses [the ones Coleridge has been outlining] refer solely to one of the two Polar Sciences, namely to that which commences with, and rigorously confines itself within, the subjective, leaving the objective (as far as it is exclusively objective) to natural philosophy, which is its opposite pole … The result of both the sciences, or their equatorial point, would be the principle of a total and undivided philosophy."[14]

As Richard Eldridge explains in *The Persistence of Romanticism*, we require the resources of poetry in pursuing this task.[15] For Kant, the form of aesthetic agency that might create a bridge between nature and freedom is the genius; the genius works free from conventional rules, hence appears to be a form of human agency acting with the force of nature;[16] in part for this reason, art must appear like nature (CJ § 45).

Kant's effort to discern the *subjective finality* of nature in the second half of the "Critique of Judgement" (CJII 3–5) proceeds toward this same end, albeit along more technical routes. His argument depends, first, on a clear distinction between subjective and objective finality. Kant gives the example of a bird to demonstrate that nature has no objective finality; it just happens that by the hollow formation of its bones, by the position of its wings, and by the nature of its tail, a bird is suited for flying; but nature might have fashioned itself in a thousand other ways to achieve this end (CJII 4). (One might offer a related characterization of artworks, each one of which could of course have been made a thousand different ways, or not at all—though in the case of artworks we are also driven to say of each one in its particularity that it must *absolutely* have been made the very way it was: artworks ask us to treat them as concrete universals.[17]) As regards nature, it is what Kant calls "subjective finality" that we can and ought to recover; and part of what I wish to suggest is that the "Romantic" hope for art turns on just this, a sense that nature may be *for us*, that it answers us with an acknowledgment of our ends:

> we do not need to look beyond the critical explanation of the pos-
> sibility of knowledge to find ample reason for assuming a subjec-
> tive finality on the part of nature in its particular laws. This is a
> finality relative to comprehensibility ... We may further anticipate
> the possible existence of some among the many products of nature
> that, as if put there with quite a special regard to our judgment, are
> of a form particularly adapted to that faculty."
>
> (CJII 3).[18]

Though some of this is not in Cavell, much of it is intimated and echoed in essays that comprise the book on skepticism and romanticism (IQO) and in a passage from SW, which I quote here: " 'The universe constantly and obediently answers to our conceptions' " (SW 97). In its compact-ness, this sentence asks us to think about the relationship between Kant's first *Critique* and the second part of the third.

The questions regarding subjective finality are not only whether and why, but how, and in what form this may be found—recognizing that the response cannot be in nature itself, not even for Thoreau. (As Cavell is quick to point out, *Walden* is first and foremost about a book, about its own writing and reading (SW xiii).) For Kant the answers lie in happi-ness and culture and, in the case of culture, in what I would describe as "works," or what Kant calls "organized products" (CJII 22–23).[19] Kant points out that individual happiness is not a final end of creation, and "not even an end of nature as regards man in preference to other crea-tures" (CJII 100, n.) It is nothing that any one of us is guaranteed; it is a *conditional* end insofar as it is only as a *moral* being that we humans can be regarded as the final end of creation. The pursuit of happiness must, moreover, be pursued through culture, which Kant glosses as "the pro-duction in a rational being of an aptitude for any ends whatever of his own choosing, consequently of the aptitude of a being in his freedom" (CJII 94). "It is only *culture* that can be the ultimate end which we have cause to attribute to nature in respect of the human race. His *individual* happiness on earth, and, we may say, the mere fact that he is the chief instrument for instituting order and harmony in irrational external nature, are ruled out" (CJII 94–95; italics mine).

But there are wrinkles even within the framework of the conditions that Kant places around happiness and culture, and these alone ought to alert us to the fact that the ways in which Kant might be said to posit a "romantic" response to the disenchantment of the world are already pregnant with the possibilities of modernism in criticism and the arts. First and foremost, art is not nature, and by Kant's own account needs constraints that come from its materials and its mechanisms. Art needs a material body if it is to be capable of eliciting sensuous responses of pleasure and pain, but this body is also *not a natural body*. By the same token, art cannot evaporate into the realm of pure freedom (see CJ § 43). What is realized in the work of art is not nature, nor experience as a whole, but the *semblance* of a world and the *semblance* of experience as a whole. (Kant uses the term "analogue" to describe what "semblance" covers here; in a remarkable formulation, he calls *nature* the analogue of *art* (CJII 23).) At its most self-conscious moments, modernist art and the criticism it calls for are supremely aware of these facts. Modernism works in light of and against the temptation of the whole, in light of and against attempts to assign art the task of realigning nature and happiness—recognizing that such a task could never be accomplished by the sheer force of wishing, or of saying. It seems to be modernism's aim to suggest that art involves *work*, and sometimes the emphatically *contrary work*, of resisting facile promises of happiness produced by facile forms of culture. The corresponding task of criticism is to meet these challenges. Its work is not simply to draw out the ways in which words in works of art ought to respond to the demand that they be thoroughly *meant*, but also to draw attention to the fact that they need not necessarily mean *anything*, because *meaning* is not a necessity of nature at all, however much it is an inescapable promise of human experience and possibly of happiness as well.

5   Cavell and Wittgenstein on Morality
The Limits of Acknowledgment
Charles Altieri

We answer by *consents or non-consents* and not by words.
> (William James, *Psychology: The Briefer Course*)

The fact that life is problematic shows that the shape of your life does not fit into life's mould. So you must change the way you live and, once your life does fit into the mould, what is problematic will disappear.
> (Wittgenstein, *Culture and Value*)

Understanding oneself properly is difficult, because an action to which one might be prompted by good generous motives is something one also may be doing out of cowardice or indifference. ... And only if I were able to submerge myself in religion could these doubts be stilled. Because only religion would have the power to destroy vanity and penetrate all the nooks and crannies.
> (*Culture and Value*)

Imagine Wittgenstein coming upon this passage from *The Claim of Reason*:

In philosophizing, I have to bring my own language and life into imagination. What I require is a convening of my culture's criteria, in order to confront them and my words and life as I pursue them with the life my culture's words may imagine for me; to confront the culture with itself, along the lines in which it meets in me. ... This seems to me a task that warrants the name of philosophy.
> (CR 125)

My projected Wittgenstein would have to admire the originality and the power of the arguments that ground the quoted passage. Moral behavior takes on rationality not from following deontological principles but from "following the methods which lead to a knowledge of our own position, of where we stand; in short to a knowledge and definition of ourselves" (CR 312). Only then do we honor the knowledge at the core of "acknowledgment." The primal scene is mutual exposure where we have only our limited grasp of ourselves to offer to others, and with which to attract possible responses from the other. Exposure in turn brings out the possibility of therapeutic efforts to know the self better, which also entails knowing the other better, which entails also knowing both parties' limitations. In other words, Cavell extends the figure of the couple basic to his work on remarriage comedies to provide an emblem both of our need for mutual exposure and of a path for the kind of dialectic that can sustain hope the remarriage will not repeat the failures of the first. In offering what Cavell calls "elaboratives" (CR 324) of one's own effort to confront the conventional aspects of the culture, one acknowledges one's limitations, offers to others what one can make of those limitations, recognizes dealing with these limitations as the development of self-knowledge, and realizes that the task is difficult because one must come to terms with a typically internalized and self-defensive skepticism about what we might share with those other minds.[1]

Yet one can grant Cavell's brilliance and still be bothered by how deeply American Cavell is in his setting the "I" over against society so that it can represent possibilities for coming to own a self who resists conformity in order to enter what we might call a dialectic of mutual exposure. My Wittgenstein would even agree with Cavell that one fundamental challenge for philosophy is to explore the degree to which it can "become literature and still know itself" (CR 496). But I doubt Wittgenstein would think that the way for philosophy still to know itself is for it to turn to confronting the culture with itself along the lines in which it meets in the philosopher. Wittgenstein would probably point out that if there are to be public moral judgments one cannot remain suspicious of the criteria making such judgments intelligible. That is, moral theory, if it is to exist at all, must have a kind of independence from the vicissitudes of self-figuration on the part of any individual subject. And, more important, I think the author of *Philosophical Investigations* and *On Certainty* would be wary of the entire effort to establish a coherent moral position in philosophy capable of judgments about good and bad character. Only individuals can make those judgments about themselves, and the appropriate theater would have more to do with religious confession than moral assessment according to principles or according to any kind of public dramatic standard like the quality of the agent's capacities to take in the complexity of moral situations.

That Wittgenstein would not agree with Cavell does not make Cavell "wrong." It would also be odd to call someone who has written so many compelling dramatic analyses of the values at stake in particular situations "wrong" about the terms of his judgments. But by Wittgensteinian standards Cavell may be overreaching in treating these analyses as contributions *to moral philosophy* (rather than contributions to states of fundamentally aesthetic awareness that should trouble efforts to involve the language of morality, with its inevitable pressure to attribute or deny authority to certain positions). Therefore Cavell's ambitions provide an ideal contrast for recovering the possible positive force of Wittgenstein's decision to have virtually nothing to say about ethics in his published philosophical work after his "Lecture on ethics" in 1930. Many philosophers and literary theorists now dismiss Wittgenstein's claims about ethics in the *Tractatus*[2] as part of his strange transcendental positivism outgrown in the later philosophy. Then they can use this later philosophy to show how moral values and moral feelings can be embedded within our linguistic practices.[3] But there is very little attention paid to the surprising fact that Wittgenstein himself did not make those extensions, perhaps because he thought ethics had to include not just a measure of awareness but also a discipline of the will that could not come from philosophy's commitments to objectivity. If we take this possibility seriously, it becomes crucial not to give the impression that the social structure of language games can encompass the intricacy and interiority of how one determines the happiness or unhappiness that comes to constitute psychological life.

Instead I will argue that Cavell brings out by contrast the force of Wittgenstein's life-long Tractarian distinction between explanation and display, a distinction wary of any effort to reconcile ethical decision-making with justification by philosophical explanation.[4] This figure of display invokes strong affinities between Wittgenstein's image of logic in his *Tractatus* and his continued refusal to develop any explicit discourse about an interpersonal ethics. There seems to Wittgenstein no compelling reason to accept the giving of reasons as an adequate model for his deeply personal sense of the ethical because the giving of reasons presumes that what is private to the self can take discursive public form, if only in the form of explanations. Giving of reasons about actions is a distinct language game involving self-justification, but that game may not give us access to the actual investments that shape behavior. If "A man can see what he has but not what he is" (CV 49), then there have to be alternatives to the ideal of ethical self-knowledge stateable in discursive terms. One must project possibilities of making visible one's values by performance or by modes of attunement that are not dependent on explanatory ideas. Who a person "is" has to be displayed by "confession" or by style. (The reasons matter, but as what is displayed of an action rather than as what points beyond the self to something like rationality—either as deontological or as offering rationales for personal interests.) And this contrast may make aspects of Wittgenstein's ascetic stance more available for fleshing out what values a person might embrace even while remaining suspicious about the ability of discursive "ethics" to shape their approaches toward social experience. So this essay will be indirectly an attempt to show why the arts are valuable precisely because they resist discursive ethics. In Shakespeare's final two plays, the most important resolutions of the action occur in an embrace and in an epilogue's request for applause—both conditions that discursive language or claims about knowledge have to oversimplify and carve into units that then rest uneasily with one another.

In order to carry out this contrast I have to begin with two caveats. I am not sure that I can replicate Cavell's thinking at its most sophisticated, so I have to settle for its most general level of assertion. I take this level to consist of his commitment to the philosophical task of being "true to oneself" (CW 11) and to making the working out of this quest a representative means of leading "the soul, imprisoned and distorted by confusion and darkness, into the freedom of the day" (CW 4). "Morally significant" here means establishing possible answers or at least attitudes responsive to the basic traditional questions of philosophy about "what kind of persons" *we* should "aspire to be" (CW 11). Second, I want to be clear that I am not so much criticizing Cavell as marking some of the limits of his very powerful and useful vision of how values are created by human efforts at mutual acknowledgment. It is obvious that in many particular cases Cavell's perspective gives brilliant illumination to works of art and to our efforts to make sense of the lives we lead that bring us into connection with other people. I quarrel only with inflating the considerations that go on in such considerations with the honorific title of "morality." And I do so largely on Cavellian grounds, since Cavell's own capacities to develop the individuality of characters and situations make it clear that in such cases he is right to be suspicious of applying public criteria. But if criteria prove problematic for the occasion (and not just difficult to locate), then these cases often call for confession rather than explicit discursive mutual acknowledgment. Cavell's ideal of mutuality easily collapses into mutual self-congratulation where the agents focus consciousness on what can be shared rather than on what may need to be confronted.

There seem to me two practical issues on which my imagined Wittgenstein would challenge Cavell in order to prepare a context in which he might strengthen the force of his Tractarian position on ethics. The first involves Cavell's claims about criteria with which I began; the second involves Cavell's resort to a discourse about knowledge and self-knowledge for cases when the philosopher finds criteria problematic and so tries to confront "the culture with itself, along the lines in which it meets in me." Cavell's treatment of criteria offers a superb way of putting the individual on stage while promising both the possibility of self-knowledge and the presentation of that self-knowledge as intimately woven into the possibilities of the culture. But Cavell also has to set the self pursuing expressiveness against a condition of ignorance that he attributes to relying on established social criteria. For him grammatical criteria prove "disappointing" and unsatisfying because they seem to bind agents to a collective enterprise that almost by definition cannot satisfy the desire for individuation. In essence grammar is the study of criteria by which we "settle judgments" (CR 31) about how a given utterance meets conditions of shared intelligibility. In its ordinary form, however, hewing to grammatical intelligibility binds the subject to those shared terms without reflecting on what one is doing in and by an utterance. Even the richest sense of community afforded by criteria cannot completely reflect what goes on in human speech, nor will it afford the kind of knowledge of oneself and openness to the other that constitute full human exposure and exchange: "Appealing to criteria is not a way of explaining or proving the fact of our attunement in words ... it is an appeal we make when the attunement is threatened or lost" (CR 34). Criteria are crucial for identifying what something is, but they do not necessarily demonstrate how that something may become significant for particular agents (CR 49). So it takes something more than operating within criteria if the philosopher is to speak significantly "for others and allow others to speak for me" (CR 28).

Speaking not only from criteria but also in an effort to reanimate them then consists in fleshing out the subject's capacities to own his or her speech by attuning it to existential circumstances and, more important, to the social circumstances that seem to demand making the claims by others on the self as fully visible as possible (CR 28). Rather than reduce acknowledgment to a matter of recognizing shared criteria, which would make morality rational and impersonal, the expressive agent makes these circumstances into "a need, to convey how perfectly, originally, I satisfy the criteria" (CR 462). In *The Claim of Reason* Cavell never loses sight of how supplementing those criteria involves an originality that is responsive and responsible to other's claims on our reasons. In fact what I think of as Cavell's Americanized existentialism gets most interesting and most useful when it grapples with how the self's drive to visibility through language becomes inseparable from the self's exposure to the claims and the scrutiny of other people. All of his talk of self and self-knowledge takes place against a backdrop of "disappointment with one's expression" (CR 350) because no words may suffice to allay the subject's neediness in relation to other people: "The brink of misunderstanding is here because the brink of emptiness is here: we do not know to whom such words are being said … . We do not know why we want to say them, what lack they will fill" (CR 339).

Grammar then is not the glue that allows language its power in society but the articulation of a conventionality that "strong" philosophers (to borrow the language of Harold Bloom) will have to set themselves against. These characters become for Cavell (but not for Bloom) representatives for everyone else of the power to supplement grammar by expressive acts that combine knowledge of the self's possible social interactions with work to define the self. One has the opportunity to face one's vulnerability before the differences represented by the other so that one can offer an effort at self-knowledge that gives the other a purchase on that self (CR 432–49, 368). This pursuit of self-knowledge affords a significant space within which the other can dwell, and perhaps offer that same kind of space in return: "All anyone knows or could know is what I am able to show them of myself" (CR 443). Words can open worlds for those who risk the necessary exposure.

I find three problems with this line of thinking.

(1) While Cavell is right in pointing to why we invoke criteria, I don't think it wise to define the range of uses of criteria by the fact that the uses only get raised to self-consciousness when disputes arise. That would be like making a quarrel between one of Cavell's reconstructed couples define the conditions of the life they have learned to share. So it seems reasonable to look for how criteria enable agreement or clarify, say, the kinds of mistakes in which philosophers impose language games derived from dealing with things on dealing with processes. As we will see in a moment, Cavell on criteria does not give sufficient place to the work "perspicuous examples" can perform.

(2) More generally, Cavell's remarks on criteria are difficult to judge because he seems to be deliberately pushing a Wittgensteinian envelope to see how far he can bend the concept of criteria to allow them to be forged by individual conversation, while at the same time he knows that criteria have to hold for more than individual conversations to apply in any given instance. For example, at one point he argues that Wittgensteinian criteria do not pertain to "what one is doing in and by an utterance." Instead, as Stephen Affeldt puts it,

such acts "constitute" the philosopher's or the speaker's own twist on public convention. One can make the private public without just submitting to the culture. Yet Wittgenstein takes great pains to teach us to recognize the difference between acts of describing situations and acts of exemplifying rules. After all, while Cavell is an American eager to resist conformity, Wittgenstein is an exile fascinated by how sociality can be sustained (c.f. *Philosophical Investigations*, p. 223e[5]). Wittgenstein has to admit that particular criteria can be called into question by inventive behavior. But there remains a huge difference between *general* claims about disappointment with criteria (so that one needs a general cure) and disappointment with specific criteria, which is a practical question. In most cases even when grammatical criteria seem to fail because there is authorial invention at stake, we identify the inventive dimension precisely by the fact that it acknowledges the criteria even as it reapplies them, just as poetry acknowledges the force of public expectations even as it alters them. Such linguistic acts rely on criteria to make manifest that our attention must be redirected to internal patterns in order to produce what intelligibility is possible. We understand why we cannot discursively understand what is involved in the final embrace between Leontes and Hermione.

(3) Yet Cavell persists in blaming criteria so that he can escape Wittgenstein's strictures about the role philosophy can play in experience. By generalizing about disappointment with criteria, Cavell makes a romantic distinction between convention and spirit as a foundation for his version of moral thinking. There is a Hegelian or at least an idealist dimension of his thinking that has to emphasize the inadequacy of attuning to established social relations because this level of attunement is not fully expressive of the full life of the spirit working through individual self-consciousness. Recognizing this inadequacy is then one step on a path of efforts to found a deeper, more authentic attunement in criteria. In effect Cavell wants a philosophical space for assessing action and for reflection that is beyond the ken of one attending only to criteria as they stand. This space must establish a dialectic where there is the expressive act, then knowledge about the self revealed in this act, and then the capacity to make public how criteria convene in making the act potentially representative. The reflective act embodied in self-exposure has the power to reshape conversation and provoke new responsiveness on the part of the audience. Ultimately Cavell can characterize this space for action in abstract terms as a negotiation with skepticism in which the philosopher can present himself as offering a heroic expo-

sure justifying the claim to be the representative of human possibilities for perfection.

Since my argument depends completely on my claims about display, I will deal very briefly with the second general criticism of Cavell that helps frame what can be at stake in distinguishing what becomes manifest in display from what becomes available for any kind of philosophical description, at least so long as we insist that philosophy has to know its own parameters and possible interventions in social life. I distrust Cavell's claims that the philosopher can "know" what is going on among dramatic agents as they try progressively to define their values and their interests. And I think he needs these claims about knowledge because he does not sufficiently trust the roles criteria play in our lives. When we are open to how criteria make subtle distinctions, we are more likely to share Wittgenstein's sense that there is a great range of human actions where we consistently make adjustments and responses to others, in which any traditional sense of knowing the other must give way to terms like "attunement" or "fit" or simply finding a way to go on.

I find myself in difficult territory here because Cavell completely accepts Wittgenstein's critique in *On Certainty*[6] of how philosophers like G. E. Moore fetishize knowledge and in the process invite skepticism. When Moore claims to know that "I have two hands," despite the fact that there is no possibility of doubt, Wittgenstein insists that he misuses the authority of philosophy, precisely because he ignores the criteria for what it is involved practically in negotiating a claim about knowledge. Moore does not provide a picture of a truth but misuses the logic of picturing to confuse it with an example of the frameworks, logical and grammatical, which we have to accept because they make our interpretive actions possible. That we cannot doubt one has two hands suggests that this statement is being used to exemplify certainty rather than to demonstrate it. Ironically Moore is in fact successfully showing what certainty might be like, precisely because he refers to a condition enabling action in the world rather than picturing a significant fact about it. But his not recognizing this betrays an anxiety about knowledge. Rather than refuting the skeptic this anxiety invites versions of skeptical doubt based on psychology rather than on epistemic grounds.

Cavell does not make this mistake. In fact in his early writing he echoes Wittgenstein's efforts to deal with "the fact that behavior is expressive of mind; and this is not something we know, but a way we treat 'behavior'" (MWM 262). But his need to sustain the authority of philosophy (despite his qualms), his desire to use psychoanalytic concepts, and his fears that acknowledgment gets dangerously sappy without some kind of test of adequate attention to actual behavior, seem to put pressure on him to return to the use of knowledge claims, albeit in contexts that are obviously not traditional epistemic ones. I am not sure how much he needs this language, but it has come to exact a cost. The connection becomes too close between what has to take the form of avowals that display states or mind rather than report on them, like "I am in pain" or "I hope he will come," and what can be captured in the giving or forming of reasons within interpersonal interactions. In such cases Cavell seems to think that we can "know" what the person means and even "know" what the agent demonstrates in an avowal that the person is in pain or hopes a friend will arrive, despite the fact that these are clearly cases of what he called "not something we know but a way we treat 'behavior'." And then it is tempting to make the reverse claim that the reasons persons give for their actions are extensions of avowals: in such cases persons express where they stand by offering reasons for their actions that are not descriptions of inner states but further articulations of their desires and senses of moral identity. After all we do depend on such expressions to decide on what our actions will be in regard to this person.

But does this mean that we are authorized to speak of knowledge in any strong sense of the term when dealing with the range of avowal behaviors?[7] What criteria do we rely on in such cases? How can we clearly resolve doubts about what a person has in mind in relation to what they do? How can we separate the agent's efforts to clarify desires from the persistence of the desire that in fact shapes the account? Again we might recall Wittgenstein's worry that "A man can see what he has but not what he is" (CV 49). For it does not take poststructuralist theories of the subject to make us distinguish between what subjects do as agents and what they propose as explanations or rationales for such behavior. Of course we often have to trust that persons offer us sufficiently intelligible behavior or want to pursue possibilities for our making sense of what their investments are. But why bring a language of knowledge to bear on something so intricate and incomplete? Yet there remains the pressure not to concede the world of behavior to the arts that concentrate on particular expressive acts. If we can say we can come to "know" what a person thinks or wants or intends, we can make rich claims about the work of acknowledgment and the possibility of mutual responsiveness even when we acknowledge the force of skepticism about other minds. Cavell's loosening of what it means to "know" can resist what is limited in skepticism's versions of "knowledge" and still allow philosophy to know itself. And because "know" is a verb with the capacity for expansion, these acts of knowledge can sponsor a perfectionist orientation without forcing perfectionism to become a theoretical position.

Wittgenstein's entire *Culture and Value* seems to contradict Cavell's orientation here, since there Wittgenstein is explicit about the fact that significant cultural expressions are manifestations of singular sensibilities that try by the work of style to afford something other than knowledge, something that can afford a model of what is possible if one sees the world or the work in a certain way. (I am using "model" in the way Section XI of Part 2 of the *Investigations* does.) Models are not pictures. Rather models elaborate particular situations but do not claim to discover that something is the case. And the most important models an individual offers become acts of confession, even where there can be little hope of acknowledgment that a particular state of being can be made representative.[8] What makes the expression worth owning by an individual may relegate it to something whose social existence remains a more problematic state than our models of knowledge can handle.[9] Confessions gain power by individuation and not by representativeness, and confessions are addressed to a range of possible responses involving languages of attention and care, for which "knowledge" is a chilling substitute. The pursuit of knowledge of what a confession displays might provide a generalizing context, but at considerable risk of losing what may be specific to the needs driving the individual behavior.

Now I have to make a positive case for the contrast I have been drawing by criticizing Cavell on criteria and on "knowledge." How can I justify preferring Wittgenstein's wariness about philosophy in the face of Cavell's efforts to dramatize how moral thinking might include much more sensitive individual efforts at mutual acknowledgment? I stress the differences between the two thinkers because I think the more moral philosophy tries to accommodate itself to how individuals compose different kinds of reasons for situations, the more it tends to impose an apparently benign responsibility for something like reasoning on situations which in the arts honor other ways of weaving individuals into their actions.

My case depends on developing the motif of display that links early and later Wittgenstein. He uses essentially the same view of foundations in the *Tractatus* for how logic takes hold and in his later work for the status of grammar. This link in turn helps us see three significant parallels between the early and the later philosophy that I view as central to assessing basic Cavellian themes. These parallels offer one large-scale framework for putting to work Wittgenstein's contrast between what can be known and what can only be exemplified or displayed; they help explain Wittgenstein's continuing fascination with religion as the alternative to ethics; and they make sense of his interest in style because style affords one paradigm for human actions that involve an irreducible particularity partially shaped by determining forces and not fully amenable to knowledge claims or open to dialogical transformation.

I have to go into some detail because I want to stress Wittgenstein's concern for the formal or exemplary aspects of learning language games that do not depend on reference. In the *Tractatus* the formal framework was the structure of logic—something that had to be displayed as a whole rather than argued for in piecemeal elements. In Wittgenstein's later writing grammar plays the same role as logic and has the same dependence on being displayed rather than discovered through argument: "Everything descriptive of a language-game is part of logic" (OC § 56). This is because language games, like logic, "did not emerge from some kind of ratiocination" (OC § 475), but are simply there like our lives. They are part of the res, not about it, as Wallace Stevens put it. So these forms do not "rest on some form of knowledge" (OC § 477) but are the indispensable medium in which to formulate what can count as knowledge.[10] These forms are given as the conditions for using various languages in the first place, so they are learned, and also developed, by further efforts to develop and assess what the language offers.

Wittgenstein's *Tractatus* shared the positivist view that logic cannot have a place for the expression of attitudes because attitudes are intensional and so depend not on how the world is but on how agents give color to their worlds. And if one dismisses attitudes, then one also dismisses the possibility of coherent assessment of values, since they too involve intentional states rather than pictorial descriptions. The best way to summarize this is Wittgenstein's image of subjects as not in the world but at its margins: "The sense of the world must lie outside the world. In the world everything is as it is, and everything happens as it does happen: in it no value exists, and if it did, it would have no value. … What makes it non-accidental cannot lie *within* the world, since it if it did it would itself be accidental" (*Tractatus* 6.41).

Values occupy the same marginal status as attitudes because they do not derive from propositions or descriptions, "ethics cannot be put into words"; rather that domain is "transcendental"(*Tractatus* 6.421). But Wittgenstein does not have a positivist attitude to this marginal status, as the respectful reference to the transcendental indicates. Wittgenstein is careful to indicate where that transcendental domain seems capable of entering the world: "If good or bad acts of the will do alter the world, it can only be the limits of the world that they alter, not the facts, and not what can be expressed by means of language. ... The world of the happy man is a different one from that of the unhappy man" (*Tractatus* 6.43).

Analogously Wittgenstein the grammarian can establish how values might be stated and intentions understood, but he can show nothing about how to evaluate values. Therefore it is not a huge jump to think that the lack of evidence to the contrary suggests that Wittgenstein never swayed from his Tractarian belief that what makes agents subjects is something still at the margin of experience where there can be showings but not meaningful assessment. What is displayed matters not because of what it refers to but because of what it exemplifies as possibilities in the language. Let me take a seemingly simple contrast from Section VIII of Part 2 of the *Investigations* to show how insistent Wittgenstein remained about that marginality. Notice here a surprising continued skepticism about knowing what other people feel emotionally (in contrast to knowing whether they are in pain):

> I say "Do *this*, and you'll get it". Can't there be a doubt here? Mustn't there be one, if it is a feeling that is meant?
> *This* looks *so*; *this* tastes *so*, *this* feels *so*. "This" and "so" must be differently explained.
> (PI Part II, p. 1863)

The primary point is grammatical. "Feels" in the sense the sentence gives it involves a different language game from the apparent form of description the sentence seems to take at first. Initially we have to interpret "this" is as a demonstrative referring to some observable particular. But the phrase as a whole gives immense force to "so" as the complement of "feels." Therefore the sentence requires recasting the force of "this." Only a "this" specified intensionally by the subject's "model" can flesh out this "so" because that task calls not for description but for illustrating how some aspect of the situation dawns on the agent. And once the agent takes on this degree of importance for determining the sense of "so," there must be doubt that one agent can understand what the other feels. This situation demands display rather than a picture, but the display does not secure lucid communication. There can be only an effort by each individual to clarify what "so" involves.

This concrete situation can become an emblem for Wittgenstein's understanding of the work style has to do in cases where a quest for knowledge might be misleading. In most circumstances we can take the expression of this dawning of an aspect as simply the work of an avowal. But it is also possible that we might ask more of this "so" than an avowal can provide. We might take the "so" as implicating full patterns of how an agent deals with the world. And then we enter conditions where confession or the making of a model must supplement the avowal (PI 222) and attempt to give substance to an attitude.[11] In such situations we want to know not just more about the agent's reactions but also about her dispositions and history. This history, though, will be particular and will also not be amenable to observation in crucial aspects: we are interested in what the character chooses as a history rather in stopping with accuracy to the facts.

It is not a huge leap to see one aspect of how the agent elaborates this "so" having less to do with efforts at mutual acknowledgment than with the production of style, the display of how an agent frames the world by composing it: "'Le style c'est l'homme'", 'Le style c'est l'homme même'". The first expression has cheap epigrammatic brevity. The second, correct version opens up quite a different perspective. It says that a man's style is a picture [*Bild*] of him. (CV 78). The second formulation says that style is a picture of the person because the self-reflexive dimension by which it frames the world makes visible how the language has been worked. One might say that style implies ownership but does not entail discursive self-consciousness about ownership or the possibility of describing the terms of that ownership. Style accomplishes this framing by accepting and displaying the individual's differences from others and not seeking any normative justification: "You have to accept the faults in your own style. Almost like the blemishes in your own face" (CV 76). Therefore while this "feels so" invites further elaboration, it is by no means clear that words will add more than they subtract from what "so" displays. Claiming knowledge or self-knowledge through these words only imposes another framework beyond the framework of language, one that is rife with normativity and temptations to make judgments. Those frameworks present "so" only in the terms that are appropriate for knowledge claims.

An intentional act need not be something shaped by meaning or overt purpose that can be stated. The act stands in the world as a showing of the person—hence the obvious connection between style as a condition of action and style in a work of art.

Agents may surround acts with reasons, but we cannot take the reasons as explanations as we would if we could treat the person as an object that explanation would suffice to clarify. There is no normative argument about values that can be presumed to have authority between the "I" and the world as I find it, or the world as I decide upon it. This does not mean our actions cannot or should not be judged; it only means that the terms of judgment are not necessarily the terms that matter for agents as they make decisions they feel they can take responsibility for.

Sometimes actions follow a Cavellian schema. They seek to issue in acknowledgment and try to pursue explicit self-knowledge that one can offer to the other. But it seems safer and less likely to induce self-evasion to be open to the degree which style, like will, extends the personal while resisting our cognitive frameworks.

There are two morals to my tale. First, Wittgenstein's sense of what is irreducibly private about values requires a corresponding wariness in our expectations about what is involved in taking up a position as audience to such individual agents. There is substantial danger in assuming that the other wants to enter a dialectic of mutual self-disclosure—dangerous because both audience and agent are likely to take up self-congratulatory poses that evade the darker or lonelier aspects of what motivates us. So Wittgenstein idealizes learning to accept differences and disciplining the self to attune to those differences by finding what in them can fascinate or instruct despite one's irreducible discomfort. One can contextualize these first-person framings—hence the role of confession—but one cannot successfully provide reasons for them that are not colored by the very conditions they propose to explain. Agents usually can only display who they have become, and perhaps seek friendships that appreciate such particular orientations. The task for an audience then in responding to style, in life and in art, is to explore different ways of looking at or playing a situation to test what might open up as a fuller mode of engagement or better way of at least accepting what remains quite different from the agent's own sensibility. One has to distinguish sharply between an appeal to friendship and the appeal to community that asks for recognition as an "ethical" being. The latter requires the giving of reasons because that is the only locus of whatever intimacy can be achieved with a group. One must elaborate one's decision in terms that allow the community to include the person within its parameters of concern. Yet, as Cavell is acutely aware, the filtering force of the conventions that form the community make it highly unlikely that it will be able to acknowledge accurately any decision not already programmed within its concerns. This is why for Wittgenstein display and confession seek a greater degree of intimacy, and a greater degree of something like grace, that cannot be demanded or explained. Wittgenstein maps a continual quest for the possibilities of friendship that can attune to what confession displays without demanding that the confession be adapted to the normative language of knowing and judging. In fact this refusal of the normative may be what drives Wittgenstein toward the transcendental as the only possible audience for what sits uncomfortably within purported explanations.[12] Even in the domain of practical behavior, grace may be the necessary condition if we desire responsiveness in relation to what must fall outside the provenance of explanatory language.

In this context Wittgenstein's fascination with Shakespeare takes on exemplary force. Wittgenstein did not "like" Shakespeare and was suspicious of people who said they "liked" Shakespeare (CV 86). Shakespeare has a distinctive power that Wittgenstein wants to identify, all the more because he knows it has the force to occupy a place in his real and imaginative world despite the fact of his "dislike":

> I could only stare in wonder at Shakespeare; never do anything with him.
>
> I am *deeply* suspicious of most of Shakespeare's admirers. The misfortune is, I believe, that he stands by himself, at least in the culture of the west, so that one can only place him by placing him wrongly.
>
> It is *not* as though Shakespeare portrayed human types well and were in that respect *true to life*. He is *not* true to life. But he has such a supple hand and his *brush strokes* are so individual, that each one of his characters looks *significant*, is worth looking at.
>
> (CV 84, original emphasis)

Cavell on the other hand writes movingly, but for me disturbingly, on the effort to own some aspects of Shakespeare's suggestive and rich engagement with issues of skepticism, as if they had a timeless philosophical world in common.

My second moral involves what this excursus may teach us about the inevitable limitations accompanying Cavell's enormous strengths as a literary critic. My line of argument hopes to make clear the cost of his effort to anchor displays of imaginative intensities within a master plot involving the recognition of skepticism as providing a normative ground for assessing imaginative power. For all of Cavell's criticism of traditional philosophy, I worry that he restores the same imperious authority to the language of knowledge with regard to selves that he criticizes when it is based on empiricist principles. He posits a determinable, at least quasi-allegorical situation for the action, and he treats the characters as mattering primarily because their actions can be interpreted in relation to how they deal with dilemmas of acknowledgment. What Cavell loses by this allegorical bent is the richness of a literary text's powers for sheer display, for articulating the capacity of particular situations to elicit values like intimacy, intensity, and wonder without soliciting psychological and moral explanation.[13]

Perhaps these differences ultimately derive from implicit competing ways of interpreting the statement "Aesthetics and ethics are one." Wittgenstein throughout his career tries to emphasize the importance of situations where we cannot "tell" anything but can only "show" what is involved in particular decisions that extend from life to the making of art works. The therapeutic bent of Cavell's work after his "discovery" of affinities with Emerson, on the other hand, makes his resistance to convention and traditional moral philosophy powerfully open to what art works do, but he has to tilt the aesthetic, in life and in art, back to the ethical where he can thematize what is displayed, and in so doing risk displacing it into what can be known.

6   The Word Viewed
Skepticism Degree Zero

Garrett Stewart

I have written elsewhere about Stanley Cavell and American writing, including verbal transference in Emerson and Thoreau, syllabic mayhem in Poe; and separately on Giorgio Agamben's sense of potentiality in regard, unpursued by him, to the neo-classic figure of syllepsis as well as to a wider range of phonetic wordplay in Romantic verse and its nineteenth-century prose legacy.[1] The venture here is to bring the metalinguistic thinking of each philosopher, and especially the relations probed between language and ontology in their explicit literary criticism, into some speculative alignment in connection with that same sylleptic figure of divided reference, remarked upon by neither but foregrounded at one point by Derrida as a touchstone for the reciprocal deconstruction of diction and syntax—and hence of the subject's being in language.[2] By way of orientation, however, let me first approach the question from another medium that is also of philosophical interest to both Cavell and Agamben.

In *The World Viewed*, cinema is defined by Cavell as "a succession of automatic world projections."[3] But succeeding each other how quickly? Projection involves the founding automaticity not only of enframed "views" wholesale but also of the serial transparencies that induce them twenty-four "successions" per second. For here—or no sooner here than there, here and gone—is the subliminal photographic impetus behind all apparitional momentum on screen. This recognition, however, need not compromise Cavell's ultimate use of film, as of Shakespearean theater before it, as a therapy for skepticism in our willing limit to participation: the acceptance of a seen and heard world upon the presence of whose drama we cannot trespass, for good or ill. What begins in a parody of doubt—there before us is a seeming world we know not to be ours, not to be real—apprentices us, after all, in emotional credence. But in cinema's laboratory for the overcoming of skepticism, why not pursue this heuristic regimen, well beyond Cavell's phenomenology, back to the film lab itself, to process as well as produced image; in other words, why not carry film's use in the practiced overcoming of skepticism all the way down and back to the file of images one knows to be only clocked photographs rather than otherwise animated bodies? Why isn't the frameline itself, the spun and backlit strip, and since then the pixel array, one of the things we are invited actively to overcome rather than simply to ignore in our vesting of conviction in the world viewed?

In fact, Cavell's work comes closer to this sense of glimpsed constitutive modularity in textual process when he writes about writing rather than film, wondering, for instance, about the intransigent "hell" found "staring out of" the name Othello or the "demon" of Desdemona.[4] More rigorous than this, though, is the linguistic undertow in an account of a single Poe story, where he is alert to the "cells" of speech, the "molecules" I find comparable to the fleeting photograms of the filmic chain. These are fugitive units of effect mostly unseen but sensed upon extrusion as the unsaid fundament of articulation. In the case of Poe's lexically dissevering wordplay, Cavell attends to certain pointed disruptions sprung from language's own material or alphabetic base. Normal writing comes clear as a series of automatic word formations projected into the axis of grammar. Only in writing like Poe's do obstreperous echoes and puns disrupt that projection with the recovered arbitrariness of their subsemantic massing as letter forms. So that the word viewed on paper exposes at times the suppressions necessary to sustain the norms of so-called ordinary language. In particular for Cavell, Poe's writing reveals by default our view of the word's typical work in the buttressing of subjectivity, which is to say language's role as the vehicle of consciousness itself.

Impotentialities

In the remarkable essay in question, "Being odd, getting even: Descartes, Emerson, Poe"—whose subtitle I will be expanding, as modestly and economically as I can, to "Descartes, Emerson, Poe, Ryle, and Agamben"—Cavell stands vigilant guard when the first noun of Poe's title in "The imp of the perverse" invades the phonemes and syllables of much other diction in the story—and I'm quoting here from Cavell's own litany of perverse recursions: "*impulse* (several times), *impels* (several times), *impatient* (twice), *important*, *impertinent*, *imperceptible*, *impossible*, *unimpressive*, and *imprisoned*."[5] In all these cases the alphabetic triad as phonemic cluster is at odds with, though never quite dismantling, the segments of morphology and syllabification at work in its respective phrasings, with the plosive "imp-words" (IQO 124) coming to attention only as intransigent blips on the screen of lexical succession. What results is a chain of entirely failed hyphenates, one useless pun after another truncated without fallout, an extreme dyslexia, a madness.

Ertinent? Erceptible? Ossible? No meaning would survive an insinuated prefix so wholly impertinent, mostly imperceptible, and strictly impossible all at once. Impotent to make meaning, these latencies are effaced in lexical motion. Or almost.

Despite these typically recessed but here obtruded alphabetic clusters, our processing the intended meaning of whole words at once depends upon "our mostly not noticing the particle (or cells) and their laws … on our not noticing their necessary recurrences," a "necessity," Cavell repeats for emphasis, that is "the most familiar property of language there could be" (IQO 125). He continues in the wordplay of his own lexical dismemberment when asserting that when and if "we do note these cells or molecules, these little moles of language (perhaps in thinking, perhaps in derangement), what we discover are word imps" (ibid.). By which mole(cules) he means "the implanted origins or constituents of words, leading lives of their own, staring back at us, calling upon one another, giving us away, alarming—because to note them is to see that they live in front of our eyes, within earshot, at every moment" (ibid.). And to see also, with these disembedded particles of the word viewed, that they don't rest easy under the concept of verbal intention, stretching it out of shape, bending it to their own impish will.

Two things there in Cavell's account offer a particularly tight grip on Poe's so-called "first person" narrative in the post-Cartesian reading to which he submits it: first the parenthetical alternative "(perhaps in thinking, perhaps in derangement)" and then the loaded, sudden, and indeed deliberately "alarming" phrase "giving us away." Evincing a psychotic break in the stream of consciousness, these disruptive "imp words" prevent us not only from saying what we mean but even from meaning it coherently. They would thus prevent my giving unified voice to what I say to myself in constituting that self in thought. These imps are not revealing in the way, say, a Freudian slip is. They don't give anything away that way, not even ourselves. Rather, they throw expressive subjectivity to the winds of the contingent. Cavell comes at this point more explicitly in the next paragraph, when generalizing such accidents of the lexeme to the "perverseness" of language at large, "working without, even against, our thought and its autonomy." Independence of mind, the law of autonomy governing expressed thought as a self-present intention: such is the first victim of the deviant signifier slipping beneath and between words, fraying them at their inner joins. In Poe's prose, this willful dispersion of apparent intent is diagnosed not just by the front-loaded phonetic imp-etuosity in this one tale, but also, here and in many another, by the traumatic gappings and overlaps of narrative grammar itself. Such writing so confounds the relation of inner or "metaphysical" voice to self-presence that it puts the "external-ity" of linguistic ciphers not just at their proper distance from any posited inwardness but at odds with dictionary meaning itself, let alone personal intent.

If, against the grain of syllabification, the title word "imp" appears (both senses: emerges and seems) to split *imp* from the likes of *ulse*, deranging all morphology in the process, it does so to remind us, more broadly, of the uncertain safety net of utterance in any intended formu-lation whatever. If our words get away from themselves, and hence our words from our thoughts, then the link between thinking and being, as tethered to inner voice, is weakened. Even the Cogito, as rephrased by Emerson in a variant quoted by Cavell—the tacit paratactic causality of "I think," "I am" (IQO 106)—harbors its own ambiguity, easily degener-ating into the non-binding subjectivism of "I think I am." Finding a dif-ferent emphasis in Poe's undermining of the Cogito, Cavell highlights the narrator's fear that "to *think* in my situation was to be lost" (IQO 123)—lost because such thinking would release not selfhood per se but its most self-annihilating urges.

Only the baroque complications of Poe's narrative can give teeth to the narrator's lament, to the full weight of its Cartesian heritage, and to the Shakespearean overtones of its perhaps oddest detail. Under Cavell's scrutiny, Poe may be found alluding to *Hamlet* in the backstory of a bizarre poisoning: not in the ear exactly (as the Ghost claims of his own murder by Claudius) but, by association, in the air of intake while listen-ing to one's own silent words in reading. For after an opening "essay" (as Cavell calls it) on a perverse willfulness at odds with desire, a self-destructive bent that goads one impetuously into catastrophe against one's better judgment, the narrator himself is indeed led to a fatal con-fession of a much earlier crime. He had killed a man with a poisonous candle planted at the victim's bedside to facilitate (but this time irrevers-ibly) the man's long-standing habit of reading himself to sleep. All this he must explain from his death-row cell, following upon a generalized account of the human perversity that led him there: "I have said thus much, that in some measure I may answer your question—that I may explain to you why *I am here*" (IQO 122). Here where? What is locally meant is quickly offered: an explanation "for my wearing these fetters, and for my tenanting this cell of the condemned" (ibid.).

Cavell leaps on this answer to a "question" no one has in fact posed, except by a tacit narrative curiosity textually occasioned, detecting in it a "fantasy of writing" (IQO 123) rather than of a speaking subject, where we are perhaps expected to assume (he puts it conjecturally) that "words are fetters and cells and that to read them, to be awake to their meaning, or effect, is to be poisoned" (ibid.). Associations continue in this interrogative vein: "Are we being told that writer and reader are one another's victims? Or is the suggestion that to arrive at the truth something in the reader as well as something in the writer must die? Does writing ward off or invite in the angel of death?" The questions are, in the context of Cavell's writing, wholly rhetorical. He expects, as he says, "nowadays little resistance" (ibid.) to this line of interrogation, since (as he lets go without saying) he is spelling all this out in the heyday of deconstruction and the Derridean thanatopraxis of the text, the deathwork of inscription. Then, too, the adverb in the carceral "I am here," indicating the speaker's (or writer's) presence here and now—comes back to haunt the story in the end, in a parallel passage Cavell doesn't quote or consider, including the story's own last elliptical phrase, when the narrator—once abruptly removed from "here" by capital punishment for his homicidal crime—will finally "be fetterless ... *but where*?" Thinking has always doomed his narrator, because the moment he is conscious of a need for self-preservation, some contradictory impulse wells up—not to do the will's bidding but to *do in* its desire. Varying Cavell's phrase about unregulated language elements undermining verbal intent, the result for the subject is to give him away, to give him up.

Yet his eventual and precipitous admission of the crime gives pause as well. Of all the perversities of will at the expense of self-interest, confession may seem the least perverse. The going public of a crime, by detection or confession, is so narratively expected that it becomes almost a law of plot: in this case trapping the sociopathic narrator unwittingly in the most conventional of ethical closures. The whole narrative arc seems reduced, in the terms of Michael's Riffaterre's semiotics, to the avoided and repressed cliché (and ethical bromide) that Shakespeare himself so narrowly skirts—and which is often misattributed to him as a coinage: the truism (phrased by Chaucer in just so many words) that "murder will out."[6] Which in turn calls up another avoided cliché at the basis of the narrator's destructive impulses, working there at odds with desire and intent. For indeed his confession is willfully blurted out, as we might ordinarily say, *accidentally on purpose*.

In *Hamlet*, however, murder needs help in being smoked out: that's what's a tragedy about it, that's the poison in the prompted ear that erodes the son's life. When he reflects on the fear of death, saying that "conscience doth make cowards of us all" (III.i.318–19), Hamlet of course famously means something more like "consciousness" than like "conscience," a sensed precariousness of being rather than an uprush of guilt, more the fear of oblivion than the threat of hellfire. But in Poe, it is precisely a more conventional sense of conscience that has, however disguised, returned through the backdoor of consciousness. The oddness of this gets parenthetical flagging by Cavell: "(That in Poe's tale the act of thinking destroys by alarming the populace and turning them against the thinker and that perverseness is noted as the confession of a crime, not the committing of it—as if the confessing and the committing were figurations of one another—mark paths of parody and perversity I cannot trace here)" (IQO 124).

But there are other such paths as well, one of which he does trace. Beyond the irony of confession as murder's true violence, part of what it means to Cavell that he is "beginning to study Poe while thinking about Hamlet" (IQO 128) is that he is uniquely alerted to the theme of delay in the second extended example of perversity given by Poe, a self-defeating procrastination (not so named in the text) in whose grips "we feel *perverse*, using the word with no comprehension of the principle" (Poe 282).[7] What Cavell doesn't mention in his turn to this passage is that this Hamlet-like delay is framed by two other examples from Poe's narrator that render it more broadly categorical, linguistic on one side, existential (even metaphysical) on the other. Call the umbrella category that of deferral per se. For the previous example by Poe, given just before that of fatal procrastination, concerns a self-defeating tendency to "circumlocution" (Poe 281) that annoys the listener and mortifies the speaker, against not just the latter's better judgment but his native talent for lucidity. Tying the tongue up in willful knots, such is the postponing of sense across "involutions and parentheses" (ibid.) of just the sort Poe's philosophical parodies are so rife with.

Verbal deferral (the open secret of literary prose), followed by protracted delay in the move to completion (the open secret of narrative plotting), is now rounded out in this trio of exemplified perversities (natural enough after all, like that which catches the narrator's own conscience in the end) by the more extreme case of a lowered guard, at cliffside, against the perverse urge to jump. Yet this temperamental quirk is introduced in a paragraph that at first would seem to be generalizing its specific setting into a treatise on philosophical skepticism. Before we realize that we've zeroed in on another isolated example of impish whim, that is, there is this Cartesian vertigo in editorial plural, itself precipitously introduced: "We stand upon the brink of a precipice. We peer into the abyss—we grow sick and dizzy" (Poe 282). The prematurely broached local instance of holding back from the plunge of disaster becomes, momentarily, the abstract figuration of one's life in time, stretched over the "abyss" of doubt.

The whole spectrum of perversities we've traversed turns out to be a strangely coherent one. From an almost negligible phonemic welt in the contagious imp words, disfiguring a lexeme by momentarily deferring its functional use, to the broadest arcs of a narrative death drive postponed by the byzantine twists and loops of story, the modes of deferred closure are both metalinguistic (circumlocution) and narratological. And at their point of intersection what I have elsewhere called narratographic.[8] As for instance at the end of the tale—when the perverse desire to plunge into the abyss returns involuntarily, with the threat of its "rushing annihilation" (Poe 282), as if it were a slip between the cracks of grammar itself; it returns, that is, following a sick joke on delivery as negative deliverance, with "the brief but *pregnant* sentences that *consigned me to the hangman and to hell*" (Poe 284; emphasis added). Syllepsis: a verb taking its direct or indirect object (by storm) in suddenly two senses at once, here a horizontal remanding to punishment and—all in the same strangled breath, before we can assimilate the shift in preposition—a vertical drop to death.

Hoist on the Gallows and His Own Petard: The Sylleptic Turn

We might say that this grammatical trope, as a kind of distended pun, deploys in reciprocal array the potential give and take of two phrasings mutually present to each other, if only by way of a logical breach. In any case syllepsis (though not vouchsafed the rhetorical term as such) has in philosophy a locus classicus. In a famous argument against Cartesian doubt, Gilbert Ryle, writing in the years just before Cavell's own work on the problematic of skepticism began appearing, gives as example a comparable grammatical oddity (uncredited) from Dickens: " 'She came home in a flood of tears and a sedan chair' is a well-known joke based on the absurdity of conjoining terms of a different type"—and thus a good model, in Ryle's thinking, not for mind-body dualism itself but for the logical disaster of its hypothesis, which is also, like syllepsis, based on a "category-mistake."[9] Dickensian comedy thus exposes the artificial parallel from which Cartesian doubt derives: as if misery and the hauling by servants can be thought to *move* a person in the same sense—now corporeal; now subjective, invisible, always in doubt. Offered up by Ryle is a trope that the Victorian novelist learned from Shakespeare and might well have passed to Poe, its grammatical disjunctions operating with equal success in the mode of comedy or macabrerie. Its splayed phrasing rests on a twofold understanding of a single subject in divided alignment with a double predicate, usually a direct object or object of the preposition taken now metaphorically, now literally, as in Pope's "stain her honor, or her new brocade." Without returning to the Dickens example in this regard, Ryle quickly concedes that one can speak reasonably of mental "processes" just as "there occur physical processes" (ibid.). But they proceed on wholly different terms, different grounds. In sum, it is "just as good or bad a joke to say 'there exist prime numbers and Wednesdays and public opinion and navies' as to say 'there exist both minds and bodies'" (CM 24). Literary comedy can thus work to expose a philosophical farce.

But there is a non-comic heritage of syllepsis as well, as taken up more obviously by Poe. Shakespeare can sound it out in the register of violent dislocation. "Thus was I"—note the inverted past tense of being itself in the speech of Hamlet's ghost (thus was I, but am no more)— "thus was I, sleeping, by a brother's hand,/Of life, of crown, of queen, at once dispatched" (I.v.74–75): instantly and all at once, according to that unprecedented use of the verb "dispatched" in passive form with the particle "of." The crown was of course not plucked from the head of the corpse, nor the queen yanked from the cadaver's side. Instead, a grammar of cause and effect figures (rather than recounts) a threefold usurpation all in one ended breath. Syllepsis again intercedes between the ghost and machine, soul and embodied life, each spirited away in a different sense. You can't take one's possessions in the way you take one's life: the first is a true removal, an absconding, the second an efface-ment that maddens any question of spatial shift.

It should be clear, then, how syllepsis, split repeatedly as it is between mind and body, emotional and material dis/positions, often figurative and literal registers (even "flood of tears" is palely metaphoric), is fre-quently in context a quasi-metaphysical wordplay. Moreover, as a syntax of two minds at once, such troping returns choice itself to the manifest level of phrasing rather than holding it to an already assimi-lated precondition of the speech act. Syllepsis thereby renders each gov-erning predicate the alternative to itself, open still to the paradigm not of morphology (the bifold verb is already spelled out) but of denotation. In Poe's story, the narrator's perverse impulse to self-destruction may send him to hell in a handbasket; but his own phrasing of his fate works to remind us—across the jolt of a traumatized grammar in "to the hangman and to hell"—that, however one strays from the path of right-eousness, and despite whatever rhetorical efforts may be imposed by a forking-path grammar, one doesn't go to church and to heaven in the same mode of transit. Nor even to the devil and to damnation. Contem-plating the inevitability of the scaffold, prose has its own trapdoor. The forking prepositions open a bottomless linguistic pit between the execu-tioner's bodily presence and his pending effect.

And so, too, with the story's closure a moment later, once the blurted confession has warranted "the fullest judicial conviction" on the part of secular justice. With that flickering pun on "conviction" sliding between the connotation of *credence* (where "fullest" makes sense) and *verdict* (where it doesn't), the story shuts down by zeroing in—and out—on an almost pointless pun straddling a faint sylleptic divide between adjectival and adverbial complements in its last four words (alluded to above): "To-day I wear these chains, and am *here*! To-morrow I shall be fetterless!–*but where?*" (Poe 286). The pivot between sentences is initially hinged, via homophonic pun, around a metaphysical shift from *wear* to(ward) *where*—as if the enchained body were the garb of the soul. What is suggested is that life comes to definition, on the brink of death, as containment itself, an emblem of self-containment, which dying decimates. Further, with its elliptical iteration of an intertextual "to be or not (to be)," the phrase "be fetterless, but [be] where" offers not just a pun on raiment and its mortal denuding, but actually a pun and a half. Before our ears, following the tripled assonance of "fetterless," the elliptical verb of being returns as an impish new prefix of its own in the slide from "wear" through "where" to the final premonitory tremors of a mordantly overdue "(be)ware!" At which point the whole cautionary cast of the narrative—with its story of life lived under the shadow of so self-perverting an impulse that the guard of consciousness is lowered only at the self's certain peril—has been encysted and eviscerated at once. What surfaces there across a single elided verb of being is a broken sylleptic framework slung between two potential grammars: an existence described as manacled and an existence posited and placed by open-ended interrogation. The self is unshackled and loosed to oblivion at once.

The Loose End of Reading

But what else has syllepsis to suggest philosophically, besides its lampoon of Cartesian symmetry across the mind/body divide? What else in connection with the imp-eriled ground of ordinary language philosophy itself? Here I turn to Giorgio Agamben, who repeatedly theorizes the ontological equivalent of a predication that would shelter rather than forbid its alternatives. By his volume title, *The End of the Poem*, Agamben means both poetry's closure and its telos as gesture, its finish and its goal.[10] Three of the included chapter titles follow suit, their linguistic force leveraged by the difference between the subjective and the objective genitive. In the context of the fictional fantasy that the first of these essays interprets, about the oneiric generation of a whole new language, "The dream of language" names at once its proleptic envisioning and its source in the linguistic strata of our own unconscious. *Mutatis mutandis*, "The thought of the voice" covers not just our philosophical understanding of voice but our sense of it as the wellspring of all thought. Similarly, "The dictation of poetry" indicates not just the writing down of phrased ideas in verse but their origin in language itself, from which all such worded ideas seem emerging not just *to* vocalization but *from* verbal potential itself, source of all poetic vocation, let alone all everyday speech.

In the two-way grammar of these entitling phrases, and perhaps most saliently in "the thought of the voice," philosophy and linguistics are found to cohabit, or at least abut, at their reciprocal limits. With such formulations being legible either according to the normal time of syntactic inscription or instead backwards (when refashioned, for instance, as "language's dream," "voice's thought," "dictation's poetry"), these genitive ambiguities maintain alternative options from within lone denominations, options all but simultaneously potentiated, hence present to each other—in, we may say, ordinary language—across a no longer absolute Aristotelian divide of non-contradiction. Alternative grammar saturates the surface features of language not as what the phrasing might have meant instead (the Aristotelian potential, always pluperfect and thus vanished in the actual, as Agamben explains), but what, still in touch with the deep being of language as potential, speech also and otherwise does right now say, does make available to meaning.

It is thus that a linguistic vagrancy of determination keeps phrasing in touch with the field of possibilities from which it has momentarily been catalyzed, never rigidly crystallized. Reveling in the no longer excluded middle, such valences of suspended contradiction sustain the both/and against the coercion of the either/or. So that it might be fair to add, in distillation of Agamben's whole metalinguistic approach to literary venture, that his philosophy is drawn to poetry—and especially in the moment of Dante's triumph in inventing the very idea of the vernacular—whenever poetry, major poetry, reaches down to the fact of language beneath the plurality of languages, whenever it finds the conditioning potential of speech still viable in given words. And when, if and when major, doesn't it? Following Agamben, literature's task—and this whether in lyric (Dante), novelistic comedy (Dickens), or gothic travesty (Poe)—is to return, insistently if not disruptively, the foundational existence of language into the epiphenomena of phrased thought.

In this very spirit, at the syntactic as well as lexical level, there is something Agambenesque about Poe's own twofold title in "The imp of the perverse," glimpsing in linguistic form both the imp that occasions perversity and the impishness that constitutes it. This genitive byplay is not unlike, for that matter, the anchoring phrase from the subtitle of Cavell's *The World Viewed: Reflections on the Ontology of Film*—since ontology, in common parlance, is both the condition of being and, more accurately, the science thereof. Implying objective and subjective genitive at once, film not only has an ontological status of its own; it *is* an ontology in view of the world, its own successively framed view. Similarly, the prepositional hinge of "the imp of the perverse" exceeds any sense of the imp as perversity's derivative or object by also lodging a so-called genitive metaphor (a matter of equivalence), with perversity refigured as in itself a demon sprite, a rogue impulse, the hellion finally come home to roost in the final consignment to hell—with a further overtone of pluralized aberrancy, as in a phrase like "the whim of the mad." The reversabilities of such entitling grammar, just like the divided syntactic loyalties of syllepsis, keep the other alive on the flipside of the same.

Whether implicitly celebrated in Agamben (by extrapolation from a linguistics of potential) or satirized in Cavell's Poe, here is the excess of virtual meaning that literature not only capitalizes on but reinvests at the level of language's own event. In this way meaning is suspended in a continuous eventuality, spinning out its possibilities in the never definitive form of the not quite (yet) said. Every unpoliced "be where" harbors a "beware," hovering free of inscription as its own phonic undercurrent—and thus witnessing to the ongoing fact of language without lending it the testimony of a determinate form; without fixing it in a local habitation and a name. This, then, is not the where, exactly, but rather the wherefore by which *is* and *might*, the one and its other, may surface in the churn of a given phrasing, whether in Poe's manic cauldron of aurality under inscription or in some other literary poetics.

Moreover, it may surface for Agamben too, more than for Cavell, in the filmic chain. As revealed at their lower limit of coherence by the cinematic experiments of Guy Debord, the "transcendentals" of film are for Agamben the founding ingredients of montage in "repetition and stoppage."[11] Here Agamben looks to the "four great thinkers of repetition in modernity," namely "Kierkegaard, Nietzsche, Heidegger, and Gilles Deleuze," for none of whom is it "the same as such that returns" (EP 330). Instead: "The force and the grace of repetition, the novelty it brings us, is its return as the possibility of what was" (EP 331). Each iteration potentiates as increment its predecessor in the series: a veritable definition of the filmic frameline, where "stoppage" is continuously overwritten and "repetitions" are incremental returns timed to a persistence of vision in just those motor and optical effects that fall beneath consideration in Cavell's film writing.

Rather than comparing the medium-deep disclosures of experimental cinema to "prose narrative" (ibid.) like that of Poe's, Agamben turns rather to verse poetics, where for him cinema deserves understanding alongside "the caesura and the enjambment (that is, the carryover to a following line)," stressing in the process Valery's "beautiful" definition of poetry as "a prolonged hesitation between sound and meaning" (ibid.).[12] That's the hesitation we've called deferral and have watched Poe thematize as procrastination as well as circumlocution—at the same time that he toys with it at the lexical level in the "imps" that slow comprehension until disappeared into it. Further, this postponement has taken form not, in our examples, just as a homophonic hesitation or its near miss, as in the waver at *wear/where/ware*, but as a lexical hesitation about syntactic deployment—or, more in the mode of enjambment, as an elliptical run-on in the elision of be-ing from "be fetterless, but/… [be] where?" So that one could bundle all the examples in this essay, from the so-called "phi effect" of cinema's flickering differentials through the stop-start mechanisms of verse enjambment to the two-way vectors and split determinations of genitive grammar and syllepsis alike under the heading of "protension/retention," where the inscribed potentiality of the other remakes the same from within.

Certainly, in the sounding of one word or phrase under reverb from its pertinent alternative, the question is what resonance is meant as the present possibility of the different. Same question at the sublexical level when latent word-sounds like Poe's put the imp back, fleetingly, in imprint. In any such hesitation over syllabic relevance, such undue prolongation of the normally subsumed, the loosened caesural stress (what marks off a semantic unit from the phonemic stream—even if only in split-second retrospect) is what, in Agamben's formulation for the delaying tactics of verse form, "causes the word and the representation to appear as such" (EP 331)—that is, as material signal en route to the sign of a represented something. At the grammatical stratum as well, meaning is also protensive and recursive at once. In its linguistic wit and its internal *edge*, the sylleptic fracture is one clear touchstone of semantic deferral by verbal return, where alternatively available meanings must be sensed there already in the differences from which they are triggered. In syllepsis, potential is the very reflex of cognition. Focusing Agamben's sense of repetition around this one salient trope, we may put it this way: Whether metrical or not, in prose as well as in poetry, when the second foot falls in syllepsis, its grammatical impress marks (this time unmistakably) "return as the possibility of what was."

All of which confronts us once more, and finally, with an important way to think of Agamben joining Cavell in the overcoming of skepticism: that is, by Agamben's finding in absence (as potential) a genuine power—as in Gilles Deleuze, a power of the virtual. Doubt is overridden by undermining the paradigm of its own condition in the either/or.

The true/false toggle is disengaged. Ontology is for Agamben the clear case of this. Though the human being can't name, in either sense of the predicate, *its being in language*—either the words for its being or the inherence of such being in those dormant words—existence is nevertheless sensed to depend at bottom on the unthought of voice: an always receding (though not demonstrably false) bottom. This might be otherwise to propose—in another flexed instance of ordinary language (Austin, Cavell), where the noun of "possibility" hovers between "condition" and "potential"—that voice before language(s) locates the *possibility of being*. Objective and subjective genitive again: the option of being and its operative manifestation as still and always (only) potential. Literature as linguistic fiction makes this phenomenon unavoidable in one sense, its worlds possible only, or plausible—never real. Major literature keeps this enactment of sheer potential from turning either obvious or complacent. And does so by actually connecting again, beneath language as style, beneath its referential and expressive function, with the paradox of a mere verbal latency retained in action. Such is a latency recovered not like a mythic source but like the continuous becoming, never finally materialized: the emergence of *what can be said to be*.

Philosophy and literary criticism keep strenuous company in the thinking of Agamben and Cavell. Exercising us (in Cavell's therapeutic sense) to the facing down of skepticism, art (literary and film art alike) proffers, in the very absence of its represented objects, the continuous possibility of a world. In this sense of the word (as well as of the world) viewed, we are positioned again—following Agamben—at the shared vanishing point of linguistics and ontology. For, at just that nodal point, we find that the *sine qua non* of consciousness—namely, *the world's being brought to mind* (-ing predicate)—operates so that (again the somersault of ordinary language) its very *being* (-ing substantive) can be apprehended. As a linguistic condition of consciousness presumed and maximized in literary fiction, any bifocal sense of verbal phrasing—now alphabetic, now semantic; now lexical, now syntactic—doesn't prompt a dim view of meaning, just a stereoscopic and mobile one, or say montaged and recursive, labile even if given no tongue.

The force of this can come through as much in parody as in rhapsody, by pun as well as epiphany. And is in no sense necessarily utopian. For as Cavell has us notice, Poe's neurasthenic prose, tapping its Cartesian intertext with imp-ish skepticism, makes the aggressive short out between lettering and wording, phrasing and syntax, throw in turn a hidden switch that brings bothersomely to light all the unnerving paranoia that is the flip side of any valorized potentiality in the work of words. Nonetheless, what Cavell gets so meticulously right about the crisis of the subject in Poe's counter-lexical punning, the slipping away of the world even in one's own wording for it, can—when turned from philosophical parody to other modes of formal experiment—offer no longer just the disaster of the unmeant but the present possibility of the unthought, exploratory rather than foreclosing.[13] To have been given philosophical terms for such moments is one of the many lessons literary scholars take, and legacies we cherish, from the writing about writing by Stanley Cavell. Further efforts in this line—speaking sylleptically, and across a ricochet of genitives—go forward only in his wake, and his honor, and his shadow, and his debt.

7   A Storied World

On Meeting and Being Met

Naomi Scheman

> It goes on one at a time,
> it starts when you care
> to act, it starts when you do
> it again after they said no,
> it starts when you say We
> and know who you mean, and each
> day you mean one more.

Marge Piercy, "The Low Road"

I

Early in *Little Did I Know* Cavell remarks on the close connection of philosophy as he understands it to autobiography, and on that connection's grounding the philosopher's speaking for others (making claims about what "we" say, for example). He finds a "trouble" with this idea, in that

> I am not sure that those who write out of a sense of history of oppression would be glad to adopt this posture. I believe that certain women I know who write philosophically would not at all be glad to adopt this posture or feel spoken for by one who does. Nor do I know that men or women who sense philosophical roots beyond American culture will be moved to test my representativeness.

What Cavell takes philosophical writing to call for is "acceptance [which] does not mean that it is agreed with, only that disagreement must claim for itself the standing of philosophy."[1] What is "troubling" in this idea of philosophy is the possibility of certain others' refusing to meet on that ground, not contesting the claim that this is what we say but disdaining the idea that there is a "we" at all. In reading that passage, in the context in which it appears, I found myself wondering whether I am among those women. It's a hard question. I don't mean whether or not Cavell would count me as among those women: that might or might not be a hard question, but it's not mine to answer. The hard question I have in mind is whether or not I would count myself among those women.

It might seem (to me, for example) that this shouldn't be a hard question at all, that I should obviously answer yes—given that much of my career has been devoted to undermining the claims of those in privileged social locations to speak for all of us, in generically human voices, and to similarly chastening those, like me, who, in the empowering rush of finding our own voices, are all too prone to do the same thing, from our own relatively privileged locations. Casting a suspicious eye on deployments of the unmarked 'we' has characterized most of feminist theory and politics since at least the 1970s. Doesn't that answer the question?

Not quite. For one, eschewing the first person plural isn't a real option: neither theory nor politics can be done in the first person singular. Nor, of course, and more deeply, can we, without an implicit first person plural, have language or even the first person singular itself; there is no *I* without a *we*. And finding/creating an appropriate, usable *we* is a task many feminist theorists and others have taken on: for whom, or with whom, am I speaking? Who are my fellow travelers? Furthermore, at the heart of much of feminist and other liberatory theory and politics are concerns about, or demands for, recognition, engagement, and acknowledgment. These are all recognizable Cavellian themes, and I will be returning to them.

But another, more personal, reason is that my experience upon first encountering philosophy—in Virginia Held's classroom during the first semester of my first year at Barnard—was of hearing my native language spoken for the first time. That was my description then, and it still haunts me. (It marks, in fact, a far easier and less vexed taking on of the identity of a philosopher than Cavell's own.) It haunts me because my own subsequent work and that of many other feminist philosophers have helped to make it less likely that other young women will have that experience, and more likely that if they do, they will fear that there's something wrong with them for *not* feeling estranged from what they are told is a problematically gendered enterprise. By contrast, when I started college, in 1964, second-wave feminism did not yet exist, and most of my undergraduate education in philosophy, after Virginia Held's class, was in the hands of Mary Mothersill and Sue Larson; I had no sense at the time that there was anything at all remarkable about women being philosophers. The feminism of Barnard consisted in the confidence that we could be anything we wanted to be, and we were expected to want to be philosophers or other academics, or doctors or lawyers or artists or writers. Very conscious of my privilege as white, as American, and as comfortably middle class—in relation to the civil rights, anti-Viet Nam war, and anti-capitalist movements—I had, along with many other similarly placed young women, no sense of gender as an axis of privilege. For women coming of age after the dawning of second-wave feminism in the 1970s, 'sexism' is an obvious part of the political vocabulary, even if they claim that it no longer exists. They know that many of us—even if they think us antediluvian, paranoid, or simply unhip—see gender, and gender privilege, pretty much everywhere.

My sense that there was some lack of fit between my gender and the philosophy I loved—that, for example, in being a philosopher, I was my father's daughter rather than my mother's, something that my parents had actually expressed for as long as I could recall—dawned on me slowly, as feminist philosophy came into existence in the 1970s. But one crystallizing moment was my reading *The Claim of Reason* and being struck by what Cavell said about Othello in relation to skepticism. What I took away was a deep sense of confusion: I loved this account of skepticism, loved the grounding in human feelings, the palpable anxiety, the way in which bringing philosophical problems home brought home the fears. But I didn't know how to find myself in the story.

In one sense, the sense in which philosophy felt like my native language, I found myself just where Cavell found himself, found *us*. But it's not as though Othello's gender doesn't matter to the play. It is as a man that he is a celebrated war hero and as a black man that he is an outsider to Venetian life. And it is as a woman that Desdemona holds his humanness: she responds to his stories not by marveling at his heroism but by "pitying" his ordeals; she loves him, and in that love he finds himself as a (fragile, mortal, beloved) man. She recognizes, acknowledges, him; and in recognizing himself in her eyes, he acknowledges her. Iago (on my account more of a plot device than—as he was, for example, for Auden—the most compelling character in the play) convinces Othello that such dependence is stupid (unmanly): if Desdemona is to matter to Othello, what is needed is solid proof of her fidelity; knowledge needs to replace acknowledgment. What Othello should demand is ocular evidence, not the blindness of love. Convincing Othello of this demand is what really matters; it is the "decisive move in the conjuring trick": Iago's tampering with the evidence is almost beside the point. Just so, philosophical questions about the possibility of knowing how it is with others promise (falsely, it turns out) to allay our anxieties about our ability and willingness to acknowledge them, or theirs to acknowledge us. But the demand for knowledge cannot be met: I cannot fill the gap between us with facts about you.

I am deeply moved by this story, but I have trouble finding myself in it. With philosophy as my native language, as my father's daughter, I am the (humanly flawed and doomed) hero. But for all my claiming that place—and here is as good a time as any to acknowledge the fact that my claim has only rarely, to my knowledge, been disputed by my male teachers or colleagues[2]—it remains that Othello is importantly in the story's terms a *man*, and I am not. What I am, of course, is a woman; and the problem is not that of inserting a woman into the place occupied by a man, as though the gender difference didn't matter (as liberal approaches to gender difference would have it). Women are, after all, hardly absent from the story; Desdemona isn't a plot device, and she dies at Othello's hands, the evidence being against her, as evidence inevitably would be. Othello, of course, dies as well by his own hands, but his is a (fatally flawed) hero's death; following the anguished recognition of his own efforts to escape being human, his death is an expression of his subjectivity unmoored from its grounding. Desdemona dies a victim, her subjectivity having been ruled out of order, inadequate to Othello's demands for proof.

The paper I wrote in response to Cavell, "Othello's doubt, Desdemona's death: The engendering of skepticism,"[3] characterizes skepticism itself as a distinctively male response to distinctively male anxieties. It is, I argued, the privileged (as generic) modern subject who needs to found his subjectivity on the distancing of everything that marks his dependency, vulnerability, embodiment, and mortality. Since such a subject is expected to outsource the labor of keeping body and soul together, it is not surprising that he will pose their connection as an intellectual puzzle. Since he is also expected to police the boundaries between himself and others, as well as between himself and the world of things, it is not surprising that he will experience those others and that world as distanced, problematic objects of knowledge. Philosophical problems, I argued, were the neuroses of privilege, the irresolvable residues of the construction of modern privileged subjectivity. Those problems were mine insofar as I identified with the privileges I had—some, as it were, by courtesy—as well with those I was expected to take up; but it was a matter of political solidarity to distance myself from those privileges, hence from those problems, to disidentify with the subject of philosophy.

But as Wittgenstein and Cavell remind us, being suspicious of the enterprise of philosophy hardly disqualifies one as a philosopher. Quite the contrary for Cavell, for whom such suspicion is at the heart of what it is to do philosophy, to be a philosopher. In a discussion of the relationship of philosophy to psychoanalysis, Cavell says of himself that he is one of those for whom the question whether philosophy exists seems the only question philosophy is bound to, that to cease caring what philosophy is and whether it exists—amid whatever tasks and in whatever forms philosophy may appear in a given historical moment—is to abandon philosophy, to cede it to logic or to science or to poetry or to politics or to religion. ... [T]he question of philosophy is the only business of philosophy ...[4]

But the suspicion cannot come from the outside: it's what *we* (philosophers) do that is problematic: philosophy poses the question to itself; philosophers pose it to themselves. Where am I standing when I distance myself from the skepticism that I agree with Cavell is at the heart of philosophy as we know it? And, in raising the particular sorts of questions about saying *we*, am I turning philosophy into politics?

II

What I want to suggest is that the anxieties about saying *we* that face feminists and other liberatory theorists inherit the problems of skepticism, though in transmuted form, and that those anxieties raise the question of whether philosophy can—or should—exist. Further, I want to suggest that we (who?) need to attend to *you*, the pronoun largely missing from philosophy, the one that stands between *I* and *we*.

To start, it will help to think of Cavell's *we* as distinctively humanist, a decidedly vexed term these days. What vexes it, I think, is the charge that humanism sees human beings as too like each other and too unlike everything else. Cavell does not, however, take humanness for granted: it is a project, not a given. As Judith Butler says about gender, it is something we *do*, not something we *are*. (The echo of Austin here is not, of course, a coincidence.) And gender has for Cavell a lot to do with it. Think, for one example among many, of Cavell's discussion of the end of *Adam's Rib*, and the complexities of meaning behind Tracy's saying to Hepburn, "*vive la différence!*" One way of thinking about the troubling of the philosophical *we* is in terms of the possibilities for, and significance of, the category of the human, whether as fact or as project, and the alternatives to it.

The alternative Cavell refers to in relation to the "troubling" posed by women's relationship to the philosophical *we* is the demographic one: the claim to be speaking not for everyone, but just for those who share with me some list of significant characteristics. A frequent response to such invocations as: "I'm speaking as a white, middle class, mostly heterosexual, late middle-aged, relatively able-bodied and minded, secular Jewish, normatively gendered, American academic woman" is to ask where the list ends and whether its logic leads inexorably to a class of one. That's not an especially *good* response: the elements on my list are all axes of significant differences in social power and privilege, and elements have been added to such lists not haphazardly but as particular groups have drawn attention to problematically overlooked axes. My having brown hair doesn't appear on the list, though its being increasingly grey might show up as a marker of the social invisibility that tends to accompany, especially female, aging.

But the demographic response is not the only possible one. Another, better, response begins with the recognition that any use of "we" more or less explicitly presumes some relevant *connection* between me and whomever else I mean to include, whether I'm presuming that you too are dismayed at the current state of U.S. politics, or arguing that we need to be concerned about the corporatization of universities. That is, *we* are up to something; there's something we are or might be doing together, something we do or might share or are implicated in, and I'm either relying on this fact and your recognition of it, or I'm soliciting your participation or urging you to recognize that you are already in this boat with me and some more or less specified others. [5]

Thus, at the end of an early paper of mine, "Individualism and the objects of psychology"[6] I added an "Apologia," addressing my assumption that the arguments in the paper would make sense, let alone be persuasive, only to those who shared with me a certain estrangement from commonly taken for granted ways of understanding persons and their mental states. I was speaking, that is, to "fellow travelers," to those who felt—or might come to feel—such estrangement, not, as I noted, as philosophers were supposed to speak—to any rational reader. And, later, in "Forms of life: Mapping the rough ground"[7] I discussed the film *Torch Song Trilogy* as appealing to a liberally generous humanism that would not exact conformity as the price of acceptance, a humanism that I suggested was a hopeful fantasy even at the time of the film and, for many, an object of nostalgia later on. My own concerns about saying "we" have been most prompted by the challenges of women of color to white feminists, and it would not have helped matters in the slightest if I had demographically limited the voice in which I responded, in part because the challenges concerned the nature of the relationship between us, between, that is, me and those who were challenging me. The question wasn't fundamentally about saying "we": it was about saying—and meaning—"you."[8]

Philosophers have until recently been oddly neglectful of second personhood, jumping from the position of the subject to that of the object, as though those were the only available options for perspectives on the world.[9] The characteristic questions of the skeptic pose the problem concerning a possibly inscrutable object of knowledge, but "(how) can I know how it is with him or her?" is not the same question as "(how) can I know how it is with *you*?"

One way of thinking about the difference between knowing and acknowledging is the difference between the third and second person. I can, of course, know (about) you and acknowledge him or her, but in each case I'm moving away from the characteristic stance I have toward, on the one hand, an object of knowledge, and, on the other, another subject. The difference comes out in the diagnosis María Lugones gives to the problematic response of white feminist theorists to the charge of racial solipsism, a response that consisted largely of learning more about the lives of women of color and incorporating what we learned into our theorizing: it was a response in the third person, learning more about *them*, when what was needed was a response in the second person: recognition, engagement—not knowledge but acknowledgment. Part of acknowledgment is recognizing that you hold part of my identity; you know me in a way I cannot, without your help, know myself. María Lugones refers to this recognition as our regarding the other as a "credible mirror," showing us one of the selves we truly are (as Desdemona was at the start of the play a credible mirror for Othello). And one inappropriate use of "we" is to include those we do not acknowledge, those in whose eyes we are too afraid to find ourselves, or too disdainful to think that anything we found would actually be ourselves, or simply too ignorant of the necessity to look.[10]

In this sense saying "we" has little to do with similarity: it does not mean "those like me." It has to do with being connected and being attentive and responsive to those connections. It starts with the recognition that connection isn't optional: it is an essential part of the human condition. As Annette Baier puts it, we are all second persons before we are first persons: one becomes an *I* through being a *you*, and through being taught by other persons "the arts of personhood."[11] Replacing one's mother with a policeman, Althusser speaks of *interpellation* as a calling into subjectivity: we become who we are by responding when called, responding as that person who was called.[12] More benignly, Iris Marion Young puts *greeting* at the heart of civic life, as a public acknowledgment of personhood, building on Charles Taylor's work on the importance of *recognition*, in particular, recognition of group identities, of language and culture.[13] In a recent book Rebecca Kukla and Mark Lance put hailing at the heart of language use: our addressing each other directly and pointing out things located in our shared space are what make possible our saying anything at all.[14] These accounts are not all the same and not wholly consistent with each other, but I want to focus on what they all share: I become the person I am through being recognized by others, taking up what I want to call a "me-shaped" place in the world. The world (or some part of it) knows what to make of me; I am intelligible in its terms. I'll call this "being met" by the world.

There is a sense in which all these accounts are transcendental in Kant's sense, in drawing attention to what underlies the possibility of our ordinary lives. But, as Cavell reminds us, the ordinariness of our lives cannot be taken for granted; skepticism looms as the *modus tollens* of the transcendentalist's *modus ponens*. We may not be able to say what it would be like to lose our way with each other, not to be met by the world, but that is no guarantor of continuing intelligibility.[15] It's rather a measure of the magnitude of the threatened loss.

There are two broad streams of feminist and other liberatory theorizing about what I'm calling "being met." While both agree on its subject-constituting nature, they differ in drawing particular attention to the positive or negative valence, to whether the shapes the world has for us are cradling or procrustean. More attention has gone toward the Procrustean: there may be no subjectivity or agency unframed by what the world takes us to be, but we can find ways of raveling the edges, flirting with unintelligibility. I want to focus instead on the positive valence, on the importance of finding—and the pain of not finding—a me-shaped place in the world.

One way of understanding what I mean by a me-shaped place is through a wonderful children's book by Debra Frasier called *On the Day You Were Born*.[16] The book describes the ways in which the earth and things around and on it have prepared a place for you: the sun creates the warmth and energy you need, the mass of the earth promises not to let you drift away, the trees make oxygen for you to breathe, and, finally, a circle of people bids you " 'Welcome to the spinning world,' … as they washed your new, tiny hands. 'Welcome to the green Earth,'… as they wrapped your wet, slippery body. And as they hugged you close they whispered into your open, curving ear, 'We are so glad you've come!' " When I talk about a me- or you-shaped place as a matter of being intelligible, this is what I have in mind—a sense of intelligibility that is not an exclusively human, discursive affair. Rather, I mean all the ways in which we fit in our surroundings, in which we are, for example, subject to the pull of gravity or symbiotically related to trees or, for that matter, to the bacteria and other organisms that account for more than 90 percent of the cells in our body. We are in this sense *met* by the world: it greets, hails, addresses, interpellates us as physical objects, as animals; we belong here, it is our home.

III

The gendering of skepticism, especially given the centrality of skepticism to Cavell's understanding of philosophy, troubles the figure of the woman philosopher, who—in a parallel to my baffled attempts to find myself in *The Claim of Reason*—haunts Cavell's work. There is no question that women are important to Cavell, and that he takes them very seriously. Women live vividly in Cavell's writing, from the real women in the pages of *Little Did I Know*—from Cavell's mother to his daughter Rachel, with others strikingly in between—to the women at the hearts of the comedies of remarriage and the melodramas of the other woman. And gender, both symbolically and as lived reality, makes frequent appearances, most notably in the essays about movies and in Cavell's writing about his own ways of being in the world. But women philosophers pose what I think is a deep, structural problem: As a teacher and colleague, Cavell, along with (many, not all) deeply principled, liberal male philosophers, has been committed to taking women philosophers seriously, when all that was available for that to mean is treating them (us) as the same as his male students and colleagues. But, unlike most other liberal male philosophers, and to his credit, Cavell doesn't write as though he really believes that gender simply doesn't matter. There is, consequently, nowhere for a woman philosopher to fully find herself in his texts: we catch glimpses of ourselves—as women or as philosophers (and occasionally as women philosophers, in parentheses or in troubling queries, such as the one with which this essay begins)—but we haunt the texts, rather than inhabiting them fully. Such, at least, has been my experience.[17]

After trying—with, for whatever reason, little success—to bring these questions out into the open,[18] I moved away from directly engaging with Cavell, and am now pleasantly surprised, although a little disconcerted, to discover the ways in which he has been haunting my texts. In particular, my thoughts about being met by the world echo Cavell's thoughts about animism and its relation to skepticism, as Josh Wilner's paper in this volume (Chapter 11) led me to see. The context of Cavell's discussion of animism in "Texts of recovery"[19] is his returning to the final part of *The Claim of Reason* and to the suggestion of "taking Othello's (other minds) relation to Desdemona as an allegory (call it) of material-object skepticism," a move that "invites the thought that skeptical doubt is to be interpreted as jealousy and that our relation to the world that remains is as to something that has died at our hands" (IQO 55). In suggesting that we read *Othello* as a parable of the modern scientific way of seeing the world, which we inherited in its starkest form from Descartes, I argued that the hands at which the world has become dead are gendered; but that doesn't mean that it is only for men that the world is disenchanted. That world—the world of modern scientific rationality—has become the world we all live in, a matter taken up by feminists as well as by postcolonial theorists and others who theorize from diverse social locations diversely uneasy with the world of scientific modernity.

In Cavell's account it is Kant, rather than Descartes, who leaves us uneasy. It is uneasiness with Kant's "bargain" (what Cavell elsewhere calls the Kantian "settlement") with skepticism, "buying back the knowledge of objects by giving up things in themselves," that prompts the "taking on" of animism (IQO 55). One of the texts in which Cavell explores this taking on is Heidegger's "*Das Ding,*" which (according to Cavell) reverses the Kantian dependency of the world on our abilities to know it, replacing it with our need to find and accept ourselves as—finite, mortal—things in a world of things. Cavell goes on to consider what it means that for him, as for most American philosophers, there has been a barrier to his understanding Heidegger, and specifically to understanding him as a philosopher. I confess that, unlike Cavell, I have not attempted to surmount that barrier, but this is an occasion, among others, when someone has presented a thought of Heidegger's that has seemed congenial to me, or told me that I seemed to be channeling Heidegger (talk about feeling haunted …).

Cavell goes on to suggest, through a discussion of John Wisdom's paper "Gods" (which Cavell takes to be the only place where, within Anglo-American philosophy, the notion of animism is given rational justification), that animism be thought of as an attitude rather than as a factual claim, a suggestion that echoes Wittgenstein's remark that "My attitude towards him is an attitude towards a soul. I am not of the opinion that he has a soul."[20] It also echoes the remark of Eve Kosofsky Sedgwick's that Josh Wilner uses as the epigraph for his essay in this volume: "[t]hat the universe along with the things in it are alive and therefore good … does not record a certainty or a belief but an orientation, the structure of a need, and a mode of perception."[21] This conjunction of remarks suggests that the springs of skepticism lie in the demand that something—another person or the world—be an object of knowledge, and that this demand in turn springs from the fearful awareness that our own existence—certainly our intelligibility—rests on our acknowledging and, importantly, being acknowledged by the other, and by the world—what I am calling being met by the world. Our being what we are—persons, but also animals and physical objects—rests on there being a world in which such kinds of things are intelligible, meaning that the world and the other things in it recognize us as, for example, objects subject to the laws of gravity, or breathers of oxygen and exhalers of carbon dioxide. The world is, as Wittgenstein put it in the *Tractatus*, my world, but not by metaphysical fiat, nor by logical guarantee.

Thinking of things in this way suggests that it is not exactly jealousy that spurs Othello (or modern man) to kill literally or symbolically, but rather that jealousy is a screen for a deeper threat, that of dependency. Othello comes to believe that if his jealous thoughts could be laid to rest he could be happy in having his soul bound up in Desdemona's love, but the conditions he places on relieving his jealousy are incompatible with Desdemona's separate existence. Turning the other (Desdemona or the "external world") into an object of knowledge is aimed at maintaining the necessary relationship (as Othello says, his life is bound up with Desdemona: "But there, where I have garner'd up my heart,/Where either I must live, or bear no life;/The fountain from the which my current runs,/Or else dries up," IV, ii, 57–59) while convincing oneself that one controls that on which one has felt intolerably dependent. Thinking of the world as an object of knowledge and ourselves (or our surrogate, God) as the only source of meaning obscures the ways in which our existence in the world rests on the world's making (creating) sense, to its having places for us—to its recognizing, meeting us.

IV

But, to return to *On the Day You Were Born*, the story doesn't stop with the earth's gravity or the tree's oxygen and, outside that book, not all babies are met with loving hands and joyous calls of welcome. And as they grow, not all of them make sense to the people around them; in important ways—notably around gender and sexuality—they may be to others, even to themselves, simply unintelligible, or intelligible in ways that, too often far too literally, they cannot live with. In a video Dan Savage made with his partner as part of an online project called *It Gets Better*, addressed to GLBT youths, he refers to the song, "Somewhere" from *West Side Story*, which speaks of a time and a place in which to "find a new way of living." The video is oriented toward the future that the makers of the videos are imploring the children to stay alive for, but it also shapes the space of address: "I'm speaking to *you*. I know you are not a monster or an unnatural thing. I understand your pain—I went through it myself—and I am now part of a world that meets me as the person I am, and that world is waiting to meet you."

An organization in Minneapolis called RECLAIM provides mental health support to GLBT youth, and in the letter Janet Bystrom, the director, sends to contributors she tells us that she begins every individual, family, or group session by stating, "People you have never met and may never know have given of themselves to make this support possible. They want you to know you are beautiful just as you are. Whenever you are feeling alone or unloved, please remember this." Bystrom reports that youth in the program typically have these words memorized, and call on them for inspiration and motivation. As she puts is, "having been met/received in this way not only creates connection but it also creates agency."[22]

One can read *Hamlet* as portraying the painful disorientation of someone's failing to find a place in the world in which he fits, failing to be recognized or "met" by his world. On Francis Barker's reading of the play, Hamlet has the inward subjectivity of a modern individual *avant la lettre*, that is, before there was such a thing to be.[23] His madness·is neither wholly feigned nor wholly real: in the liminal space that he occupies, it is the best he can do by way of meaning what he says. Strikingly, it is with Horatio that he comes closest to speaking words he can mean: friendship, in its relatively unscripted intimacy, can shape a social space undefined enough to allow us to "find ourselves." Friendship is, for example, unusual among intimate relationships in having only one word for both people (unlike parent and child, or husband and wife): the improvisational quality Cavell finds in, especially, Tracy and Hepburn's screen relationships can be seen as marking them (not only but importantly) as friends.

Ontology (in the straightforward Quinean sense, concerning what sorts of things we take to exist) is an ineliminably normative enterprise (a claim Quine would not, of course, agree with). The things we take to exist are those we are prepared to meet, those whose shapes we take the world as we know it to hold. Consider, for example, meat. Carol Adams makes the point that those who are vegetarians on the grounds of the moral wrongness of eating animals should say, not that they don't eat meat, but that they don't believe in meat, they do not admit it into their ontology.[24] To disbelieve in meat is to refuse to participate in the practices in relation to which parts of dead animals count as meat. Meat is meat only in relation to (in the context of) those practices, and there is no meat in Carol Adams' world—no beef or pork, lambs but no lamb.

What I want to be getting at here is our need to be met, to be intelligible, to be acknowledged, the necessity of our taking responsibility for whom (and what) we are willing and able to meet, to whom we say "you" and with whom we say "we", and the unavoidable moral and political normativity of all these questions. There is a politics of intelligibility, maps of power and privilege that set the terms on which some are called on to make themselves intelligible to others who face no reciprocal demand. [25]

If philosophy is about the conditions of its own existence, then questions about saying *we* are quintessentially philosophical. So while I may
be (or think I ought to be) uncomfortable with Cavell's speaking for me,
the ground on which I pose that discomfort is itself philosophical. The
reasons for the fear of being incomprehensible may differ, but the fear
itself may be central to what it is to be human—it is in relation to those
with whom I share a language that I fear falling out of sense—or resent
having to make myself intelligible.

The *we* at stake here is not necessarily all-embracing—and is frequently necessarily *not* so: as in the Marge Piercy poem that serves as
my essay's epigraph, it is a matter of ethical and political commitment
to create a usable *we*. But I do find myself—I would hazard a guess that
we (everyone, not just philosophers) not infrequently find ourselves—
saying "we" and meaning, or wanting to mean, everyone. It is true, for
example, that we, all of us, began life inside a woman's body, we
remained for a long time after birth physically and socially nearly totally
dependent and may well become so again, and to a significant extent we
are still dependent no matter how ably embodied and minded we might
now be. It is a striking fact about modern Western philosophy that the
philosophical *we* is explicitly grounded in purported commonalities,
notably those of reason and rationality, that are at best oblivious to these
genuinely shared facts of human life and typically explicitly hostile to
them: it is one of Cavell's tasks, as it was one of Wittgenstein's, to bring
us back to our embodied, social dependencies. But as embodied social
beings we are differently placed in the world: we have no access to an
experience of the unmarked human; we live our shared dependencies
differently.

But if, as I have suggested, saying "we" is a matter not of similarity,
but of connection, of recognition, it isn't some generic humanness that
would make possible an all-embracing *we*. In another context, I have
described the quest for such a *we* as *diasporic*, not a return to some earlier
home, but a commitment to working toward a future one: for Jews the
name for this commitment is *tikun olam*: healing the world.[26] As diasporic,
the achievement of a *we* lies beyond a rolling horizon, and part of what
moves us toward that horizon is attentiveness to those who are excluded
from the *we*'s that shape our practices, excluded by our culpable ignorance, indifference, fear, or contempt.

A philosophical claim isn't an empirical claim about what some—or
even all—people think (or would say); it's a claim I make on your behalf,
and there's nothing I can appeal to against your rejecting what I say: I
can appeal only to *you*. And whether I can actually do that depends not
just on the content of what I say but, crucially, on the relationship

between us, on whether we can meet each other, be each other's companion,[27] whether you can—or should—trust me, and me you. And when it comes to *that*, such things as race, gender, and sexuality are clearly relevant, and properly chasten the scope of our philosophizing.

It is, I want to suggest, an open and vexed question whether there are unbounded philosophical claims, whether any one of us *can* speak for all of us, whether there is, in any interesting sense, an unbounded, human *we* at all. Many would answer that "no," and some would go on to say that, perhaps for that reason, there cannot and should not be philosophy in the way we have known it. (Some anti-humanist arguments are of this sort.) Vicky Spelman, in *Inessential Woman*, in an under-cited passage in an often-cited book on the arrogant overreaching of white feminist theorizing, marks as a final "roost" of privilege the giving up on the possibility of any general claims: "If my picture is biased, then so is everyone else's, in just the same way, and to just the same degree."[28] The possibility she points us toward is that, in Cavell's words, "those who write out of a sense of history of oppression" may be better placed to initiate the forms of acknowledgment and recognition that would allow any of us to speak for all of us.

8 Skepticism and the Idea of an Other

Reflections on Cavell and Postcolonialism

Simona Bertacco and John Gibson

Introduction

One point at which the concerns of philosophy and literary theory have intersected is in both parties' interest in the idea of otherness. Some of us might approach otherness by way of the problem of other minds, others by way of the idea of radical alterity, and if certain regions of philosophy and cultural studies are not cured of their current obsessions, for many the problem of otherness might soon become a chapter in the study of zombies. Whatever else makes otherness philosophically and literarily interesting, it at least has to do with the fact that the idea of an Other is unsettling, and it is unsettling because it calls into question the ability of our language and ultimately our community to reach out fully to those around us. The idea of a genuine Other is the idea of someone with whom our shared tongue cannot be shared, at least not fully, authentically, or without one of us changing in a quite basic way. One would like to think that the things we have the greatest chance of knowing would be the things most like us, namely, other people; that our intimate biological likeness should entail a kind of epistemological familiarity. If philosophical skepticism is unsettling because it raises the possibility that reality is ultimately beyond our reach, the idea of an Other is unsettling because it makes imaginable the possibility that certain humans, despite presumably sharing in our kind of body and mind, can in effect remain as unavailable to us as the fabled thing-in-itself.

There are many ways of thinking about otherness, and few terms have been given such a vast array of senses in philosophy and theory of the past fifty years. In some traditions of thought otherness is cast as an inescapable and constantly encountered fact of social life: the other as whatever is not I, that is, anyone I might happen to meet. While there are reasons for speaking of otherness in such a way,[1] it has the unfortunate consequence of making it impossible to draw a meaningful distinction between one being Other and simply another, and so it fails to isolate that very particular phenomenon essential to many of the forms

of oppression and denial the feminist, philosopher of race, postcolonial-
ist, and many others besides, bring to our attention. This is the phenomenon that shall interest us here. As it will concern us, otherness designates
an exceptional—though not for that uncommon—kind of experience. To
play on Levinas' terminology, it is not the Other we encounter in the
face-to-face but the Other as one in whom we do not quite see a human
face at all.[2] It is this queer capacity we possess, certainly on occasion, to
look at another and see something alien, incomprehensible, inhuman—
something *other*—that we are interested in here, a capacity that under-
writes a great many of our stories of tragedy, fictional or otherwise.
How does one pass from a state of mere anotherness to one of genuine
otherness, and what are the conditions of mind and culture that make
such a passage possible?

   The work of Stanley Cavell is especially helpful for thinking through
these issues, and it would be good for both philosophy and literary
theory if his work on the conditions of, as he often puts it, "human separateness"[3] occupied a much more central place in thinking about otherness. Cavell's work can show us how to tame the concept of the Other,
focusing it such that it reveals why the idea of otherness is both inescapable and deeply problematic. As we shall put him to use here, Cavell can
help us to see two very different ways in which the idea of otherness is
significant. One, we shall argue, is significant in a wholly negative sense:
otherness as a result of a skeptical stance we take towards other people,
the result of which is often to banish them to a state of impenetrability
because we make a rather big deal of the ways in which they differ from
us. The second sense of otherness is more interesting. It concerns a way
of conceiving otherness that has been immensely popular in certain
corners of literary theory but that Anglo-American philosophy has
almost entirely ignored: the conception of otherness that arises with
special clarity in the discussion of the so-called "postcolonial subject,"
though its significance extends far beyond the postcolonial. It is interesting not only because it helps us see what is vicious in the skeptical conception of otherness; it also brings to view a genuinely *non-skeptical* way
of thinking about otherness, that is, of understanding otherness not as
inevitably a projection of the skeptical imagination but as a kind of lived
condition to which one can very much bear witness. These two conceptions of otherness, we shall argue, are essential for understanding the
representations of the unfamiliar so central to what one might just as
well call the modern novel of otherness. In Anglophone literature this
novel begins to appear in the early nineteenth century with Mary Shelley's *Frankenstein; or the Modern Prometheus* (1818) and Charlotte Brontë's
Jane Eyre (1847); it develops into the troubled and troubling vision of the

colonized we find in turn-of-the-century works such as Joseph Conrad's *Heart of Darkness* (1899) and Rudyard Kipling's *Kim* (1901), and in ever more complex terms it is now being written by authors as diverse as Jean Rhys, Chinua Achebe, George Lamming, Wole Soyinka, Athol Fugard, and J. M. Coetzee, among, of course, many others.

The Sense of Separation

Cavell's thought cannot be understood without first getting clear about the basic philosophical story he tells about skepticism and human separateness. What we need to understand is that for Cavell the sense of separation arises from something deeply paradoxical about the human situation. The very thing that brings us into a shared world can also provoke in us a sense of alienation from that world, even an urge to withdraw from it. And as we will see, the casting of one as an Other can amount to one such mode of withdrawal.

Cavell often explains this paradoxical human situation in terms of language and the peculiar way in which we inherit it. One thing language does is hold out the promise of community—of a mutually intelligible way to "word the world together"[4]—but of course there are no assurances that this promise is actually kept. The skeptical impulse begins to appear when we ask how we *know* that the world is as our inherited language presents it to us, that those shared "linguistic criteria," as Cavell often puts it, actually count the objects in the world aright, getting them as they are.[5] We experience, at least in our skeptical moments, the very things that give us access to a common world as barriers to that world, seeing language, even our form of life, as empty of whatever it is we think necessary to establishing a satisfying connection to that world. For Cavell, without the intervention of another stance—that of acknowledgment—the sense of separation the skeptical voice prompts in us runs the risk of becoming a sense of *comprehensive* isolation and, ultimately, of undoing meaningful ways of being invested in the very world we wish to know.

But there is also something odd about the kind of disappointment with our condition the skeptic registers. The skeptic experiences whatever it is that grounds our relation to the world not as a point of entry but as a limitation, an obstacle, and this reveals something uncanny about the skeptic's stance. Consider the following passage from *The Claim of Reason* (and for our purposes one might replace talk of "mind and world" with that of "ourselves and others"):

> The gap between mind and world is closed, or the distortion between them straightened, in the apprehension and acceptance

of particular human forms of life, human "convention". This implies that the sense of the gap originates in an attempt, or wish, to escape (to remain a "stranger" to, "alienated" from) those shared forms of life, to give up the responsibility of their maintenance.[6]

And another, this time from *Must We Mean What we Say*: "Philosophy comes to grief not in denying what we all know to be true, but in its effort to escape those human forms of life which alone provide the coherence of our expressions. [Wittgenstein] wishes an acknowledgment of human limitation which does not leave us chafed by our skin, by a sense of powerlessness to penetrate beyond the human conditions of knowledge."[7]

The idea of feeling "chafed by our skin" is powerful. As with Socrates, who at times speaks of death as necessary for the attainment of knowledge, in this mood the body unfortunately makes knowledge impossible: the skeptic in effect experiences the fact of *embodiment* as an obstacle to be overcome. The skeptic is right that my flesh, as it were, presents a kind of barrier to what is external to me. This is hardly surprising. But then again, without our skin we wouldn't have much of a chance of experiencing anything at all, and so we find ourselves in the strange position of regarding that which grounds the possibility of having a purchase on the world (cultural, linguistic, or even personal embodiment) as making us "powerless," as Cavell puts it, to penetrate into that world, in this respect feeling very much chafed by our skin.

It is here that the philosophically familiar picture of a "gap," of a division in kind, between mind and world, language and reality, indeed between another and an Other, can begin to appear, though in a problematic and suspicious form. What is troubling about this picture is that we soon find that not just the objects of knowledge—this makes it sound merely epistemological—but nearly the entire range of objects of human concern, of *value*, can be placed on the other side of this gap. It doesn't matter if one is Bishop Berkeley wondering skeptically about the existence of physical reality or Othello about Desdemona's fidelity. What this picture does is place the objects to which we wish to be brought closer in a kind of elsewhere, and it makes impossible the satisfaction of conditions for knowing precisely what is happening there. How do I *know* that reality is as I think it is, that morality demands what I understand it to demand, or that my friends are really that? This picture of separation can strike us as inescapable because "the sense of the gap," as Cavell puts it, is conjured up by the very act of asking the skeptic's question. For we can always wonder whether the world and those in it are as we think they are. And to realize that nothing can voice an assurance that they actually are is to experience our relationship to these objects as disappointing, because shot through with a sense of insurmountable distance.

How we might overcome this—always imperfectly but effectively enough to keep our relationship to the world intact—is the topic that occupies much of Cavell's thought. What is unique about Cavell's work on skepticism and acknowledgment is that he insists that the taming (if never conquering) of this sense of separation cannot be carried out in the same tenor of mind that prompts it. We might recall Wittgenstein's claim that "knowledge is in the end based on acknowledgment."[8] For Cavell, as for Wittgenstein, acknowledgment holds near with one hand what the skeptic in us pushes away with the other. It is through our various acts of recognition and acknowledgment that we keep the objects of human concern tethered to us *here*. This shows us something important about our relations to others, and for his part the skeptic helps us see this. In Cavell's own words, "our primary relation to the world is not one of knowing (understood as achieving certainty of it based on the senses). This is the truth of skepticism."[9]

Acknowledgment is not a *response* to skepticism, if by this we mean that it answers the question skepticism raises, at least on the skeptic's terms. It rather acts as a kind of corrective, or countermovement, to the motion of mind that gives rise to the skeptical question itself. As Cavell often puts it, acknowledgment is an *inflection* of knowledge, not a separate route to arriving at its objects.[10] If we do not hang our knowledge on the appropriate hook of response, to this extent we create the conditions that give rise to the feeling of distance between ourselves and those regions of the world that interest us, for we inevitably experience them as "queer," removed. As such, we experience them apart from the ways in which they can make a claim on us and so bring us into a kind of community with them.

Of course, we can always make mistakes, acknowledging what should be avoided and believing what turns out to be false. The point is that the further skeptical error, both epistemic and moral, is to allow local mistakes and failures of knowledge to give rise to a generalized sense that the world and others in it might be systematically beyond us, at least, as the skeptic says, "as far as we know." It is at this point that skepticism can become "world-annihilating," removing the conditions under which we can experience it as *ours*. Put differently, the problem with the skeptic is that the kind of stance he takes towards the world makes it impossible to *hear* the various claims to community the world issues; these invitations can be received only when we take the world to be an object of *interest*, concern, and care, and not as a mere object of knowledge. Skepticism of this sort is, in its most terrible manifestations, tragic, as Cavell shows us when he looks to Shakespeare to achieve a sense of what it means to *live* skepticism,[11] leading us as it can to undo our connection to those to whom we most wish to be brought closer: Cordelia, Hermione, Desdemona, and all the other unfortunate characters who suffer because they find themselves on the receiving end of the skeptic's question.

The Skeptical Conception of Otherness

One lesson is obvious. The problem of otherness is both insoluble and vicious if cast skeptically, that is, as a problem of *knowledge* of whether others are as we are. One does not experience a sense of otherness of the philosophically interesting sort if one is merely skeptical about some feature of a person, say his or her love for us (though this can pave the way to this comprehensive sense of estrangement). If the idea of otherness is to register something more than the dull fact that other people can conceal their beliefs, desires, and histories from us—and everyone can, the Other and the mere Another alike—it must mean something more than this. To be interesting, it must give voice to a more thorough sense of concealment, not the sense of some one truth another might hide from us but some grander thing that shakes our confidence in the possibility that another could be understood even if perfectly forthcoming about who she or he is. Skepticism interprets the sense of an Other's impenetrability as a kind of *cognitive* impenetrability, imagining all others as in some sense inscrutable to a mind like one's own. If this is not quite tantamount to denying the humanity of another, it does, as skepticism generally does, create the conditions for tragic avoidance, for regarding another *as though* fully alien.

A work whose title perfectly expresses this skeptical conception of otherness is Primo Levi's *If This is a Man,* and note that in the original— *Se questo è un uomo*—one hears not only a doubt about whether one is a man but, lingering behind it, a human. Much of what Levi does is recount the forms of madness that not only gave rise to the question but that allow us to respond to it as though we have discovered its answer. One thinks here of Levi's coming to understand that many acts of humiliation in the camps were not, or not just, forms of torture; they were a kind of training. To make one eat on all fours like a dog is to make it possible to see another as an animal and so as other than human, in this way creating the condition of mind that makes the question "if this is a man" seem intelligible, legitimate, and even as clearing the ground for a kind of revelation. A home-grown example of this is James Baldwin's "Going to meet the man," which represents lynching as a horrible but effective social ritual, at least in an oppressively racist culture.

The members of the (white) community pack picnics, dress in their Sunday best, gather their children, and meet in a shared social space to watch a man be castrated and set aflame, until the body no longer bears the mark of the human, as if to say, "behold the answer to our question; this is *not* a man."

It would be unfair to say that philosophers and theorists who interpret the problem of otherness as a *skeptical* problem are always on the side of the devil, though Levi and Baldwin might wish to disagree. There are, after all, many who appear to cast the concept of otherness skeptically and then go on to try to derive a powerful ethics from it. (There is good reason to doubt that Levinas does this, though many of his commentators seem happy to regard him as going about his business this way.[12]) But what Cavell helps us to see is that the worry here lies not in the prospect of answering the skeptical question negatively. We go astray with the way we ask the question itself. This is why the concept of acknowledgment is not enlisted as a *response* to the skeptic's question but as indicating what we must do to prevent ourselves from succumbing fully to its all but inevitable pull: from allowing it to give rise to the sense of overwhelming separateness that places an impossible burden on our capacity to recognize others as *fellow*, at least in such a way that they could make a claim on our response. Interpreted skeptically, otherness is never discovered; it is never found, as it were, in the world itself. It is generated by the queer and potentially annihilating question the skeptic in us raises. In this respect *we* create the very conditions of mind and culture that permit another to pass into a state of otherness.

Otherness Without Skepticism

It would be to err in the opposite direction to dismiss the idea of otherness on account of these arguments, as though Cavell reveals that the notion is inherently confused and can be disregarded. Indeed, the denial of otherness would indicate just a different kind of failure of acknowledgement, not the skeptic's but the crank's. But what might it mean to acknowledge otherness non-skeptically, and how do we respond to otherness so conceived?

Recall that the skeptic generates the sense of separation by his very question and the realization that no answer is forthcoming. It isn't that the world stands up and says "I am not as you think I am." This is why it is skepticism: it is created by a doubt we raise and not some item in the world that claims to be otherwise than we think it is. Put differently, on the skeptical interpretation there is nothing that really *bears witness* to the gap we sense running between ourselves and others. But when one looks beyond philosophy to those corners of the humanities that study otherness as a kind of literary and cultural phenomenon, one can find an exception to the skeptical way of conceiving otherness. We find examples of a kind of subject who on account of usually terrible social facts *is* precisely in a position to *bear witness* to this; in this sense, we find an example of something in the world standing up and pointing to the distance between ourselves and them.

We can see something that amounts to this in certain strands of feminist and Marxist thought, and critical race theory, among many others. And we see this perhaps most perfectly in the idea of a postcolonial subject and the critique of the colonial imagination. The colonial here can often be read just as the embodiment of the skeptical sense of otherness, of the very stance that gives life to Levi's question: of the native as Caliban, capable only of swearing and expressing the desire to sleep with the daughters of Europe; of terrible and incomprehensible savagery existing beyond the final colonial outposts, and so on. In the various forms of postcolonial 'writing back,' one often finds the attempt, carried out as though guided by a moral imperative, to unravel the skeptical imagining of the colonized subject *yet* doing so by embracing and indeed insisting upon the distance between the two worlds. One thinks here of Franz Fanon waging war against the Western canon in his own mind.[13] Among other things, this is a struggle to achieve a kind of authentic and free expressivity—of *voice*, as Cavell might put it—that is premised on the knowledge that this cannot be done, at least not exclusively, in the colonial language. What all this gives us is a feel for the sorts of situation—political, sexual, and cultural—in which one can be compelled to say "I am not as you think I am, and your words can't be mine," and to say so sincerely, as a kind of testimony.

What Cavell helps us see is that a legitimate idea of otherness might be reserved for cases such as these, cases in which the sense of distance and incommensurability is too significant to be got at by speaking vaguely and sloppily of "cultural difference" or "diversity of lifestyles." In this respect, the notion of otherness designates the point at which we can't undo the sense of difference simply by speaking to one another in a common tongue, at least not without one of us changing in basic and significant ways. The idea of otherness one gets from this is not a skeptical worry about zombies. It is in effect a conception of otherness as a problem of specific *opacities of embodiment*, cultural, linguistic, religious, "racial"[14] and otherwise, without the *a priori* skeptical packaging. It is the obvious possibility of being specifically embodied differently that gives the truth to the idea of otherness, for the sense of separation this provokes can at times be thorough enough to undermine the prospect of any sharable community.

The kind of communication that is impossible here has little to do with the conveying of discrete bits of information—we can translate "facts" of the everyday sort and share them with the other—and it would be silliness to speak baldly of the impossibility of making ourselves understood to an Other, so conceived. But as Cavell helps us to see, when we speak we do not simply utter words that bear "cognitive" meaning; we attempt to conjure up a very precise environment of thought and feeling in which our words are meant to be received. We attempt to convey a sense of the world as textured with aesthetic, affective, moral, and perhaps spiritual qualities: as expressive of routes of interest and concern, of how and why what we say *matters*. This is a fundamental respect in which what I can say can constitute an act of acknowledgment. The sharing of all this, more than anything else, is what makes language capable of establishing community, since it is here that we create a space we can potentially share with others, as well as enact a sense of how one is that can be issued as an invitation others might accept or refuse. The sense of separation that otherness provokes in us arises from the awareness that our words can at times fail to establish this, that at present our words are idle in *this* respect: the words I am bound to use will not suffice to bring you any nearer. The mere expressing of propositional attitudes and stating of facts-of-the-matter are not especially helpful here, and so while this kind of factual communication is possible with an Other, it fails to help us confront the sense of separation we wish to overcome.[15]

The Two Faces of Otherness

We can see both senses of otherness at play in a great many colonial and postcolonial literary works, and indeed writers have arguably done more than philosophers to think through them, study their manifestations, and attempt to understand their entanglements. For it is arguable that each is part of our experience of the unfamiliar: otherness as a problem of skepticism and of embodiment. At any rate, consider as illustrations of the skeptical interpretation of otherness these two famous passages taken, respectively, from Charlotte Brontë's *Jane Eyre* and Joseph Conrad's *Heart of Darkness*. In the former, the readers, along with Jane Eyre herself, are introduced for the first time to Mr. Rochester's Jamaican and Creole wife, Bertha Mason. The passage is long, but it is worth quoting in full:

> He lifted the hangings from the wall, uncovering the second door: this, too, he opened. In a room without a window, there burnt a fire guarded by a high and strong fender, and a lamp suspended

from the ceiling by a chain. Grace Poole bent over the fire, apparently cooking something in a saucepan. In the deep shade, at the farther end of the room, a figure ran backwards and forwards. What it was, whether beast or human being, one could not, at first sight, tell: it grovelled, seemingly, on all fours; it snatched and growled like some strange wild animal: but it was covered with clothing, and a quantity of dark, grizzled hair, wild as a mane, hid its head and face. [...]

"Ware!" cried Grace. The three gentlemen retreated simultaneously. Mr. Rochester flung me behind him: the lunatic sprang and grappled his throat viciously, and laid her teeth to his cheek: they struggled. She was a big woman, in stature almost equalling her husband, and corpulent besides: she showed virile force in the contest -- more than once she almost throttled him, athletic as he was. He could have settled her with a well-planted blow; but he would not strike: he would only wrestle. At last he mastered her arms; Grace Poole gave him a cord, and he pinioned them behind her: with more rope, which was at hand, he bound her to a chair. The operation was performed amidst the fiercest yells and the most convulsive plunges. Mr. Rochester then turned to the spectators: he looked at them with a smile both acrid and desolate.

"That is MY WIFE," said he.[16]

The description of Bertha Mason exemplifies the extent to which the construction of the colonial subject and indeed colonialist rhetoric itself were predicated upon the skeptical idea of otherness. Bertha Mason embodies the most widespread stereotypes of the colonial subject as bestial, inhuman, instinctual, wild, and indeed in need of physical and moral restraint. The choice of deictic in the last line—"that" instead of "this"—to refer to the woman, who is tied to a chair and in full view of those present, reinforces with brilliant literary simplicity the insurmountable distance between the two cultural worlds represented in the work, despite, or precisely on account of, their physical proximity.

In Conrad's novella *Heart of Darkness*, written at a time when the very idea of colonization was coming under intense scrutiny, we see a more complex reflection on the same felt sense of separateness between colonizer and colonized, embodied especially in the figure of Mistah Kurtz. Examples abound in the text of natives constructed as "black shapes," as "barbarous" and "savage," but one of the most deeply troubling and literarily complex moments is when Marlow recounts the death of his helmsman:

The man had rolled on his back and stared straight up at me; both his hands clutched that cane. It was the shaft of a spear that, either thrown or lunged through the opening, had caught him in the side, just below the ribs; the blade had gone in out of sight, after making a frightful gash; my shoes were full; a pool of blood lay very still, gleaming dark-red under the wheel; his eyes shone with an amazing lustre. The fusillade burst out again. He looked at me anxiously, gripping the spear like something precious, with an air of being afraid I would try to take it away from him. I had to make an effort to free my eyes from his gaze and attend to the steering. […] We two whites stood over him, and his lustrous and inquiring glance enveloped us both. I declare it looked as though he would presently put to us some questions in an understandable language; but he died without uttering a sound, without moving a limb, without twitching a muscle. Only in the very last moment, as though in response to some sign we could not see, to some whisper we could not hear, he frowned heavily, and that frown gave to his black death-mask an inconceivably sombre, brooding, and menacing expression. The lustre of inquiring glance faded swiftly into vacant glassiness.[17]

What is troubling about the helmsman's gaze is the allusion that it seems to make to the existence of a shared language between the European man and the African man, as if there were something deep—that we might call human nature—bringing them together. Later in the text, in fact, Marlow explicitly states that he "had to look after him" and that there was "a subtle bond" between the two of them, and this is clearly meant to debunk the prejudice that the helmsman was "of no more account than a grain of sand in a black Sahara." Most significantly, he says that he cannot forget "the intimate profundity of that look he gave me when he received his hurt […] like a claim of distant kinship affirmed in a supreme moment."[18] Yet, despite his critical attitude towards colonial imperialism, Marlow is not ready to embrace the consequences of such an acknowledgment, an acknowledgment that would ultimately signify the demise of his world and his civilization. At any rate, what Conrad's text captures well is the troubled consciousness that colonialism faces in turn-of-the-century Europe and America and the growing interest in finding new ways of understanding and making sense of otherness. Above all else, this work explores the entanglement of the two visions of otherness discussed here: the skeptical one and what in this context we might simply call the postcolonial conception of otherness. In passages such as these one can witness a consciousness shift, often chaotically and violently, between these two ways of grasping otherness, as though to say that the experience of otherness for the colonizer is destabilizing, mad, and carries with it the potential for both annihilation and liberation.

The South African novelist J. M. Coetzee is arguably the contemporary author whose treatment of these issues is among the subtlest one can find in either recent literature or philosophy. In Coetzee's fiction, otherness is thematized as a central moral and political issue, and it reveals itself in a continuous struggle to acknowledge alterity without recourse to the stereotypical representations of colonialist discourse exemplified in the works discussed above. *Waiting for the Barbarians* (1980) and *Foe* (1986) are each exemplary in this respect. In these novels we find a thorough exploration of the issue of unspeakable otherness, otherness that cannot be bridged by words or language or the establishment of a shared life, and yet these books speak, as works of art, of the inevitability of such explorations in order to make sense of our world, echoing in this respect Cavell's own views on skepticism.

Coetzee's treatment of otherness in these works tallies to the positions the postcolonial theorist Gayatri Spivak exposed in her essay "Three women's texts": "No perspective *critical* to imperialism can turn the Other into a self, because the project of imperialism has always already historically refracted what might have been the absolute Other into a domesticated Other that consolidates the imperialist self."[19] In other words, the category of the other in postcolonial discourse can only be explored through and in the other's own language, a language that is radically different from the colonialist one and its core values and that enables the absolute other to speak outside of what is considered the accepted and canonized modes. The characters of Friday in *Foe* and the Barbarian Girl in *Waiting for the Barbarians* well exemplify this idea of the irreducible otherness of the postcolonial subject. They make demands on the reader simply by being there: they become inescapable and call out for an act of recognition. In Derek Attridge's words, they are "two figures of alterity who respond to the task of conveying their resistance to the discourses of the ruling culture, and also find means of representing the claims they make upon those who inhabit that culture."[20]

In *Foe*, Friday—unlike the original Friday in Defoe's *Robinson Crusoe*—cannot be tamed, trained, or educated. His tongue has been removed, therefore he can neither speak nor tell his own story. But, more than that, he seems to be totally indifferent to Susan Barton's language (English), despite her efforts to educate him, as well as to her displays of human affection. Friday's missing tongue becomes *the* central problem of the text.

Friday has no command of words and therefore no defence against being re-shaped day by day in conformity with the desires of others. I say he is a cannibal and he becomes a cannibal; I say he is a laundryman and he becomes a laundryman. What is the truth of Friday? You will respond: he is neither a cannibal nor laundryman, these are mere names, they do not touch his essence, he is a substantial body, he is himself, Friday is Friday. But that is not so. No matter what he is to himself (is he anything to himself?—How can he tell us?), what he is to the world is what I make of him.[21]

What Susan Barton is trying to do here is turn Friday's radical otherness into something familiar—what Spivak refers to as "turning the Other into a self"—with which she can establish a relationship along the master–servant lines. She is trying to make Friday intelligible to her and her potential readers, shaping him into a domesticated Other.

Textually, Friday's incommensurable separateness is signified by the complex narrative structure of the novel *Foe*, by an ambiguous use of inverted commas at the beginning of each paragraph, and, most importantly, by the prose poem that occupies Part IV of the novel that forces us to re-read the book as a whole. In a poetic prose reminiscent of Caliban's lyricism when celebrating the sounds of the islands to Stephano and Trinculo in Shakespeare's *Tempest* (III,ii), Part IV closes the novel with Friday's "faraway roar"[22] and leaves the reader wondering about the secret meaning of that roar. "This is not a place of words," we read at the end. Instead, "This is a place where bodies are their own signs. It is the home of Friday."[23] Friday's story, when it finally gets told, is not given through an abstract system of signs. It is delivered, instead, through his body, to an audience that can only try to understand him by finding a way to acknowledge the humanness of his body and the signs it bears:

His mouth opens. From inside him comes a slow stream, without breath, without interruption. It flows up through his body and out upon me; it passes through the cabin, through the wreck; washing the cliffs and shores of the island, it runs northward and southward to the ends of the earth. Soft and cold, dark and unending, it beats against my eyelids, against the skin of my face.[24]

That is the story that Susan Barton most wished to hear and write about. But, as Derek Attridge points out, "[f]or her, there can be no assurance that all silences will eventually be made to resound with the words of the dominant language, and to tell their stories in canonized narratives."[25] We are left, then, with the act of bearing witness to otherness, not as a skeptical projection but as, quite literally here, the problem of embodiment, in the form of Friday sending out his song not, as it were, to but upon Susan Barton.

Conclusion

We have had much to say about how the two senses of otherness we have explored are generated and very little to say about how they are overcome. A good story is owed here, and we don't have a good story to tell about this. But if one were to look to Cavell to find a hint, we suspect one would find it not just in his writing on skepticism and avoidance but perhaps especially in his work on moral perfectionism, and that this would be excellent way of putting Cavell in touch with those areas of literary theory that explore otherness.[26] That is, we suspect that understanding how we form a community with the other is for Cavell in certain key respects akin to understanding how we form it with ourselves. We've known since romanticism that alienation is not simply from nature or others but that it can be internalized such that we experience *ourselves* as foreign, as, in effect, Other—and that the world does its part to make this a constant threat. For Cavell the self is not a kind of thing but a sort of achievement, and we come to possess it by engaging in a certain project, Emersonian at root. For Cavell there is no ideal specifiable in advance, no rule to guide us, when we pursue selfhood. It is a kind of improvised, fragmentary, exploratory affair in which we constantly test and push against whatever provokes a sense of being unfamiliar, even unavailable, to ourselves. It strikes us as reasonable to cast the attempt to create community with another in at least some of this light. If we take it to be an unscripted project of good will and not an attempt to render another in terms already intelligible to us, we at least diminish the chances that at the end of our project we'll have inevitably done another harm by, as it is said, totalizing or rendering the other as the same. The story will be infinitely more complex than this, of course. But it would be productive to look closer at Cavell's work on moral perfectionism to figure how to tell this story.

II Practices

9 William Shakespeare and Stanley Cavell

Acknowledging, Confessing, and Tragedy

Sarah Beckwith

A very good actor once said to me that your role as an actor in preparation for a script is to find out why your character says what she says when she says it. If you know that, you will know the lines. You will have no anxiety about learning them because they will feel obvious, natural; you will see the point of the words you are saying and be able to say them with conviction.[1]

Anyone who has read Stanley Cavell's extraordinary essay "King Lear and the avoidance of love" can see or intuit that just this kind of loving attention and thought has gone into motivating every line of that harrowing play.[2] Now in his newly published memoir, *Little Did I Know: Excerpts from Memory*, Cavell tells his readers about his participation in a "memorably, extravagantly successful production" of *King Lear* at Berkeley in 1946, a production that had as a cast young students and returning soldiers on the GI Bill, a production that allowed him to "weigh every word with others in it," and about which he could claim: "no experience of theater I have been exposed to in my life has made a greater lasting impression on me."[3] It is not simply that working on a production of a play makes for an intimate, intricate, and lengthy exposure to the play's words, but that it

> overtly and continuously demands explicit and systematic exercises of imagination and articulation, from being thrown into the analysis and interpretation by the initial and fundamental practicalities of tryouts and the fatefulness and surprises in casting the various parts of a work for the stage, to the eventual and perpetual considerations of the possibilities of mood and condition into which each line can be delivered then and there, and responded to then and there.[4]

Such work involves not merely considering what each line means, a question of imagining the motivation and setting, but also how to "materialize the expression of what you say it means."[5]

After his reprise of the demands and discoveries of the *Lear* production it can come as no surprise that Cavell should inform us that this life in theater was nothing more or less than a preparation for his sense of the importance of "Austin's practice of a philosophizing out of a perpetual imagination of, as Austin put the matter, 'what is said when', why a thing is said, hence how, in what context."[6]

For Cavell, one might say, theater is a form of ordinary language philosophy. It requires us to ask: why does Edgar, Goneril, or Coriolanus say just this just now, in response to what, and inciting what response? On what do they stake their authority for saying what they say? Is that authority contested, interrupted, countermanded, exposed as fraudulent, ill-founded? Is it assumed, insisted upon, arrogated, risked? (I will go on to argue later that Shakespearean theater explores both what happens when a whole series of speech acts are unmoored from their authorized speakers and contexts, and the anxiety and creativity unleashed in such unmoorings.) In pursuing just these questions we will not only be doing what good criticism requires—making the work available to just response—but also imagining precisely, concretely, the simple, difficult fact that words are said and meant by particular people in particular situations.[7] Theater can thus aid in the consequential flight from particularity, from the world-denying, and self-forgetful elimination of the contexts in which words have a use. It may be therapeutic, redemptive, for it may return us to ourselves and bring words home, may "free the soul from its self-imposed bondage."[8]

In Cavell's intellectual journey moreover, *Endgame* and *King Lear* provide the structure of *Must We Mean What We Say?* and so convinced Cavell that his collection of texts "added up to a book."[9] The distinction, that is, between knowing and acknowledging takes its shape through the logic of Cordelia's "What shall Cordelia speak? Love and be silent" and would not have been available but for Cavell's pressing inquiries into the logic of that silence. I take it that when Cavell claims that *Endgame* and *King Lear* are integral to the insights he came to, he is insisting that that they are not illustrative of concepts formed independently of their logic.

The intuition that "I know" needs to stretch beyond its narrow confining of sureness, of certainty, of the purely cognitive, to the practice of acknowledgment as the mode in which human beings come to know and disown their knowledge of each other comes by way of *King Lear*: "What the advance required in my case was coming upon a way to make sense of the mysteries and grave events of *King Lear*." (LDIK 322) And just as "King Lear and the avoidance of love" is the culmination of *Must We Mean What We Say?*, so *Othello* is integral to the lived skepticism of tragedy, as tragedy is to the way skepticism tempts, incites, and compels us to disown the risky, self-exposing knowledge we have. Employing his novel interpretation of skepticism, Cavell develops stunning readings of Shakespearean tragedy, but his reading of Shakespearean tragedy also informs his definition, and brilliant re-definition, of skepticism.

What follows in this essay is neither explication nor application of Cavell's brilliant, illuminating writing on Shakespeare. The one has been admirably performed in different places; the other is a way of disowning the knowledge we have, an evasion of our own response to the plays at hand.[10] Rather I hope to trace out some patterns of, and paths to, acknowledgment in Shakespeare's plays by way of some field-work on confession.[11] Here it is as much Cavell's extension of Austin's work in his essays on "Performative and passionate utterance" and "Counter-philosophy and the pawn of voice," as any of his own readings of Shakespearean tragedy that I want to put into play. Confession is as important as acknowledgment in Cavell's reading of Wittgenstein.[12] Indeed, for Cavell the *Philosophical Investigations* partici-pates in the genre of confession: the voices in PI express wish, desire, temptation; they search for the acknowledgment of others; they search for recognition.

In our own culture confession has come to be mistaken for a self-revelation granted out of the mind's own (infallible) self-knowledge and thus become another instance of the privatization of the world. Wittgen-stein, Cavell, and Shakespeare all explore the tragic costs of such pictures. I will rather show the depth, complexity, and history of acknowledgment in some of Shakespeare's plays and cultural inheritance.

Here then are two thoroughly complementary versions of confession. The first: "confession is a speech act that seeks its completion in the acknowledgment of another."[13] The second: "confession, unlike dogma, is not to be believed but tested, and accepted or rejected. Nor is it the occasion for accusation, except of yourself, and by implication those who find themselves in you."[14] (The first is James Wetzel's: the second Stanley Cavell's.) How does my confession find the one who can, who will, acknowledge it? What happens when confession is both radically contracted and radically expanded as, I shall argue here, happened in the English Reformation? My claim is that Shakespearean dramaturgy is a search for forgiveness and that in the process confession becomes a vehicle of conversion and acknowledgment, as new forms of drama inherit the burdens of language in making and breaking human com-munities. Above all, a change of the heart is articulated through acts of speech, in which all have equal authority. I will not have time to chart out the complex inheritances of confession in Shakespeare's late plays. Instead I will try to show how confession is both "lost" and expanded in Shakespeare's time, how we need a much more nuanced picture of the work of ritual language than that found in the functionalist models still operative in the world of Shakespeare Studies, and how Shakespearean tragedy painfully uses confession in its complex charting of failures of acknowledgment.

Shakespeare's post-tragic plays cannot forgo what they have acknowledged: our ceaseless, relentless exposure to the consequences of our own passions and actions. But the group of post-tragic plays we have come to know as romances stage the recovery from tragedy in the renewed possibility of mutual acknowledgment. The medieval home of the language of acknowledgment is the sacrament of penance, and the earliest usages of the word "acknowe" are intimately bound up with the histories of this sacrament, especially in the act of confession. (The first definition given for confession in the OED is "to acknowledge," the second "to make oneself known.") What acknowledgment comes to be in the late plays is bound up with the investigation there of the languages of penitence.

For just over three hundred years the language of forgiveness had been adjudicated by priests in the care of souls and linked to a compulsory annual confession to a local parish priest at Easter. Forgiveness was declared on God's behalf by his authorized officers. The priest's absolution declared the sinner relieved of the *"culpa"* and the *"poena"* of sin.[15] But the reformations in Europe began, almost accidentally, as David Steinmetz suggests, as a debate about the word for "penitence."[16] Penance was to be not so much a set of actions (the *agite poenitentiam* of the Vulgate) but repentance, translating *metanoia*, the turning or returning of the whole mind and soul and life to God. "There is therefore, none other use of these outward ceremonies, but *as far forth as we are stirred up by them*, and (they) do serve the glory of God" (my italics), says the Elizabethan homily on "Repentance and True Reconciliation unto God."[17] All life, says, Luther, is a baptism declaring that we are not initiated once and for all but rather that we are always beginning.[18] What ensued was not the tidy replacement of one doctrine or practice by another, but a long conversation and conflict about the conventions of forgiveness.

In Shakespeare's theater there are almost countless instances of the word "confession" and its cognates, yet only three instances in the entire corpus of the word "absolution," even though both terms were once an intrinsic part of the sacrament of penance. Consider some of the following uses of "confession":

"Dear daughter, I confess that I am old" (Lear to Regan, *King Lear*, II.iv.154)[19]

"Therefore confess thee freely of thy sin" (Othello to Desdemona, *Othello*, V.ii. 53)

"I will hereupon confess I am in love" (Armado, *Love's Labor's Lost*, I.ii.57)

"I confess nothing, nor I deny nothing" (Beatrice in *Much Ado about Nothing*, IV.i.273)

"… scarce confesses/That his blood flows" (Angelo in *Measure for Measure*, I.iii.50–51)

To hear these words in these circumstances (to take a bare few examples) is to be exposed to: Lear's ironizing of the rites of confession in the face of Regan's demands for amends; the grim usurpations of the role of confessor trying to enforce the admittance of truths Othello can hardly bear to hear; the inevitable coming to awareness of truths the rest of us had known long ago, and long awaited, all the more delicious in being uttered by the one who has in denying them, denied his nature; the jocular denial of a woman outed in her emergent, despite-herself love; the wedding of a mind to its own fierce purity here seen as a denial of a human capacity to feel. In short, to confess is to begin to chart paths to self-knowledge, commitments made to different futures and claims, callings out in the light of these avowals and admittances which risk and require response, and in kind.

Consider, by contrast, the three instances of absolution. The first instance is the jocular black humor by which Cardinal Wolsey's execution of Buckingham is referred to as an absolution with an axe in *Henry VIII*. The second is in the same play when Katherine of Aragon interrupts the same Cardinal's Latin to declare "the willing'st sin I ever yet committed/May be absolved in English" (III.i.48–49), thereby depriving him of his Latinate authority and restoring the task of absolution to the common vernacular. The third instance is in *Romeo and Juliet* when Juliet asks her nurse to tell her mother that she's going to Friar Laurence's cell to confess and be absolved of the sin of having displeased her father (III.ii.231–33). And here it is a ruse to put them off the scent of her real mission to the friar to find a remedy for the consummation of her forbidden love for Romeo. So the putative confession and absolution are a disguise to ward off discovery. In Shakespeare's corpus, then, absolution is either punishment, joke, or disguise. The post-tragic plays on the other hand chart paths to forgiveness, paths that seem essential to the ability of the communities therein to find their feet with each other, to go on at all.

The transformation of the languages of penance and repentance were at the very center of an unprecedented, astonishing revolution in the forms and conventions of speaking, hence of modes of human relating. Confessing, forgiving, absolving, initiating, swearing, blessing, baptizing, ordaining—these are a mere few of the speech acts so transformed in the English Reformation. We might say that it is not clear any longer how any of these speech acts count as performative utterances at all, how, to use the scholastic jargon, they are to count as efficacious signs. It is not just that the conventional procedures were altered in the careful revisions of the *Book of Common Prayer* (1549, 1552, 1560), but that the question of what is effected by means of such acts and who has the authority to say and so perform them remained fundamentally uncertain and always open to judgment. Shakespeare's theater, I want to argue, charts from first to last, with huge clarity and remorselessness, the transformed work of language in human relating that follows from this revolution in language. When authority is no longer assumed in the speech acts of a sacramental priesthood, it must be found, and re-found in the claims, calls, and judgments of individuals who must single themselves and others out in these calls, who grant them the authority in each particular instance. So Shakespeare's theater is a search for community, a community neither given nor possessed but in constant formation and deformation. This puts him in powerful continuity, of course, with a theater he is often thought to have entirely superseded and overturned.

The result in Shakespeare's writing is an extraordinary, unprecedented expansion in the expressive range, precision, and flexibility of language as it takes up this terrible burden and gift of human relating when nothing but language secures or grounds human relations. His plays explore the finding, losing, and re-finding of community through the path from performative to passionate utterance, finding and seizing words unmoored from their conventions and open to the "disorders of desire" rather than "the order of law."[20] Given the new vulnerability of certain ways of speaking, hence relating, to the improvisations of desire, the late, post-tragic plays seem particularly overcome by a consequent sense both of the depth and of the fragility of human bonds.[21] Such bonds seem to rest on nothing at all but mutual intelligibility and this seems too insecure a foundation, too liable to breakage, fracture, betrayal, and rejection. They must be forged anew and through each conversation. That is the miracle in an age where all miracles are past.

This is a picture of language which insists on the dependence of reference on expression.[22] The risks involved in the acknowledgment of this dependence may feel overwhelming, for it is a picture that makes mutual reliance in a world of unreliable others unavoidable. It is no wonder that there are concerted, serious, utterly well-meaning attempts to bypass the necessity of such voicing. If the relation of word and world could only depend on anything more reliable than our voicing, our expression of that relation, we might feel more secure in the world and we might be released from the frightening contingency and variability, the unpredictability, of the actions of the others in our lives, from their fearful autonomy. But if the relation of word to world has to be established and re-established through our own voicing of it, then our responsibility in meaning might threaten to overwhelm us completely. Early moderns inherited and espoused at least two ways of evading this responsibility, both of which Shakespeare rejects. Language might operate magically outside of my particular contribution to it: this formula was precisely the object of much reformation polemic, which attacked Catholic versions of a language that worked *ex opere operato*, the core delusion here being the "hocus pocus" of the mass itself. But Protestant polemic had its own way of bypassing human expression: this emerged in the disdain and suspicion of all forms of human mediation. Some Reformation theology for example insisted that it was only by eradicating all human mediations that we could be sure of the God-sidedness of grace; all human interventions stain and contaminate, and infringe the sovereignty of God. The theological warrant comes along with the eradication of the human—and human acknowledgment. Forgiveness was not the province of priesthood; rather it was a speech act that had already happened. Luther's assurance was quickly undermined by the disastrous pastoral implications of the Calvinist understanding of double predestination; and Protestant "practical divinity" had to find ways of dealing with the epistemological fallout of this doctrine, one that rapidly became intellectualized as a problem of knowledge: how will we know if we are saved? The epistemological anxieties notoriously focused on this unknown but quite fundamental aspect of an unmediated relation with God. Shakespeare inherits these massive quandaries and questions and attends to them in terms of *human* speech as what makes or breaks the bonds between people. For Shakespeare, forgiveness *is* acknowledgment.

In her philosophical contemplation of the nature of human action, Hannah Arendt talks about the boundlessness, the irreversibility of action. We do things in the world utterly unsure of their effects; they are taken up by others in ways we can neither determine nor predict.[23] Such effects stemming from our actions are nevertheless uncertain and quite uncontainable. In her attempt to develop democratic and politically sustainable and just frames for action, Arendt suggested that there are two speech acts that make the boundlessness and irreversibility of action bearable: promising and forgiving. In an unpredictable world the promise is the foundation of trust, of dependability. In a world of harm the act of forgiveness allows a way of going on to new futures. It is through such acts of speech that the risk and uncertainty of action can be addressed. Both speech acts go through different conceptualizations in the course of the Reformation.

> Bud Welch's daughter died in the Oklahoma bombings of the Murrah Federal Building in April 1995. "About a year before the execution," he says, "I found it in my heart to forgive Tim McVeigh. It was a release for me rather than for him."

Mary Kayitesi Blewitt lost fifty members of her family in the Rwandan massacre of Tutsi in 1994:

> I met a woman who, after watching her husband and son being killed, was raped alongside one of her daughters. Her other daughters were killed at roadblocks. She was on the run for 100 days, meeting different people on the way, and was repeatedly raped. Finally she went mad and ended up in a mental hospital where she discovered she had AIDS. Now, if there was one person who had done all this and that person was found and apologized, perhaps you could forgive. But if there are hundreds who have hurt you, how can you forgive? ... You can't heal without feeling that justice has been done.

Simon Wilson was permanently disabled in a hit and run accident. Afterwards, he trained for the ministry:

> Some people within the church believe you can't forgive unless the other person repents but to me repentance isn't a condition of forgiveness because ultimately forgiveness comes from within. Only I know whether I can forgive or not ... Some people think I'm being pious telling people to forgive but actually I don't tell anyone to do anything. I simply tell people that the place I've reached is better than the place I was before.

These comments are all taken from *The Forgiveness Project*, a charity that explores forgiveness through the telling of stories. They rehearse—so painfully and particularly—the moral, social, spiritual and legal dimensions of forgiveness.[24] Who is to be the agent of forgiveness, which is an act of release as well as judgment? Each of the people I quote struggles with the extraordinary demands and possibilities of forgiveness. Each of them is confronted with questions of justice, with the terrible logic of the reciprocity of the hurt and the hurter in the same irrevocable act. Mary Blewitt would agree with Hannah Arendt: we can only forgive what we can punish. For Simon Wilson and Bud Welch, their own forgiveness cannot wait on the acknowledgment of the other no matter how desirable that act would be. They might agree with Avishai Margalit: forgiveness is not a voluntary mental act but rather a mental change.[25]

In medieval culture each of these elements—the moral, social, spiritual, legal and juridical dimensions of forgiveness—were bound together in the sacrament of penance, and medieval penitential and pastoral theology provides an extraordinarily capacious meditation on the social and psychic effects of sin and the remedies for sin. In this thinking it is impossible to separate the idea that sin is an offense against God, self and neighbor at one and the same time. The charity whereby we love our neighbor *is* a participation in Divine charity.[26] The sacrament of penance is fundamentally concerned with justice and therefore with the machinery of punishment and correction in the cure of souls, but it is also profoundly concerned with friendship.[27] Penance, suggests Thomas Aquinas, is concerned with justice but it differs from vindictive justice

> because in vindictive justice the atonement is made according to the judge's decision, and not according to the discretion of the offender and the person offended; whereas, in Penance, the offense is atoned according to the will of the sinner, and the judgment of God against Whom the sin was committed, because in the latter case we seek not only the restoration of the equality of justice, as in vindictive justice, but also and still more the reconciliation of friendship.[28]

The Reformation was an argument about the very nature of forgiveness. "If there is anything in the whole of religion that we should most certainly know, we ought most surely to grasp by what reason, with what law, under what condition, with what ease or difficulty, forgiveness of sins may be obtained!" declares Calvin in the *Institutes*.[29] Luther declared that no word had been as bitter to him as penitence; now, after he had formulated his understanding of man as justified by God, "nothing sounds sweeter or more agreeable to me than penitence."[30] Sins had been counted and classified in the massive encyclopedic compilations of the pastoral manuals of the thirteenth and fourteenth centuries; they were the subject of recounting in the mandatory practice of annual auricular confession before communion at Easter. In the reformed doctrine of justification, sins were no longer counted against the sinner and it was in virtue alone of Christ's imputation of righteousness to the undeserving sinner that sin was gratuitously, graciously, divinely given. The eleventh of the Thirty Nine Articles (1563, revised 1571) proclaimed it as an article of faith that: "We are accounted righteous before God only for the merit of our Lord and saviour Jesus Christ by faith, and not for our own works or deservings. Wherefore, that we are justified *by faith only*, is a *most wholesome doctrine*, and very full of comfort."[31]

Can there be an *office* of forgiveness? Don't we learn the meaning of forgiveness (if not how to do it) when we learn how to speak? Surely there can be no special office in which the forgiver is formally initiated? It is a speech act that must be risked, or not, in individual encounters.[32] This kind of talk is unobjectionable if we forget that the forgiveness under discussion is forgiveness for sin. Sin is an ontological category; it stains the soul, alienates it from its maker. It is, as I have suggested, inseparably an offense against God, self and neighbor. How is that offense to each party to be rectified, how mended? And who will or can judge such offenses? It is precisely in virtue of the category of *sin* that there is an office of forgiveness and a rite of initiation into that office.

Shakespearean theater is everywhere marked by the transformation of confession and absolution. When people confess and forgive in the absence of an office of forgiveness they are newly exposed in their words. For if the work of ritual is to make explicit what the force of an utterance is, then absent the ritual assurance that makes explicit the force of a performative, conferred in the precisely detailed conventions of the rites of confession, the act of forgiveness is both no one's and everyone's to bestow. It is no one's because the priesthood is no longer authorized to speak in God's name and his intention is no longer "covered" by the intention of the Church. And it is everyone's for the same reason. But precisely because priestly authority is contested there can no longer be a clear-cut distinction between what words do *in* the act of speaking and *by* the act of speaking, between the conventional and the consequential effects of the words, or in Austin's parlance, between illocutionary force and perlocutionary effect.[33]

Supposing you are a priest and you confess and absolve me. Your absolution might make me cry with relief and joy, or perhaps I resent your authority but require its effect, in which case my relief will be tinged with resentment. In either case you will have absolved me regardless of the perlocutionary effects your words have on me. But supposing you are not a priest, but you care about me. You think that I have been making some egregious and harmful decisions and you want to bring me to an awareness of them. You will in short be trying to confess me. But now because you have no authority to do this except for the authority I grant you in this particular instance, your attempts to confess me cannot be isolated in the same way from my response to you; there is no longer any conventional procedure whose conditions can be satisfied. We are both "singled out" in this exchange, exposed in our words to each other. Our judgment of each other is laid bare. We will be improvising, and the words we choose to address each other will be loaded with consequence: the future of our relationship might depend on them. I might refuse the position you are assuming in speaking with me and tell you have no right to set yourself up as judge; you might feel that our friendship is thereby shallower and frailer that you had thought. This might be called a "rediscovery of speech," and it is the essential medium of Shakespeare's theater.[34]

In the complex transformations from penance to repentance, some of whose contours I have attempted to trace here, there can be no simple model of replacement, no blanket functionalism which defines and adjudicates cultural losses. Rather, as J. L. Austin says, "the total speech act in the total speech situation is the only actual phenomenon which … we are engaged in elucidating."[35] This kind of an approach requires a sensitivity to occasion; it entails that ethics pervades every act of speech.[36]

I barely have time to trace out two examples from the world of Shakespearean tragedy. Let these two examples form part of a complex mapping of stifled speech in the plays in which they appear.

First, then, let us look at "Hamlet's confession" to see how questions of responsibility in meaning crowd into the scene in the absence of the office of confessor. The closet scene begins in mutual accusation as Hamlet and his mother each attempt to claim moral authority and the right to call the offense:

Queen: Hamlet, thou hast thy father much offended.

Ham: Mother, you have my father much offended.

(III.iv.9–10)

These accusations involve an attempt by both characters to reposition themselves in relation to each other. Gertrude speaks as Claudius' wife; Hamlet as King Hamlet's son; both claim the name of father. When

Hamlet sets up a "glass/Where you may see the inmost part of you" (III. iv.19–20), he is laying title to the role of confessor: his task is to bring Gertrude to shame and contrition and then to confession: "Confess yourself to heaven,/Repent what's past, avoid what is to come" (III. iv.149–50). Hamlet has not been formally invested with the role of confessor; there has been no ordination. He claims the role by virtue of what he has seen, by the burden of his knowledge: that the king is a murderous usurper. So his claim is deeply revelatory of his desires for justice, his own inheritance, and moral authority, claims that can at any point be rebuffed and refused by Gertrude. Whether or not she will grant him the role of confessor on this particular occasion is precisely what is at issue, and it will involve her in the most painful revelations about herself: that she is colluding with the murderer of her husband, supping at his table and sleeping in his bed, sharing the fruits of usurpation. Hamlet as "ghostly father" (a common word for priest or friar) rests the authority for the confession of Gertrude on his own "ghostly father," the ghost of King Hamlet whose provenance is notoriously unknown, and who now interrupts the scene. But not before the confession has been punctuated by the killing of Polonius behind the arras; the confessor is now guilty of a bloody deed "almost as bad, good mother,/As kill a king and marry with his brother" (III.iv.27–28). Where is Hamlet's moral authority now? In this scene, the "ghostly father" is one that he alone can see; as far as Gertrude is concerned he is staring fixedly into the vacant air and he looks like a madman. As he catechizes Gertrude about her congress with Claudius it seems as if his object is now not so much to soul-search Gertrude as to evince his own appalled disgust at her sexual depravity.

I am not so much claiming that Hamlet can confess Gertrude but not absolve her, nor that they inhabit a culture that has lost the rites of confession, as of mourning and marriage. Such accounts tend to posit too straightforward, and too functionalist, a relation between ritual and theater.[37] Rather I want to show how in the claims to confession as a language in which they are not formally invested as priest and confessor, Hamlet and Gertrude have constantly to take up their responsibility in assuming these incessantly changing roles. In that endless and uncertain terrain, there is a persistent struggle over where authority might lie, and who can lay claim to the "ghostly father" is continually in play. In such play each character is newly and continually exposed to the other and to his or her own judgment of the other.

Shakespeare gives us a further instance of "tragic" confession in Othello's deathbed confession of Desdemona. In the last act of *Othello*, Othello seeks to confess Desdemona. Acting as a demonic agency of justice, he believes that it is Desdemona's acknowledgment of guilt in confession that will make his killing an act of sacrifice and not murder. Confession is what links truth to reconciliation, and yet here we are given a scene in which it is impossible for Othello to hear any truth because he has convicted Desdemona in his mind. Only her admittance of guilt will count as a confession for him and so Desdemona is rendered dumb. There is nothing she can say that might count as a confession except that which would be a lie. So the scene appears as a hideous quasi-blasphemous travesty of confession in which Othello is a usurper of the role of priest. If you confess someone you must grant them authority in their own speech act—that is the whole point of confession and it is why confession is seen to be so necessary in the travesties of justice we call show trials and also why we feel the terrible injustice in such attempts. Othello will only accept as confession what we already know is blatantly untrue. There is simply nothing Desdemona can say—her words are rendered utterly impotent because she has been granted no authority in their saying. And before she is stifled, her speech is. Desdemona might here say with Hermione: "My life stands in the level of your dreams" (III.ii78), as Othello might say with Leontes: "I have said. She's an adulteress." Both have turned language itself into a private possession.[38]

We might say that Shakespeare's tragic heroes, such as Othello and Leontes, are would-be private linguists, denying the shared nature of language, imagining that they can define a world from their viewpoint only. The tragedies thus diagnose the relentless cost of imagining that language can be a private property of the mind—the protagonists of those plays define a world from their single perspective and lose it along with everyone they love. Unless we can see why this is a position to which any one of us is tempted, that it is internal to our existence as linguistic creatures, we will fail to see what is at stake in Shakespearean tragedy. Unless we also see why such a position may lead to violence and court unintelligibility, we will fail to see why the fates of Shakespeare's private linguists should be of such concern to us.

If theater, like ordinary language philosophy, asks us to pay such close attention to the particularities of speech, it is also where we show how necessary are our responses to each other, and how deep our mutual dependence, as we sit or stand, as actor and audience, waiting on each other's words, cueing each other unendingly for acknowledgment, for recognition.[39]

10 Competing for the Soul
Cavell on Shakespeare[1]

Lawrence F. Rhu

It is tempting to couch this essay in terms of a letter beginning like this: "Dear Stanley, I have received your letters and would like to say, 'Thanks.' They mean a lot to me, and I have been meaning to get back to you about some of the things you said." I would continue this way until I signed off, as in previous emails, "Your friend, Larry." Stanley Cavell sometimes describes his own manner of writing in ways that would make opening with such a letter no more indecorous than he has often dared to be, but I choose to begin somewhat more formally with the simple question "What is a letter?" I also promise to provide a relatively simple answer. That answer will lead, in turn, to further thoughts about Cavell's ways of reading Shakespeare and his impulses in doing so, about why they matter, and about what they mean to me and might mean to us.

Stephen Mulhall has already addressed the question of letters with regard to *Cities of Words*, so I do not need to rehearse the apposite antecedents that he brings to bear, such as Plato, St. Paul, and Friedrich Schiller.[2] Rather, I'd like briefly to remember how Tudor culture would have considered this question, when Shakespeare was a Warwickshire grammar-school boy at the King's New School in Stratford-upon-Avon. Erasmus's famous book of instruction, *De Conscribendis Epistulis* (*On Writing Letters*), would have been the likeliest source of such guidance, which would in turn lead us to classical definitions of the letter found in Demetrius and Cicero.[3] Simply put, they conceive of a letter as a means of continuing a conversation between friends who are separated by a distance that makes it impossible for them to get together and talk. You might say that the "dearness" of the addressee signifies at the start an effort to overcome what keeps them apart and asserts a nearness in spirit that abides despite any such obstacle. As with Emerson's assertion of spiritual affinity, it also suggests an awareness of our poverty, in the sense of enduring realities of human finitude that constrain us all.[4]

Erasmus himself is exceptional in his directives for composing a letter inasmuch as he expects letters to be written in accordance with

rhetorical models for giving a speech rather than in more casually structured prose, as his classical exemplars recommend. This odd feature,
which may arise from the fact that he is addressing grammar-school
students, can remind us not only that Cavell describes some of his writings as "pedagogical letters" and "love letters of nightmare," but also
that those so described derive from lectures given mainly to undergraduates. Moreover, chief among the classical models that Erasmus recommends is the collection of Cicero's letters entitled *Ad Familiares* (*To
Family and Friends*). After a long season of oblivion, these letters from the
time of the late Roman republic were rediscovered in the fifteenth
century, and they acquired their title from a fourteenth-century collection of letters by Petrarch. Perhaps this anachronistic misnomer can
demonstrate a version of something revisionary that Cavell observes
about Emerson. This sort of writing at its best does not merely represent.
It reanimates, like Julio Romano's art in *The Winter's Tale*.

Cavell emphasizes what he calls the origins of the American difference in philosophy, when he explains the apparent oddness of leading
off a series of lectures that includes Plato, Aristotle, Shakespeare, and
Locke among its particular topics with a lecture on Emerson. That
American difference makes such "monsters of fame" themselves look
different. In the process, philosophy becomes something we take by surprise, discovering it for ourselves, as if philosophy exists only in its discovery, not in some pre-established structure of time or thought,
however grand or authoritative it may seem (CW 7; ETE 133). Such an
event of discovery is the kind of interpretation of *The Winter's Tale* that
Cavell offers in his latest essay on Shakespeare, "Shakespeare and
Rohmer" (CW 421–43), although this approach has its beginnings in
Cavell's earliest writings on the plays. "Approach, " however, is, in a
pertinent sense, precisely the wrong word because, in Cavell's way of
thinking, we are already where we need to be if we only awaken to a
fresh understanding of the place where we happen to find ourselves: a
Shakespeare play or an Emerson essay, for example; or the country to
which most Americans pledge their allegiance (or the place in our hearts
that the idea of it still holds).

Given the subject of this essay and the book of which it is part, let me
add that by philosophy I mean the interpretation of texts, or reading, as
Cavell presents that activity in "The philosopher in American life,"
where he claims for it, when responsibly done, the name of philosophy
(ETE 33–58 (45–46)). By Cavell's way of thinking I mean what is nomi-
nally left out of Stephen Mulhall's essay "What Heidegger and Cavell
call thinking," which is Emerson.[5] When Mulhall traces an affinity
between Cavell and Heidegger in various passages, their clear debt to

Emerson is never mentioned. Thus, Mulhall effectively perpetuates the repression of Emerson's influence, as a philosopher, that Cavell has endeavored to expose and undo. Yet we might fairly say that what Emerson calls thinking amounts to an unacknowledged forerunner and kindred spirit of the thinkers whose affinity Mulhall seeks to elucidate in that essay. Moreover, when Cavell mentions the significant disagreement among Shakespeareans about whether the final scene in *The Winter's Tale* works dramatically, he notably does not seek to resolve the issue one way or another for the experts. Rather, he allows a very particular response to that play to stand for, as he puts it, what Emerson calls thinking—a whole-hearted receptivity to an intuition or whim that, in this instance, affirms a conviction previously shaken and inspires patience in seeing it through. In Emerson's terms that intuition requires a tuition, which, in this particular case, amounts to living in hope (CW 427).

To inflect a favorite word of Cavell's and to encourage the frame of mind that that word suggests, it warrants saying that Cavell's influence on Shakespeare studies is considerable (LDIK 529). It appears in recent work by Sarah Beckwith, Harry Berger, David Miller, Stephen Orgel, and Robert Watson, to name only a handful of estimable Renaissance scholars responsive to Cavell's writing on the plays. No one would deny, however, that Cavell's essays on Shakespeare come from a distinctive source, unrepresentative of the main streams of such criticism. Cavell is a philosopher whose commitment to what is commonly called ordinary language philosophy has prompted him to believe that he can write about anything—or at least anything in the humanities as they are routinely understood nowadays—and Shakespeare has figured largely in his work.[6] Cavell's belief is the sort of conviction that we (Cavell included) often seek to instill in undergraduates whom inexperience as readers, or skittishness about academic specialization, sometimes threatens to rob of a voice in their study of the humanities.

While taking these facts about Cavell into consideration, this essay seeks to distinguish key features of Cavell's approach to Shakespeare and to trace the trajectory of his writings on the plays from the beginning to his more recent essays. Basically, I will argue that Cavell is a sort of allegorist who senses a spiritual affinity between the skeptic's dilemma and the agons of tragic protagonists in Shakespeare.[7] In representing the feel of such ordeals, he becomes, like Emerson, an epistemologist of moods and a writer of a prose that competes with poetry in the experience that it seeks to effect in its readers, which is nothing less than "[making] things happen to the soul" (CHU 7). Such efforts both risk indecorum and aspire to provocation that will open fresh conversations. I will especially focus on how several of Cavell's responses to Shakespeare fit into his later philosophy, where Emerson and film increasingly preoccupy and inspire Cavell. These responses include most prominently the essays that are collected in *Disowning Knowledge in Seven Plays of Shakespeare*, though they are not confined to that collection of essays on individual plays.

Whether the quest for a comprehensive take on Cavell's readings of Shakespeare amounts to the best way to approach them should remain an open question. Cavell himself has commented on the fragment as a dominant, indeed necessary, mode of literary and philosophical expression since the Romantic era; and such reflections about his precursors suggest conditions and criteria pertinent to his own writing (NYUA 59; ETE 132–33). Moreover, he has increasingly become a writer of essays and occasional prose in the spirit of Emerson. In Emerson's essays and talks, overall coherence often cedes priority to provocation in transit from one turn of thought, phrase, or feeling to the next; and the materials of their composition can be found, in Emerson's phrase, "strown along the ground."[8]

Cavell admits that his writing perhaps makes exceptional demands and, as chief among them, he specifies the "friendship" of the reader (CT 12). If this sounds like an inordinate demand, it may also be a necessary one. Cavell borrows from Luther and earlier biblical exegetes to suggest that much of what we read in the humanities requires belief prior to understanding.[9] The mind's journey or, if you will, further reading of this sort, requires trust to proceed. It shares the vulnerabilities of trial and error that give the essay its name as a particular kind of writing; and the persona of the essayist invites us temporarily to share in his open efforts at thinking or, as Cavell puts it, at conducting his education in public (NYUA 8). Of course, if the scholar's profession requires conducting the education of others in public, such a scholar may not be performing his office. But then he may have found a more companionable way of handling that job, an epistolary style that encourages conversation despite various degrees of separation.

In first collecting his essays on Shakespeare, Cavell remarks that his essay on *King Lear* "bears scars of our period in Vietnam; its strange second part is not in control of its asides and orations and love letters of nightmare." Then, in updating that collection, he notes that no essay of his on Shakespeare has been more often requested for reprinting, yet "without exception the request has been to use only its first part, and even from that to excise everything 'philosophical' …, which in practice meant everything not contributing to a fairly direct recounting of the interpretation of the play's narrative" (DK xii–xiii). Perhaps in Cavell's two presentations of this essay, separated as they are by over fifteen years, we can chart a course that runs from apology to self-defense, where responsibility for its shortcomings and imperfections shifts from source to destination, as those limitations themselves change in kind. From either angle, however, we can sense a concern for decorum, for the appropriateness or fit of certain words at certain times. It is a general concern that recurs in Cavell's writings on Shakespeare. Notably, *Disowning Knowledge* concludes in the interrogative mood, where this disclaimer sets the stage for those final queries: "In emphasizing, rather than Shakespeare's sources, Shakespeare's writing as a source variously open to appropriation, I may find my own provocation in it, without claiming to speak for it" (DK 249–50).

This concern about professional authority echoes similar challenges that Cavell acknowledges, not only in writing about movies, but also in writing philosophy, where we might think he would be on surer ground. He describes the first step in speaking philosophically as the arrogation of voice and even as touching one's own lips—on the model of a call to prophesy, but without divine intervention (PoP 3–5; SW 29). He suggests that in writing about film and philosophy he may be courting outrageousness; and in bringing Shakespeare to bear upon a moment in classical Hollywood comedy, he defends himself against the charge of being hysterically indecorous (PH 73; TOS 15). Such questions of decorum arise during the period of campus unrest, when Cavell published his essay on *King Lear*, in which he managed (as he puts it) temporarily "to *suppress* questions about movies entirely" (WV xii, my emphasis). Shortly thereafter, "with America so under attack from the young," Cavell says,

> I wanted something America could do at its best and most generous: provide entertainment and education and valuable aspiration across class and generational and national lines. America could create these films that recognize simultaneously a human desire for schmaltz and for chic and that turn out to demand moral imagination and intellectual refinement in distinctly unacademic environments, indeed in definitively democratic relationships.[10]

Cavell's concerns about decorum overlap with his interest in provocation. His remarks about both of these issues derive from different moments in time that deserve their own placement in history—whether in Cavell's evolution or in the development of Shakespeare studies or film studies or in the history of philosophy. But that is precisely the problem (or one of them) that arises in discussing a writer who has ventured into such various fields. In undertaking these adventures, Cavell himself has been keenly aware of challenges that they pose, and he often acknowledges them as he proceeds. For example, he character- izes his essays on Shakespeare as "amateur forays" and describes himself as writing them "without professional thoroughness" (DK 179, xiii). In granting the losses entailed due to such limitations, however, he also speaks of the gain that comes from "being allowed to leave things incomplete, as it were uncovered, until [he feels he has] something inter- esting and urgent enough to say in his circumstances." Furthermore, Cavell locates these limitations of his readings of Shakespeare in his own disposition and in his academic formation when he declares that by "instinct and training [his] mode has been that of careful ignorance" (DK xii).

Such a mode brings to mind distinguished ancestors, and the most obvious among them, Socrates, can remind us of the defining arc of Cavell's career: that is, from skepticism to perfectionism, the latter of which he exemplifies by appealing to Plato, though Cavell derives his primary inspiration as a perfectionist from Emerson. This transit occurs over time and could be given an historical account; but it also can occur in a moment, any moment, of foundering and finding one's way. More reductively, the defining arc of Cavell's career could also be described as a development from Shakespeare to Emerson, with particular attention appositely paid to how Emerson begins to enter Cavell's interpretations of Shakespeare. And, to continue with drastically partial views, it can be seen as a passage from tragedy to romance, akin to what we can witness in *Antony and Cleopatra* and in *The Winter's Tale*, as Cavell reads these plays.

In a reading of *The Winter's Tale*, lodged within his essay "Shake- speare and Rohmer," Cavell finds the phrase "instinctive science" to describe the source of that reading; and he sees this kind of response as exemplifying "what Emerson calls thinking," the move from intuition to tuition (CW 427–28). Revealingly, in this context, Cavell becomes a reader of Shakespeare not merely through the perspective of a film's relation to *The Winter's Tale* but specifically through an interpretive response to the play's final scene as it is experienced by the film's pro- tagonist, Félicie (Charlotte Véry), a young woman with no special train- ing in such an activity. Thus, Cavell addresses a notorious moment of dramaturgical risk by identifying with an utterly "amateur foray" into Shakespeare interpretation. Or should we say "utterably"? Cavell's response to an interpretive crux in the reception of Shakespeare's romance becomes speakable or, rather, publishable, via the thoughtful convictions of a relatively uneducated character in a movie.

It bears repeating that Cavell's writing on Shakespeare, early and late, derives from teaching large undergraduate lecture courses in the Program in General Education and the Core Curriculum at Harvard. The long essay on *King Lear*, in good part, derives from lectures in an introductory humanities course; "Shakespeare and Rohmer" appears in *Cities of Words* as the finale in an entire course-worth of lectures transcribed into what the book's subtitle terms "Pedagogical Letters on a Register of the Moral Life" and Cavell further describes as "documents of a certain intimacy" (CW x). In Rohmer's *Conte d'hiver*, whose title in English is *A Tale of Winter*, Félicie represents the enactment of a youthful response to her experience in the theatre such as Emerson celebrates in his characterization of the "nonchalance of boys" in "Self-reliance" and such as Cavell may have hoped not only to encourage among undergraduates during his decades of teaching but also to sustain in his own capacity as a reader. "A boy is in the parlor what the pit is in the playhouse," Emerson pertinently remarks—or perhaps impertinently, with decorum and provocation keeping company here too.[11] Cavell's recounting of Félicie's decisive role in this film's meditation upon *The Winter's Tale* casts her in various parts in that play but most explicitly as Perdita or, as Félicie puts it, "the girl no one can find" (CW 430). Cavell's discovering, via Félicie, his own voice for reading the climactic scene in Shakespeare's play complements his previous turn as an unknown woman via impersonating Bette Davis in *Now, Voyager* in his essay on that movie in *Contesting Tears* (CT 132). With these personae in mind perhaps we can better appreciate the refreshing mobility of this writer's voice, the various subject positions that his subjectivity often seems to outstrip.

Finding Perdita, as he does in "Shakespeare and Rohmer," also complements Cavell's taking memorable note of how Shakespeare's romance loses Mamillius virtually without final notice or memorial, after the announcement of his death proves so decisive in the protagonist Leontes's repentance. Taken abstractly, finding and losing (or vice versa) readily pose the question of allegory with regard both to *The Winter's Tale* and to Cavell's philosophy overall, its moments of transition from tragedy to romantic comedy and from skepticism to perfectionism. If philosophy is education for adults, may we not see the loss of Mamillius, whose name itself suggests a nursing child, as a sign of becoming a grown up and putting away childish things? Such a change comes at a cost, but it brings a reward: finding Perdita, whose name itself suggests the soul we have lost in the process of growing up. Cavell explicitly rejects such a reading, however, and wants nothing to do with subliming away this play's avoidance of an honest reckoning with the death of

Mamillius. Even though he sometimes understands the stages along life's way as dimensions of the self, a perspective that encourages allegory, he rejects that view in his essay on *The Winter's Tale* (CHU 52).

Cavell insists upon the play's ultimate obliviousness to the loss of this boy in *Disowning Knowledge*'s sixth chapter, "Recounting gains, showing losses: A reading of *The Winter's Tale*." This title morphs unobtrusively into the running head for the chapter, "Counting and recounting," which initially sounds like a typo (Shouldn't it be "Recounting and showing"?) but actually highlights key aspects of Cavell's understanding of skepticism and its manifestation in this play. What counts as an instance of something is a key factor in determining our criteria of knowledge, disappointing as they may sometimes be; and "recounting" emphasizes both the mathematical and economic concerns within *The Winter's Tale* and the importance of narration to this play's dramatic action and its skepticism. Moreover, when you tell the story again, on the lookout for particular details, you are likelier to notice that Mamillius remains unaccounted for.

These central issues are duly elevated to a prominent position, the running head, to indicate their importance, but their form also signifies. Indeed, as with Emerson, the manner of Cavell's writing often registers or reinforces the gist of the claims he makes. His prose features a distinctive diction and phrasing, and an allusive resonance uncommon in academic writing. Cavell also makes dramatic use of a stunning talent for aphorism, which has been celebrated, though some have demurred.[12] Robert Watson, for example, acknowledges his profound debt to Cavell for inspiring the Cartesian reading of *The Winter's Tale* in *Back to Nature*, but Watson explicitly forbears from trying "to match" what he describes as Cavell's "oracular style."[13]

This arch demurral provokes further inquiry. Of course, emulation often turns into rivalry, but the personal animus here is negligible compared with the professional or disciplinary stakes. The claim to speak philosophically invites accusations of charlatanry, as Cavell knows full well and satirizes in himself by recounting his friends' parodic revulsion to "Stanley's deep responses" (LDIK 391, 498–505). Moreover, when the discoveries we seek to make frequently pertain to matters that we cannot simply *not* know, we are in a region where the obvious and the esoteric, the banal and the pretentious, may haunt and undo one another in both earnest and ironic efforts to inhabit a shareable world on meaningful grounds. Yet, if we cannot meet upon these words, Cavell asks of Shakespeare's plays, where can we meet (DK 19–20)? Pious fantasies of inter-disciplinarity abound, but the challenges of frank exchange and mutual intelligibility abide.

An affinity with Emerson as an epistemologist of moods comes through Cavell's prose in the way he deploys the grammatical moods of verbs, especially the interrogative, when questions flood the page with compulsive skepticism, and the imperative, when we are urged honestly to encounter the withering assault of shame (DK 193–94, 58). It may be, however, the indicative, the mood of simple assertion, that accounts for reactions like Watson's, and perhaps what he overhears is the arrogance that (Cavell himself takes pains to acknowledge) comes with the territory that Cavell pretends to inhabit. Pretends? Yes, he puts himself forth as a philosopher and arrogates the sort of voice that is sometimes required by such a role in order to get conversations going and to take matters into consideration that may otherwise be overlooked.

Given the banality of Emerson's popular reputation as the sage of Concord (or worse), Cavell's open affiliation with his legacy may risk further such misrecognitions, even though Cavell's philosophy is often expressed indirectly, in terms that are hardly prepossessing and can easily go unnoticed. For example, Cavell's agreement with Emerson's refusal to split the difference between subject and object informs the grammatical play of genitives (objective and subjective) in several titles to Cavell essays, like "Thinking of Emerson" and "The thought of movies." Likewise, the inflected form in the running head of Cavell's reading of *The Winter's Tale* is meant further to distinguish its philosophical content. The words in question ("counting" and "recounting") are gerunds, or verbal nouns, which is a grammatical sign of Cavell's effort in his writing to exemplify processes of thought—the paths we follow mindfully in a moment's attention, not just the destinations we finally reach.

"This one fact the world hates; the soul *becomes*" might be Emerson's gloss on the onwardness of Cavell's thinking, and what becomes of the soul is the prize that perfectionist philosophy competes with poetry to win, both in Emerson and in Cavell.[14] It is also what Shakespearean theatre competes with religion to win in Cavell's reading of *The Winter's Tale*, a play whose presence Cavell detects in Emerson's "Experience," where Emerson's struggle to grieve over the death of his five year-old son, Waldo, constitutes the nearly unutterable loss at the heart of that essay (ETE 126). Surprisingly, what Cavell finds in Shakespeare, tragedy and skepticism, turns out to be what Cavell also finds in Emerson in his effort to identify Emerson's claim to the name of philosopher and, ultimately, to designate him as the inventor of the tragic essay (ETE 207).

In one of his love letters of nightmare to his native land, in his *Lear* essay, Cavell avers that, in Shakespeare, tragedy comes upon an audience as it learns patiently to attend to the action of such a play and thus becomes present not only to the sufferings undergone by the characters in the drama but to its own powerlessness to influence their outcome. Moved to such emotions as compassion and fear,[15] the audience becomes alert to its separateness from the sufferers. Initially, in his reading of *King Lear*, this awakening of heart and mind to the conditions of tragic experience becomes Cavell's subject within the context of national tragedy, the Vietnam war; but his findings there sound akin to Emerson's process of writing as Cavell later seeks to elucidate it in his reading of "Experience." In that essay Emerson's distance from his own grief eventually leads him to acknowledge the unapproachability of America. This sense of blocked access signals the necessity of change within our country's current tenants, not the discovery of some new place on the globe or in the cosmos, but of a place in the heart. Cavell expresses similar convictions about philosophy when he writes "There is no itinerary, say no approach, to philosophy. Rather philosophy comes upon me, approaches me, like a conversion." Cavell then singles out for his attention "that strain or moment of philosophizing when philosophy does not recognize itself as having a history" (CT 64).

Perhaps Cavell's decisive response to a momentary impulse where history seems hardly to matter is the scandal (if there is one) of his writing on Shakespeare; or, at least, it is the scandal most readily discernible to chroniclers of philosophy and literature. Cavell finds something like Cartesian skepticism at work in Shakespearean tragedy, and he concludes that the precipitousness and unappeasability of Othello's doubt is akin to the hyperbolic and extreme skepticism of Descartes, not the mitigated variety of Montaigne. However provisional and incomplete Cavell's mode of writing may need to be, it also seeks to follow thoughts out to their conclusions, wherever they may lead. Explanations come to an end somewhere in this way of thinking.

This proleptic claim about Shakespearean tragedy and the history of philosophy becomes central to Cavell's readings of Shakespeare. It may run aground most obviously due to anachronism, but insistence upon that feature of Cavell's argument can quickly blow it far out of proportion. For Cavell is not primarily an historian of philosophy nor is he an historian of literature. Rather, he is, as I said before, an allegorist who senses a spiritual affinity between the skeptic's dilemma (or, more specifically, the philosophical problem of other minds) and the agons of tragic protagonists in Shakespeare. Putting it this way emphasizes not only Cavell's alertness to the spirit in which Shakespeare's words may be said, but also an obliquity in Cavell's way of hearing them. Strike too directly, and you miss. Grip too hard, and they slip away. In dramatizing the feel of such an ordeal, which he dubs the skeptic's recital, Cavell lets the questions pour in, and he becomes, like Emerson, an epistemologist of moods—in this case, the interrogative—and a writer of prose that competes with poetry in the experience that it seeks to effect in its readers.

To find an analogue for such ambitions in Shakespeare and the history of philosophy pertinent to *The Winter's Tale* and to Renaissance thought such as Shakespeare would have known it, we can turn to that culture's most influential perfectionist text, *The Book of the Courtier*, by Baldesar Castiglione. The Platonism that sets the terms of exchange in this dialogue launches a quest for the perfect courtier and culminates in the ecstasy of union with the Summum Bonum. Cavell's commitment to conversation and exemplarity as means of taking steps in the soul's journey maps reasonably well onto the overall structure of Castiglione's dialogue, though finding a conclusion in every step is, in Cavell, a sign of our finitude revealed in the provisionality, incompleteness, and fragmentariness of the ends we can reach. Moreover, Cavell's hearkening to the transcendental voice that he hears in Emerson and Thoreau leaves an opening for ecstasy, at least as those Concord writers characterize it—for example, "this new yet unapproachable America" in Emerson and "being beside oneself in a sane sense" in Thoreau.[16]

The Renaissance has a pervasive understanding of the relationship between poetry and philosophy that coincides in part with Cavell's evolving project as a philosopher and with Shakespeare's as a dramatist, especially in *The Winter's Tale*. Widely circulated paraphrases of a handful of lines from Lucretius effectively formulate this understanding. The fourth and final book of Castiglione's *Book of the Courtier* decisively registers their currency when the purpose of courtiership comes under discussion. At the least, this turn in the conversation provides the courtier with a high-minded cover story for otherwise suspiciously exclusive devotion to self-cultivation and the paths to advancement it might open at court. On the fourth night of conversation, Ottaviano Fregoso, a Genoese nobleman, leads the discussion and appeals to a rhetorical commonplace drawn from *De Rerum Natura* that most of us know nowadays from P. L. Travers and Julie Andrews. Renaissance literati would know it not only from Castiglione's frequently reprinted and often translated book, but also from the proem to Torquato Tasso's celebrated epic, *Gerusalemme Liberata*, and from Sir Philip Sidney's *Defense of Poesy*, among many other sixteenth-century texts of literary theory.[17] In Sidney this topos illustrates how poetry succeeds in moral education where philosophy fails; in Tasso it describes how the Muse helps the poet charm readers into learning otherwise difficult lessons; in Castiglione it shows how gracious courtiers persuade powerful princes to do the right thing. All of them, poets and courtiers, are like wise physicians who smear the rim of a cup with honey and trick sick children into swallowing bitter medicine and getting better.

We can also hear allusions to this trope in Giambattista Guarini's discourses on the sort of play that Shakespeare has written in *The Winter's Tale*, tragicomedy, when Guarini seeks to respond to the Aristotelian question Why does tragedy give us pleasure? Even more to our immediate point, the language, imagery, and sentiments of these verses pervade Shakespeare's tragicomedy, *The Winter's Tale*, not only in the drama of counsel at court that features Camillo and Paulina most prominently, but also during one of the play's most conspicuously metatheatrical moments. When Leontes implores Paulina to proceed with the business of the statue, however much it may afflict him, "Do, Paulina," he pleads, "For this affliction has a taste as sweet/As any cordial comfort" (V.iii.75–77).[18]

These Renaissance reprises of this originally Lucretian formulation treat the pleasure of poetry as instrumental, while philosophy, though generally ineffective, is considered a higher order of understanding whose achievement justifies the deployment of artful means on its behalf. Cavell, however, wonders if poetry and philosophy can change places, become one another, and still know themselves (CR 496). He sees them in competition so that philosophy can "claim for itself the work that poetry does in making things happen to the soul, so far as that work has rights." Though it may feel otherwise, such writing "does not seek to banish poetry from the just city" (CW 447). Even in Urbino, the "little city," which serves in its way like Plato's and Cavell's "cities of words," sonneteering is rejected as a game for the evening, but vernacular eloquence is central to the idea of the perfect courtier.

In *The Winter's Tale* there are three named characters who play the courtier's role. Camillo performs ideally and disobeys his king's command to administer poison to a visiting monarch whom he serves as cup-bearer. Antigonus does ill and exits pursued by a bear. His wife Paulina ultimately replaces both him and Camillo as chief advisor to the king by peremptorily intruding upon him. She promises explicitly not to be "honey-mouthed" but to speak "words as medicinal as true,/ Honest as either" (II.ii.31; II.iii.37–38). This Lucretian imagery of honey and wormwood is hardly confined to the court, whose stifling constraints *The Winter's Tale* so tellingly dramatizes. In Shakespeare's England it is standard homiletic fare; and, as Gail Paster memorably demonstrates, everyday practices of childrearing, specifically the weaning of children, made it fare indeed of the most aversive kind.[19] Moreover, Cavell's central interest in "the body's fate under skepticism" makes her line of thought particularly pertinent to his reading of this play, which seeks to locate the origins of Leontes's jealousy in a man's (any man's) biologically predetermined uncertainty about paternity.

The theme of grace is key to *The Winter's Tale* from the outset, as it is in Castiglione's dialogue. It is introduced in the most ordinary language imaginable in the play's first scene when Camillo remarks to a departing courtier from Bohemia "You pay a great deal too much for what is given freely" (I.1. 17–18). This theme centrally figures in the competition between institutions as Cavell sees it in *The Winter's Tale*. Paulina's name and many of her lines give away her connection to the Pauline theology of grace crucial to Reformation religion, and the boy who played this complex role must have been an extraordinarily "gracious" actor in his mimetic accomplishments. Lady Macbeth, Cleopatra, and Volumnia were likely to have been three of his recent roles. The stakes competed for remain nothing less than the souls of the audience, our souls; and when Cavell uses Rohmer's *Conte d'hiver* as a meditation upon *The Winter's Tale*, he adds another art to the competition, film.

Cavell's turn to film is his quintessentially Lucretian gesture, inviting those who might need or seek the consolations of philosophy to go to a show. It is a gesture that challenges standards of decorum in its embrace of ordinary experience as worthy of such demands. When Cavell makes this move, Shakespeare and Northrop Frye figure prominently in the process; but, in Cavell's cities of words, those eventual communities of his making and perception, we also find on screen unlikely philosophers. Sometimes they are specifically identified as such, and they are in therapeutic conversation with isolated and disappointed interlocutors— Cary Grant, the man from dream city himself, with Katharine Hepburn in *The Philadelphia Story*; Barbara Stanwyck with Henry Fonda in *The Lady Eve*; Claude Rains with Bette Davis in *Now, Voyager*. Their philosophical virtues include patience, practicality, and the refusal to play the role of the sage; and the pleasure and satisfaction of their company can come as a delightful surprise, especially to students who were previously unfamiliar with such films. They might lead students to do some serious reading or to read on, if they have previously grown weary or confused. Such films, and Cavell's use of them, might even inspire some in the classroom to write themes out of school composed, to a degree, as criticism of the academy from within, by a loyal opposition.

Or, as Sir Philip Sidney says, if we are already philosophers, we may not need poetry of any kind—cinematic, dramatic, etc. We may already know what such arts deployed in the interest of moral education strive to make palatable to consumers otherwise indisposed. But that's one of the dangers of *sprezzatura* or nonchalance, as Castiglione's courtiers famously commend it, as Sidney deftly puts it into play, and as Emerson praises it in boys. Nonchalance can become disedifying smugness and make even churlishness seem almost refreshing. In his increasingly Emersonian mode, Cavell emphasizes the questionable inheritability, by an American philosopher, of what he often calls the edifice of European philosophy;[20] and that would include the systematic terminology that comes with those grand structures of thought. Cavell celebrates Emerson's skill with ordinary language, and he explores various of Emerson's entanglements with European philosophy. They are not necessarily systematic but they are scrupulously accountable for their own ways of wording the world. In Cavell's later writing on Shakespeare, Emerson becomes a decisive touchstone; but, from the late 1970s, he is already coming upon Cavell like a conversion to which there will be many sequels.

Emerson is the first philosopher discussed in *Cities of Words*; Plato and Aristotle are the last. The cover of that book further illustrates its perspective on the history of philosophy in the suggestive relation between the two images it displays. It features a smaller photo inset against a larger background photo of hats worn by barely discernible men. The hats in the cover's background photo suggest a moment from the second of Descartes's *Meditations on First Philosophy*, where the philosopher notes in passing a tangential thought that arises from an accidental memory of glancing out the window. "By chance I remember that, when looking from a window and saying I see men who pass in the street, I really do not see them but infer that what I see is men ... And yet what do I see from the window but hats and coats which may cover automatic machines?" Even though Descartes proceeds to resolve the problem of his potential aloneness in the universe by an appeal to the nature of God, we can hear in these words an intimation of the philosophical problem of other minds that Cavell explores from myriad angles throughout his writings. Most notably, his interpretation of *Othello* reveals how the General's murderous distrust of Desdemona camouflages a willful denial, his death-dealing skepticism and avoidance of love.[21]

Although the background photo indicates how solitude threatens to strand us in a sea of unknown and perhaps unknowable others, the inset photo offers what Cavell claims Othello tragically lacks when he describes the play of that title as a failed comedy of remarriage (PH 120). It pictures Katharine Hepburn, Cary Grant, and James Stewart, as they appear in *The Philadelphia Story* (dir. George Cukor, 1940), and it offers a glimpse of a world where individuals and couples manage to recover from threats of such a catastrophe. With apposite vagueness, Cavell has termed the desired goals of their Emersonian quests "happiness" or "mutual intelligibility," which is always a transient achievement and often a renewable challenge. The conversations of classic Hollywood comedies of remarriage, like *The Philadelphia Story*, have served Cavell as texts to interpret in an effort to explore such possibilities of human relations, though Beatrice and Benedick in Shakespeare's *Much Ado about Nothing* could provide a pertinent analogue. This inset photo, however, is precisely *not* a best case, or example, of overcoming the threats of skepticism. That is part of the problem, which only hastens the breathtaking momentum of Othello's murderous turn: he has an example in mind which is too good, "the divine Desdemona." No human being can measure up to that fixated ideal. Rather, the inset photo simply offers a glimpse of a world where lively alternatives to isolation are imaginable, where intimacy between word and world, self and other, body and soul may be attained, however temporarily, time and again. But the logic of tragedy, like that of Cartesian skepticism, is inexorable. It is inconceivable that such a sight, or the considerations that it might raise or represent, could stop Othello in his tracks, once he has given himself over to the absolute demands of jealousy and doubt. How could you do that? The play, after all, is a tragedy.

In Shakespeare's tragicomedy, however, there *is* a moment that stops people in their tracks. This turn of events in *The Winter's Tale* blatantly amounts to a set-up, so that even skeptics are being encouraged knowingly to drop their guards and to awake their faith, to let it happen to them too. Moreover, it is a typically romantic moment in terms of the genre whose name we have come to apply to Shakespeare's late, post-tragic plays. Canonical Renaissance instances of romance routinely traffic in marvels and commonplaces. If we shift from a lower to an upper case "r," it is also a claimably Romantic moment in which a kind of sublimity breaks through everydayness when we read it along with Cavell through the figure of Félicie in Rohmer's *Conte d'hiver*. Such changes of character—from lower to upper case—can serve as a sign of the soul's journey in perfectionism, as Cavell inherits it primarily from Emerson. This work of genius brings back to Félicie her afternoon's meditation, her own thoughts in their alienated majesty.[22]

Thus, in *Conte d'hiver* Félicie's interpretation of the last scene of *The Winter's Tale* represents for Cavell what Emerson calls thinking, and it is subject to all the attendant risks of such a process. "It may prove whim at last," as Emerson is the first to admit, "but [she] cannot spend the day in explanation." For Félicie, that risk proves worth taking, and, in the final scenes of the movie, it also serves as a prelude to her happy reunion with Charles (Frédéric van den Driessche), her lost love and the father of her child. Their getting together again mirrors the plot structure of such remarriage comedies as *The Philadelphia Story*, where, you may recall, Dexter Havens (Cary Grant) ironically describes Tracy Lord (Katharine Hepburn)'s leading characteristic as her horror of men who wear their hats in the house, like Macaulay "Mike" Conner (James Stewart), the skeptical newsman, at that very moment. The reunion of Hermione and Leontes in Shakespeare's romance does not hold nearly as much promise of happiness as these movie endings, especially if we remember the absence of their son, Mamillius, who remains unaccounted for. Although wonder is the keynote of romance, both as a genre and in this play's practice of that form, it is hard to imagine that the King of Sicilia will, like the man from Chicago, dance with his wife. Still, the play is over, so, at the Globe, there will at least be a jig. Inspired by Shakespeare's play and Cavell's philosophy, clearer acknowledgment of both our skepticism and our hope in such affairs becomes possible. That strikes me as a possibility worthy of a Gene Kelly kick on the streets of Paris.

11 "Communicating with Objects"

Romanticism, Skepticism, and "The Specter of Animism" in Cavell and Wordsworth

Joshua Wilner

That the universe along with the things in it are alive and therefore good: here, I think, is a crux of Proust's mysticism. Moreover, the formulation does not record a certainty or a belief but an orientation, the structure of a need, and a mode of perception. It is possible for the universe to be dead and worthless; but if it does not live, neither do the things in it, including oneself and one's own contents. So put it comparatively: the universe itself is *as* alive as anything it holds.

Eve Kosofsky Sedgwick, "The Weather in Proust"[1]

My aims in what follows are both limited and tentative. First, I will offer a sketch of Cavell's portrayal of Romanticism as expressing a disappointment with the Kantian settlement with skepticism and of its embrace of "something like animism" as pivotal in its reclaiming of a human relationship to things, *things in themselves*. Next, I turn to "Tintern Abbey," a poem that Cavell does not discuss but which his account of Romanticism, I suggest, centrally alludes to, to reflect on one extended passage in particular in the light of that account and vice versa. Finally, I will briefly consider the role that the term "pathetic fallacy" plays in Cavell's characterization of Romantic "animism," and its relation to the perhaps more technical, but in any case more rhetorical, term, "apostrophe."

The "issue, or specter, of animism" turns up by name in the introductory pages to "Texts of Recovery," the third of the 1983 Beckman lectures that constitute the first and principal part of *In Quest of the Ordinary: Lines of Skepticism and Romanticism*. By Cavell's own account, however, it had made "a momentary, somewhat disguised or frightened appearance in a late speculation in the final part of *The Claim of Reason*" (IQO 55).

In that earlier discussion, having worked through a series of symmetries and asymmetries between material-objects skepticism—the denial that I can have knowledge of the external world[2]—and other minds skepticism—the denial that I know (there are) minds outside my own, Cavell entertains the possibility, though not in so many (or so few) words and while careful to place its demonstration beyond the limits of his present undertaking, that other-minds skepticism underlies material-objects skepticism, or, in his own more guarded formulation, that "my discoveries in the regions of the skeptical problem of the other are, rightly understood, further characterizations of (material-objects) skepticism ..." (CR 451). Momentarily continuing in this direction, Cavell proposes that we find in Othello's relation to Desdemona an "allegory" of "the human being's [skeptical] relation to the world," rather than "a phase in its career"(ibid.).[3] Looking back on this speculation from the perspective of In Quest of the Ordinary, Cavell characterizes it as *explicitly* "show[ing] material-object skepticism to be derivable from other-minds skepticisms, hence perhaps, on this line, less fundamental,"[4] and *implicitly* "invit[ing] the thought"—from which Cavell writes of himself as having "shrank"— "that skeptical doubt is to be interpreted as jealousy and that our relation to the world that remains is to something that has died at our hands" (IQO 55).[5]

As the thought of skeptical doubt as jealousy is now, in "Texts of recovery," allowed to surface, it does so accompanied by what Cavell calls a "new misgiving," specifically the sense that he has "transformed the issue of skepticism into the issue of animism, exchanged one form of craziness for another" (ibid.). That is to say, if skeptical doubt is to be understood as at bottom a death-dealing jealousy toward the world in "its progress beyond our knowledge" (CR 52), then the condition of that interpretation is the belief that the (material) world is, or had been, instinct with life.[6] I offer as a touchstone both for the orientation Cavell finds himself espousing and for its quintessentially Romantic nature these words from the closing book of The Prelude:

Witness, ye solitudes ...
—whatever falls my better mind,
Revolving with the accidents of life,
May have sustained ...

[I] rather did with jealousy shrink back
From every combination that might aid
The tendency, too potent in itself,
Of habit to enslave the mind, I mean
Oppress it by the laws of vulgar sense,
And substitute a universe of death,
The falsest of all worlds, in place of that
Which is divine and true ...

(XIII, 128–30, 136–43[7])

True, Wordsworth speaks of the threat to our sense of the life of the world posed by "habit" rather than skepticism, and of "shrinking back" from that threat "*with* jealousy," while Cavell writes of shrinking back *from* (the thought of) a life-negating jealousy. But it seems to me that the tendency and prospect they envision and recoil from is virtually the same—as though it is the alliance of jealousy with habit that is the catastrophic "combination" Wordsworth guards against and which Cavell sees the skeptic's stance as consolidating.

If what distinguishes Romantic animism in a general way from those older animistic beliefs we have "to a greater or lesser extent surmounted" (Freud, 248[8]) is its occurrence as a response to the threat of skepticism, then Cavell proposes more specifically that Romantic animism be read as the expression of a disappointment with "the Kantian settlement" by means of which philosophy had come to terms with that threat: granting the human mind its claim to knowledge of the phenomenal world of objects, on condition that it relinquish to the domain of the unknowable the thing in itself (IQO 31, 52 *passim*). Recalling the discussion in the *Theaetetus* of perceptual knowledge as the "offspring" of an encounter between mind and world, each in perpetual flux, we might say that under the terms of this settlement, we get the children, but skepticism keeps the house.

Now, to cite a different philosopher, comes "the bit when we bog down." Having glossed or recast the idea that "the thing in itself is off the limits of human knowledge"[9] as the "den[ial] that you can experience the world as world, things as things; face to face, as it were, call this the life of things ..." (IQO 53), Cavell pauses to "note a characteristic difficulty in the way [he finds himself] setting out to think," and then imagines a "philosopher" or simply "someone" asking that he explain exactly what he means by "experiencing things as things face to face" and how he defines "the life of things," i.e. that he translate these formulations into some presumably stricter, more *controlled*, manner of speaking. But having conjured this interlocutor, whom I take to voice disciplinary expectations, and in particular the expectation that one "define one's terms" (an expectation from which Cavell by no means simply feels exempt or this brief encounter wouldn't have even been staged), Cavell *bridles*, declaring that "Such words mean nothing whatever, or I have no interest in their meaning anything apart from their accuracy in wording an intuition ... concerning something like a prohibition of knowledge, a limitation of it from the outside" (ibid.).

Cavell's imagined interlocutor is of course likely to find "the wording of an intuition" as elusive a phrase as those whose, let us say, logical status it is meant to characterize, nor do I propose to elucidate it. Rather,

I want to point out that these *particular* "wordings of intuitions" also involve citations, most transparently of St. Paul—For now we see through a glass, darkly; but then face to face—but also, if less distinctly, of Wordsworth, who writes in "Tintern Abbey" of

> ... that serene and blessed mood,
> In which the affections gently lead us on –
>
> While with an eye made quiet by the power
> Of harmony, and the deep power of joy
> We see into the life of things.
>
> (41–42, 46–49)[10]

In July of 1798, when "Tintern Abbey" is composed, there can be no question of Wordsworth directly responding to Kant or expressing a "disappointment with the Kantian settlement." As is well known (and as Cavell acknowledges in "Emerson, Coleridge, Kant," the lecture preceding and laying some of the groundwork for "Texts of Recovery" (IQO 47)), Coleridge's own serious engagement with Kant was not to begin until he and William and Dorothy travelled to Germany in December of that year, and as for Wordsworth himself, he is reported to have declared himself some years later "utterly ignorant of everything connected either with Kant or his philosophy."[11] On the other hand, and to stay for the moment with the biographical record, that "Tintern Abbey" is composed in recovery from a skeptical crisis that can be dated to 1796, thus to the heart of the "(f)ive years ... five summers, with the/Length of five long winters" that had passed between Wordsworth's visit to the Wye Valley in 1793 with Robert Jones and his return there with Dorothy in 1798, we have on Wordsworth's own testimony in *The Prelude*:[12]

> ... Thus I fared,
> Dragging all passions, notions, shapes of faith
> Like culprits to the bar, suspiciously
> Calling the mind to establish in plain day
> Her titles and her honors, now believing,
> Now disbelieving, endlessly perplexed
> With impulse, motive, right and wrong,
> Of moral obligation – what the rule, the ground
> And what the sanction – till, demanding proof,
> And seeking it in everything, I lost
> All feeling of conviction, and, in fine,
> Sick, wearied out with contrarieties,

Yielded up moral questions in despair,
And for my future studies, as the sole
Employment of the inquiring faculty,
Turned toward mathematics and their clear
And solid evidence.

(X, 888–904[13])

What *The Prelude* thus figures in retrospect as an acute but passing crisis ("I was no further changed/Than as a clouded, not a waning moon" [X, 916–17]) presents in "Tintern Abbey" as a more intermittent, but also recurrent and ongoing heaviness at heart, as:

... when the fretful stir
Unprofitable, and the fever of the world,
Have hung upon the beatings of my heart ...

(52–54)

It may seem that the "world" that weighs on Wordsworth in these lines is not the world whose existence skepticism calls into doubt, but on the contrary the one that is "too much with us," the frenetic world of human commerce and society so distant from and mindless of "the calm/That nature breathes among the hills ..." (*Prelude* I, 287–88). But consider, first of all, how much the language of feverish but futile and wearying activity, here used to convey an image of "the world," anticipates the fever of skeptical agitation that, in the passage from Book X of *The Prelude* cited above, leaves Wordsworth "sick, wearied out with contrarieties."[14] And then recall his earlier evocation of the dead weight of "all this unintelligible world" as he moves in "Tintern Abbey" towards speaking of "the life of things":

Nor less, I trust
To them I may have owed another gift
Of aspect more sublime; that blessed mood,
In which the burthen of the mystery,
In which the heavy and the weary weight
Of all this unintelligible world
Is lightened, – that serene and blessed mood,
In which the affections gently lead us on,
Until the breath of this corporeal frame
And even the motion of our human blood
Almost suspended, we are laid asleep
In body, and become a living soul:

> While with an eye made quiet by the power
> Of harmony, and the deep power of joy,
> We see into the life of things.

$$(36-50)$$

Specifically, Cavell's portrayal of Romanticism as shadowed by a disappointment in the Kantian settlement encourages me to hear those lines about "the burthen of the mystery/The heavy and the weary weight of all/This unintelligible world" in relation to the unknowability of the thing in itself as a major burden of the critical philosophy. Not, to repeat, as a matter of supposing some allusion to Kant, but of according the poet's language its full philosophical resonance, and the philosopher's gravity its undertow of melancholy. If these possibilities are allowed, then the development of the passage as a whole, the "lightening" that takes us from "the weight of all this unintelligible world" to "see[ing] into the life of things," also warrants consideration as the laying out or clearing of a path of response to the immobilizing threat of skepticism alternative to that proposed by the Kantian settlement.

In the section of the poem with which we are concerned, Wordsworth passes from describing the place to which he has returned to paying it homage, through the enumeration of what, "through a long absence" (1824), he has owed the influence of its "forms of beauty." At the same time, though this is not as immediately apparent, the lines are valedictory, spoken on the occasion of a parting, for Wordsworth revisits the scene, both literally and in composing the poem, in view of more irrevocable separations than those imposed by physical absence. Thus the lines which open the section:

> Though absent long,
> These forms of beauty have not been to me,
> As is a landscape to a blind man's eye …

$$(24-26)$$

look to the future as much as the past, serving as a pledge of continuing devotion even as they intimate a more drastic severance. Not surprisingly, Harold Bloom interprets the "blind man's eye" as Milton's, thus as the visionary poetry that Wordsworth is foreswearing (72–73). Whether we want to be that specific, this seems to me correct insofar as it associates the question of separation with Wordsworth's dedication of himself to poetry, an association that, on the one hand, approaches explicitness when Wordsworth, having declared himself "changed, no doubt, from what I was, when first/I came among these hills" (67–68), finds "for such loss…/Abundant recompense" (88–89) in a new capacity to hear "the still, sad music of humanity" (92). The question of renewed separation and the association of that question with language may be seen, moreover, to involve the structure of the poem as a whole, and are reflected in Wordsworth's decision to change the title of the poem in 1815 from "Lines written a few miles above Tintern Abbey" to "Lines. Composed a few miles above Tintern Abbey," at least in part, one suspects, because he knew that the poem's "scene of writing" and the banks of the Wye were *not* the same place.[15] Thus so simple—and central—a formulation as the clause "While here I stand" splits between a "here" and a "standing" on the banks "of this delightful stream," and a "here" and a "standing" less determinately anchored but which clearly find their place within iterable—let us say, memorable—utterance.[16]

Returning now from these general considerations to the specifics of the mood and process of the passage with which we are concerned, we might note, to start with, that it is both the first and the main passage in the poem where the language slips into the first person plural, a first person plural that becomes, indeed, all but hieratic: "the affections gently lead *us* on … the motion of *our* human blood [is] almost suspended … *we* are laid asleep in body and become a living soul… *We* see into the life of things." In a related way, the simple fact that Wordsworth's sentence repeats its gesture of identification—"that blessed mood,/In which …" "that serene and blessed mood,/In which …" and that the repetition is expansive and processual, where the initial formulation is dense and compressed, also suggests something about what it might mean for the "burthen of the mystery" to be "lightened." While the burden of unintelligibility isolates, the mood in which it is lightened is shared, and that sharing is continuous with the sharing of language, the circulation or circumambience of a specifically human power of communication.

Yet, in a movement that would seem to run contrary to the emphasis I have been placing on the shift from "I" to "we" occurring in these lines and on the accompanying flow of the mood that is being summoned into the process of its rhetorical dilation, the experience Wordsworth articulates is described, at the same time, as developing through a succession of suspensions of activity to arrive at a rapt state of contemplation, a trance state, that appears totally withdrawn from the field of human intercourse and even perception of the external world as we usually think of it: The "breath of this corporeal frame," which sustains our being in continual interchange with the world around us, is "almost suspended"; as alike "the motion of our human blood," the inner circulation that keeps us alive and whole; "we are laid asleep in body" and, in a striking oxymoron, the "eye [is] made quiet." It is under these conditions that "we become a living soul" and "see into the life of things."

I observe first of all how close we are with this sequence to the well-known line from the "Intimations Ode" on which Cavell dwells, "Our birth is but a sleep and a forgetting," and thus how the former might be enlisted in his undertaking to read the latter "philosophically … as a statement about the conditions of human birth, of the birth of the human, one that we, as we stand, might still suffer, sometimes called a second birth" (IQO 73). But I also find myself led by that association beyond, or perhaps via, what Cavell speaks of as "participation in childhood's birth" (ibid.) to consider how, in "Tintern Abbey," in order to "become a living soul" we first must verge on becoming inanimate—on becoming a thing.

Christian ideas about death, rebirth, and resurrection of course play a role here in what reads, in a certain light and up to a certain point, as a prefiguration or rehearsal of the death of the body and the freeing of the soul. But the words which complete the sequence, and around which we have been circling—"we see into the life of things"—point towards an immersion in that life, not its transcendence. More specifically, I would suggest that what is here called "seeing … with an eye made quiet," and which is neither simply seeing nor the "blind man's eye" of the opening to which it harkens back, involves something like an *entry* into the "life of things," a sense of nearness to them in their "uninscribed and mute"[17] condition and which the infant child, not yet fully inducted into the community of human speakers amidst which it finds itself, may especially share, happily or unhappily. This is one direction in which I take Cavell's understanding, still *à propos* the Intimations Ode, that we (we adults) are to "participat[e] in [childhood] by participating in what it participated in" (p. 73). Taken further, it suggests the thought that the movement by which we see into, or enter into, or participate in, "the life of things," cross that line, is not in essence different from the way that things are implicated in one another.

Is this going too far? That Wordsworth feels that his words test the limits of the allowable seems clear from how ready he is to retract them: "If this/Be but a vain belief …"[18] Or is he? For this voicing of doubt is also a pulling back, as of a bow drawn, in preparation for the release of the apostrophe that ensues:

How oft, in spirit, have I turned to thee
O sylvan Wye! Thou wanderer through the woods,
How often has my spirit turned to thee!

Since apostrophes, though they "make no natural or regular part"[19] of ordinary language, are thoroughly conventional poetic performances, we may wonder whence Wordsworth's turn to the Wye derives its pivotal force. Or, as Cavell suggests of Wordsworth's parting address "to preanimate nature" in the 'Intimations,' "...it seems ... worth trying philosophically to understand well, and to be part of understanding what Wordsworth meant, in the preface to the *Lyrical Ballads,* by 'communicating with objects'" (IQO 71).[20]

Cavell also observes at this point that "talking to nature ought to strike us as being nearly as crazy as being spoken to by it," a remark that should remind us of his earlier acknowledgment that "in transforming the issue of skepticism into the issue of animism," he has the sense of having "exchanged one form of craziness for another." One approach to understanding philosophically such crazy talk might be to simply declare it crazy, something Wordsworth himself comes close to doing when he characterizes his self-description as a "Worshipper of Nature" in "Tintern Abbey" as "a passionate expression uttered incautiously in the Poem upon the Wye."[21] Another, presumably more sympathetic, approach would be to understand such talk figuratively, which in the case of Wordsworth's apostrophe to the Wye, in particular, would be to understand it as indirectly targeted, either in its meaning or its effect, at the human reader.

Cavell is obviously not averse to figurative interpretation, but his method and the originality of his readings often depend on attentiveness to what he identifies early on in the Beckett essay as "hidden literality" (MWM 119), which in the present instances means taking at face value the fact that Wordsworth is "communicating with objects." Indeed it may be in doing so that Wordsworth recovers apostrophe from its conventionality. My way of trying to making sense of this, however, depends on seeing that this address to things occurs both as a turning away from or interruption of another, intersubjective circuit of communication, and, by the very form of its language, as a partial disengagement from the object to which it declares its plight. In "Tintern Abbey" this disengagement is implicit in the structural bifurcation of voice and writing, a bifurcation that is reinforced by the way in which the turning to the Wye executed by the apostrophe in language doubles but also publishes the turn "in spirit" it recalls.

My engagement with Cavell's account of Romanticism as embracing "something like animism" in response to both the threat of skepticism and its disappointment with the Kantian settlement as the decisive philosophical response to that threat has been organized so as to focus eventually on Wordsworth's use of apostrophe as manifesting "something like animism." At the same time, I have to acknowledge that the term "apostrophe" does not occur as such in "Texts of recovery," but appears to be subsumed within the broader and somewhat differently centered category of "the pathetic fallacy," as when Cavell writes that "romanticism … accepts something like animism, represented by what seems still to be called, when it is called, the pathetic fallacy" (IQO 53), or that the Intimations Ode "as a whole may be taken as a process of understanding and overcoming the unabashed pathetic fallacy that occurred in its opening stanzas" (IQO 71). I find that such moments, as Cavell says of certain propositions in Heidegger, "project a barrier for me" (IQO 68) and wonder why this should be.

When, in Volume III of *Modern Painters*, Ruskin launches the "pathetic fallacy" on its career, he starts out on a sharply polemical note, decrying "German dullness" and "English affectation" for giving currency to "two of the most objectionable words that were ever coined by the troublesomeness of metaphysicians," the words in question being "objective" and "subjective," which for himself Ruskin claims to find "exquisitely and in all points useless" (III.4.1).[22] That Kant is among his targets seems clear when he goes on to complain that the use of the distinction between "subjective" and "objective" has conduced to the further "opinion, that it does not much matter what things are in themselves, but only what they are to us" (ibid.).

From its moment of inception then, the notion of the "pathetic fallacy" was embroiled in a critique of philosophical jargon of metaphysical and continental inspiration in the name of, as Ruskin has it, "plain old English" (III.4.3) and a no-nonsense approach to the distinction between, again as Ruskin has it, "true appearances" and "false appearances" (III.4.4). Ruskin's extensive discussion of the pathetic fallacy requires of course a treatment of its own, both for its excellences and its limitations. Here I will only suggest that the inheritance of the notion by subsequent literary criticism incorporates the defensiveness of its origins towards an essential possibility of philosophy—a defensiveness that has everything to do with the threat of skepticism. Perhaps then what makes me uneasy in Cavell's recourse to the term is not that it participates in that defensiveness, of course, but that it engages with a version of literary criticism whose own counter-engagement with philosophy is not absent, but comparatively weak.

To take just a step further: With the exception of a citation from Wordsworth, what is most conspicuously missing from Ruskin's discussion of the pathetic fallacy, and what is specifically brought into focus by the ancient and modern concept of apostrophe, is attention to the vector of address as distinct from that of reference, or, in Cavell's phrasing, the impulse to communicate *with* objects as distinct from the wish to communicate about them. Why the foreclosure of that impulse, with its connection to problems of rhetoric on the one hand and to pre-Oedipal object relations on the other, from Ruskin's field of attention should occur in conjunction with a dismissal of continental philosophy is as yet obscure to me, though it seems more than coincidental. What is clear to me is the as yet unexplored affinity—which is not to say agreement—between Cavell's work on Romantic animism and deconstructive work on apostrophe and prosopopeia.

As indexing that affinity, I propose the following pair of comments, the first from "Texts of Recovery," *à propos* what Wordsworth may mean by "communicating with objects," the second from de Man's "Wordsworth and the Victorians," *à propos* Wordsworth's reference in the opening lines of Book V of *The Prelude* to "look[ing]/Upon the speaking face of Nature ...":

> A question for us becomes, Is there something we have to say to Nature if we are to say some things at all?
>
> (IQO 72)

> One can speak only because one can look upon a mode of speech which is not quite our own.[23]

What these observations share for all their differences is their philosophical attunement to Wordsworth's use of apostrophe (or, in de Man's case, apostrophe in conjunction with prosopopeia) as engaging with or in "a mode of speech" which is, at once, "not quite our own" and the condition of possibility of our "say[ing] some things at all"—and thus as something other than a more or less high-flown, more or less dated, piece of rhetoric to be overlooked or discounted if noticed at all.[24] Moreover, the sense of estrangement or disconnection on which de Man insists ("the mind gazing upon a speaking face" (de Man, p. 90)) may be seen to haunt Cavell's question as well if one catches its note of anxiety, "Is there something we have to say to Nature if we are to say some things at all?" and then attends to Cavell's continuation a sentence later: "In the lines I cited in which the poet speaks to things, what he speaks to them about is their speaking, their foreboding. He commands them, or beseeches them, not to be omens of severance" (p. 72). To say some things at all is to risk a relationship to a language not quite our own, a language which, like the world, is there before us. That this is also "our language," the language of everyday, is an insight Cavell shares with deconstruction and with which he has transformed our understanding of the reach of ordinary language philosophy.[25]

12 Emerson Discomposed

Skepticism, Naturalism, and the Search for Criteria in "Experience"

Paul Grimstad

[*In memory of Barbara Packer*]
The secret of the illusoriness [of life] is in the necessity of a
succession of moods or objects. Gladly we would anchor, but the
anchorage is quicksand. This onward trick of nature is too strong for
us. *Pero si muove.*

Emerson, "Experience"

Skepticism and Naturalism

Stanley Cavell's guiding question in *Senses of Walden*—"Why has
America never expressed itself philosophically? Or has it, in the metaphysical riot of its greatest literature?"[1]—seems both to signal his attraction to great nineteenth century American prose and to profess a
commitment to working through the "metaphysics" that the most recognizable form of philosophy to have emerged in America—classical
pragmatism—set out to reject. The tension between metaphysics and
pragmatism, though, conceals a deeper one, between skepticism and
naturalism; a difference, I want to claim here, that depends on different
understandings of experience. In what follows, though, I want not so
much to insist on the incommensurability of these two philosophical
attitudes, but to emphasize some deep affinities between Cavell's
reading of Emerson's "Experience" as an instance of what he calls the
mood or truth of skepticism, and John Dewey's naturalist inheritance of
Emerson's essay.

Cavell says that in his essay "Experience," Ralph Waldo Emerson
"explicitly challenges the … idea of experience to be found in Kant and
in the classical empiricists."[2] Both of these earlier models of experience—on the one hand, the way the making of determinate judgments
functions as the condition of possibility for objects to become intelligible
at all; on the other, the mechanism by which sense impressions come to
furnish the mind with ideas—are representationalist. That is, both are a
matter of giving an account of how outer phenomena are aligned with
inner representations. Consider this, then, in relation to what Cavell

takes to be Emerson's "challenge" to such construals of experience, particularly his line "but far be it from me the despair which prejudges the law by a paltry empiricism."[3] Cavell interprets the line as saying that what is "wrong with empiricism is not its reliance on experience but its paltry idea of experience", a reading that leads him to consider the "little argument" he takes Emerson to be having with Kant about "the nature of experience in its relation to, or revelation of, the natural world."[4] In Emerson's lines, "the secret of the illusoriness [of life] is in the necessity of a succession of moods or objects. Gladly we would anchor, but the anchorage is quicksand. This onward trick of nature is too strong for us. *Pero si muove*,"[5] Cavell finds an engagement with Kant's second Analogy of Experience, hearing in Emerson's word "anchorage" an allusion to Kant's well-known example of a boat moving down a river. We might take Cavell to be finding Emerson engaging the Kantian point that if an "anchorage" in outer succession were to turn out to be quicksand, then our inner representations would be set adrift, in such a way that they would not even be representations. That is, since the point of the boat analogy for Kant is to give a proof for the objectivity of outer succession (and thus avoid what he calls "dogmatic" idealism), the melting away of the anchorage to which Emerson alludes would seem to lead him toward an extreme form of external world skepticism.[6]

But matters are not so simple as this. Cavell rather tells us that for Emerson "the succession of moods is *not tractable* by the distinction between subjectivity and objectivity Kant proposed for experience," and that "*this* onward trick of nature is too much for us; the given bases for the self are quicksand. The fact that we are taken over by this succession … means that you can think of it as at once a succession of moods (inner matters) and a succession of objects (outer matters). This very evanescence of the world proves its existence to me; it is what vanishes from me."[7] On Cavell's account, Emerson is saying that the "secret of the illusoriness of life" is our inability to gauge the one order of succession by the other, because you can think of experience as "at once" a succession of moods or objects. And if neither order is "tractable" by the other taken as fixed, then, as Cavell puts it, the "given bases of the self are quicksand," since for Kant one of the conditions for the self's unity— what he calls the "unity of apperception" as the necessary ground for the synthesis of experience—requires and implies a certain isomorphism between inner and outer matters. Any unity of subjectivity seems prone to vanishing in this quicksand. Cavell's recognition of Emerson's "bringing to mind the characteristics of skepticism's mood,"[8] thus leads him to hear in these lines from "Experience" both an acknowledgment of one of the more formidable efforts at heading off at the pass the threat of the world's becoming alien to us, and a resistance to the idea that the skeptical mood either arises out of or is properly addressed in relation to a problem of inner representations and outer objects.[9] This wariness about the effort to provide an "answer" to skepticism—that is, a refutation of it as construed in either Descartes or Kant—is perhaps an instance of what Cavell elsewhere calls the "truth of skepticism"; as if Emerson's disappointment in the "proof" Kant offers as a way of dealing with skepticism were, not a failure to be persuaded by Kant's arguments, but a part of skepticism's mood.[10]

But while Cavell finds in Emerson a skeptical mood not so much characterized by a doubt about knowledge of the external world, but by an inability to feel satisfied with Kant's effort at "answering" the skeptic, he does so by pointing precisely to that feature of Kant's empirical realism—the boat as an emblem for the necessary objectivity of outer succession—that brings Emerson's lines back to the epistemological problem of representation. That is, if our moods "succeed" each other (even if, as Emerson has it elsewhere, they "do not believe in one another"[11]) then their "logic" remains expressible in the kind of argument that would ground the fact of their succession in something outside us. That last *Pero si muove*—an allusion to Galileo's tactful response to his persecutors that, while he did not mean to suggest that the Earth moves around the Sun, nevertheless added "and yet it does move"—while pointing ahead to Copernican turns both astronomical and epistemological, might then be read as a sort of *sotto voce* reminder of the nagging pull on us of Kant's understanding of experience as (in part) premised on the gauging of inner by outer succession. That is, the problem of imperfect or thwarted knowledge—an understanding of skepticism which, as Timothy Gould puts it, "already accepts too much of skepticism's self-interpretation"[12]—remains legible within Emerson's logic of moods. Changing course from riverboats to celestial bodies, we might say that Cavell's concern to show how Emerson both feels the gravitational pull, and the desire to get out of, the orbit of "answering" the skeptic, necessarily depends on the continuing legibility of skepticism's self-interpretation for finding in "Experience" a "little argument" with Kant.

Despite these different renderings of the role of succession in Kant and Emerson, and despite Cavell's own professed disappointment with the Kantian "settlement with skepticism"—for all the glory of transcendental idealism, it still requires that things in themselves drop out of the picture (to this gift from Kant Cavell has replied: "thanks for nothing"[13])—Cavell's reading of Emerson's lines returns "experience" to the problem of aligning "inner matters [with] outer matters"; that is, to the problem of representation, or at any rate a successor of this problem.[14] We might push this further and say that to get off the ground as a genuine problem skepticism must understand experience as some form of (however failed) representation. If we are worried about our access to the external world, or to other minds, or whether we can get a grasp on what it means to follow a rule, or whether we can have our selves reflected back to us in another's recognition, or whether or not we in fact exist; or if it is just that we have begun to wonder how a simultaneous respect for, and doubt about, efforts to "answer" the skeptic might stand for some deep truth about us—the "truth of skepticism" as, for example, the "plight of mind and circumstance within which a human being gives voice to his condition"[15]—In each case, what we are worried or wondering about is the accuracy of some set of representations in relation to a condition of life.

But consider some of the compositional steps that led to the making of the essay "Experience"—the journal entries and lectures from 1841 and up to the tragic death of Emerson's son Waldo in January 1842. Here we find Emerson appealing to the language of "succession" in ways that suggest its role in the essay might be something different from Kant's way (however disappointing to Emerson and to Cavell) of configuring the relation of inner and outer matters. A journal entry of January 1841 says "the method of advance in nature is perpetual transformation," and on September 11, 1841 Emerson says: "It is much to write sentences; it is more to add method & write out the spirit of your life symmetrically ... to arrange many reflections in their natural order so that I shall have one homogeneous piece ... this continuity is for the great."[16] Here, the role of "succession" seems not to be bound up with the problem of squaring inner with outer matters, but of arriving at a practicable method of composition; of "writing out the spirit of your life" so as to "arrange [it] in natural order" as a "continuity" between the "transformations of nature" and "sentences." The move from the "perpetual transformations" of nature to what Emerson calls "writing out the spirit of your life" is made more explicit in the lecture "The method of nature," given at Waterville College in Maine, also in 1841. In that lecture Emerson says to his audience that they (and he) will "piously celebrate this hour by exploring the method of nature. Let us see that, as nearly as we can, and try how far it is transferable to the literary life."[17] Some months later in his lecture on "The Poet," Emerson describes what the poet does as "vehicular," "fluxional" and "transitive," such that the poet's lines "flow with the flowing of nature." This celebration of the "trial" and "transfer" of the course of nature to the "literary life" imagines succession as carried forward into literary method; that is, of an inventiveness that would allow "succession" to be continued in the steps of composition itself. So rather than think of outer succession as lost to us, because of a veil or an imbalance between "inner and outer matters," or of a precariously uncreated or unacknowledged self in need of performative enactment to bring it into being (say, going through the cogito argument), Emerson wants to establish, in composition, a "continuity" running from nature to language. Given Cavell's assertion that Emerson's idea of experience is a "challenge" to both transcendental idealism and classical empiricism, I want to treat that "challenge" as the way he replaces a worry over the vicissitudes of representation with what he simply calls "method."

Emerson's concern with method clearly informs John Dewey's description of experience as the "continuity between natural events ... and the origin and development of meanings [as a] naturalistic link which does away with the often alleged necessity of dividing the objects of experience into two worlds."[18] Dewey's naturalist account of experience is premised on what he calls a "shift of emphasis from the experienced (the *what*) to the experiencing, the *how,* the method of its course."[19] Dewey later describes this emphasis on the move from the "what" to the "how" of experience as a desire to eliminate the "division of everything into nature *and* experience,"[20] encouraging us rather to think of experience, both as a form of experimentation as the "direction of natural events to meanings."[21]

All of this sounds like a belated reformulation of Emerson's "Method of nature." Indeed, in his 1903 essay on Emerson, Dewey challenges those who would accuse Emerson of being a mere amasser of charming aphorisms rather than a thinker, or of having a "lack of method."[22] Instead, Dewey praises Emerson's "movement of thought"; a thinking that happens through "art" not "metaphysics"; the way he "set out to be a maker rather than a reflector."[23] More attuned to the "surprises of reception than any fixed goal," Emerson's method is one of "following the unfolding of perception," and of the "*way* of things"; a form of making that "takes the *way* of truth ... for truth."[24] Summarizing the importance of method for Emerson, Dewey quotes from "Spiritual Laws," that a man is "a method, a plan of arrangement," and, taking literally the etymology of the word "method" (μέθοδος; road), quotes Emerson's line from "Experience," "everything good is on the highway."[25]

Despite the apparent differences between Dewey's naturalist construal of what Emerson is doing, and Cavell's skeptical one, Cavell too sees in the word "composition" a method of open-ended experimentation. In an essay written before he'd found a model pitch for his own writing in Emerson and Thoreau, Cavell asks, in his essay "Music discomposed": "What is composition, and what is it to compose?"[26] The question for Cavell amounts to asking (in keeping with the general concern in his work with the notion of criteria): What is to *count* as an example of composition? Answering his own question, he calls composition the "search for an object worthy of our attention", a process he describes as an "experimental problem."[27] By "experimentation" Cavell seems to mean an activity that takes the form of a "search"; an activity which does not know where it is going ahead of time, makes or fashions provisional goals as part of the unfolding of the process, and remains open to the surprises that emerge from an "attention" to work as it is being made.[28] When Cavell extends this idea to a discussion of Emerson and Thoreau's practice of working "up" from journal entries into lectures, essays, and books, it is just this kind of experimentation he has in mind. Where the earlier essay called this process a form of "attention," here the word is "interest": "Emerson [and Thoreau's] relation to poetry is inherently their interest in their own writing ... their interest in the fact that what they are building is writing, that their writing is, as it realizes itself daily under their hands, sentence by shunning sentence ... the making of it happen, the poetry of it."[29] If we put together some of Cavell's different claims we might say that for Cavell the words "composition," "experiment," "search," "attention," "interest," and "poetry" are related in the way they each contribute to a description of experience. And this would then be one that bears some affinity with Dewey's description of Emerson's open-ended, experimental "method." As Russell Goodman puts it, "there is a tradition running through the work of Emerson, James and Dewey to Cavell [which amounts to a] response to the epistemological mind–world relation," and one that is based on the way "Emerson shares an open-ended, experimental attitude with ... Dewey," an attitude literalized in the connection between the words experience and experiment.[30]

While we find in both Cavell's Emerson and Dewey's Emerson a notion of experience as experiment, there is still the apparent tension between Cavell's staying within the problem (or mood, or truth) of skepticism and Dewey's naturalism. Cavell acknowledges this in a recent book, *Philosophy the Day After Tomorrow*, saying of Dewey's work that it "sometimes ... demonstrates how a mass of experience can go philosophically almost nowhere (for Dewey into a hundred abstract rejections of some patently unintelligible thesis together with its obviously undesirable antithesis)."[31] An entire philosophic position is squeezed into that parenthetic aside, and it is worth unpacking a bit. The "hundred abstract rejections" are presumably the relentless critique of representationalism that is the backbone of *Experience and Nature*, and the "patently unintelligible thesis" must be that experience can (or should) be understood as a matter only of having inner representations. The obviously undesirable antithesis must be Dewey's simple assertion of a continuum running from nature to meaning, an assertion that all but suppresses the very existence of subjectivity. But given Cavell's claim that Emerson offers a challenge to the models of experience found in classical empiricism and Kant, we are left to wonder if Cavell has a still different idea of how such notions of experience might be "challenged," and in a way that would be both attuned to Emerson's literary method, and yet not fall into line with Dewey's "hundred abstract rejections" and assertions of continuities.

Here, then, we ought to turn to Cavell's essay "What's the use of calling Emerson a pragmatist?," which both develops the idea of literary composition as a form of experimentation, and offers a new set of arguments for why Emerson should not be thought of as a precursor to pragmatism. Cavell describes Emerson's writing as an appeal to "the words we are given in common," and the way the "proposals for what we say … require something like experimentation … trials that inherently run the risk of exasperation [and so lead to a] writing which is *difficult* in a way no other American philosopher's (save Thoreau's) has been, certainly not that of James and Dewey. Are these different responses to language not philosophically fundamental? They seem so to me."[32] Here the relation of philosophy to style—the Emersonian claim that philosophy is inseparable from a *way* of doing something—is used to buttress Cavell's annoyance at how "pragmatism seems designed to refuse to take skepticism seriously, as it refuses [in Dewey's case] to take metaphysical distinctions seriously."[33] That is, given Cavell's claims that in philosophy "the sound makes all the difference," and that Emerson and Dewey just sound too different for there to be a substantive philosophical link between them it is, above all, the *sound* of Dewey's prose that leads Cavell to the thought, in his essay "Thinking of Emerson," that Dewey "never took up [Emerson] philosophically."[34] But what is more telling and interesting here, I want to claim, is the deep affinity between Dewey and Cavell around the way method as composition leads to a certain construal of experience as a search for criteria, a predicament Cavell takes to be a specifically "modernist" one. It is to a discussion of this modernist understanding of the relation of composition to experience that I want to devote the remainder of this essay.

Cause, justification and composition

Dewey's naturalist understanding of experience—that you can get from causal series to linguistic meanings—has met with strong objection in the last 50 years, and particularly from those claiming to inherit the mantle of pragmatism. While Richard Rorty thinks of Dewey as one of his "principal philosophical heroes,"[35] and gets from him and the other classical pragmatists the desire to abandon representationalism in favor of process and practice (what he sometimes simply calls "conversation"), he rejects Dewey's notion of experience as a continuum bridging the causal order of nature to the normative order of linguistic meaning. Taking Dewey to task in his essay "Dewey's metaphysics," Rorty says Dewey makes the mistake of "cross[ing] the line … between causal [relations] and the self-conscious beliefs and inferences they make possible," cautioning that "nothing is to be gained for an understanding of human knowledge by running together the vocabularies in which we describe the causal antecedents of knowledge with those in which we offer justifications of our claims to knowledge."[36] In a later essay, "Dewey between Hegel and Darwin," Rorty makes more explicit this criticism of what he calls Dewey's "running together sentences with experiences."[37] This for Rorty amounts to a blurring of the "distinction between cognitive and non-cognitive states … between sensations and beliefs … the distinction between the question 'What causes our beliefs?' and the question 'What justifies our beliefs?'" Such "blurring" is, according to Rorty, "essential for any representationalist theory of knowledge."[38] In short, for analytic neo-pragmatists like Rorty, and his student Robert Brandom, it is not so simple to move from causal mechanism to linguistic meaning simply by intoning the word "experience," as they take Dewey to do. That is, you cannot set up a "continuity between natural events … and the origin and development of meanings," without accounting for the fundamental discrepancy between nature as the order of causes and the linguistic as the normative order of reason giving and justification.[39]

The analytic critique of classical pragmatism thus hinges on a notion of language as bound up with justification: the reason you can't move from the cause to the justification of a belief is because to say something meaningful is to be in what Wilfrid Sellars called the "logical space of reasons,"[40] not the space of natural processes alone. But here I want to return to Cavell's description of composition as an experimental "search," finding in it an advocacy for a use of language that would not be a matter simply of justification. Cavell says that in those objects we call "compositions," "the concept of intention does not function as a term of … justification."[41] Instead, "we follow the progress of a [composition] the way we follow what someone is saying or doing. Not however to …learn something specific, but to see what *it* says, to see what someone has been able to make out of these materials."[42] We might hear in this description a resemblance to the analytic pragmatists' critique of Dewey, which we could imagine as re-phrased in the question: What does one have to be able to *do* in order to count as *saying* something? But to claim, as Cavell does, that composition is a matter of "following what someone is saying or doing" is not to treat it as bound up with giving and asking for reasons, or of offering "justification" for this or that instance of saying. It is rather to be involved in what is for Cavell the specifically modernist predicament of searching for the criteria by which the work becomes intelligible as composition; a search which takes place *in* and *as* composition. This means that composition is a process of "trying to find the limits or essence of [its] own procedures" since it is "not clear a priori what counts, or will count" as composition.[43] Thus for Cavell the "task of the modernist artist ... is to *find* what it is his art finally depends on [such that] the criteria are something we must discover ... in the continuity of [the artwork] itself."[44] On Cavell's account, it is as if each individual work has to discover the criteria by which its particular forms of saying become intelligible.

Cavell's claim that composition entails the "discovery" of criteria immanent in the process or activity of composition seems a deepening of the description, in "Music discomposed," of composition as an "experimental problem" requiring a "search for an object worthy of our attention." Such a search would seem to be an investigation into the criteria by which some particular compositional activity aims to discover the norms by which "what *it* says" becomes meaningful and so sharable. Contrast this with the later analytic pragmatist objections to Dewey's naturalism: what a given composition "says" would not be defined as its giving and asking for reasons, nor as its place in an inferential series, but as the way its search for criteria opens onto more general questions about what the object *is*, and so to what Cavell elsewhere calls a "natural relation to existence" that is "somehow *closer* than the idea of ... knowing is made to convey."[45] Rather than "knowing" we should think of this process as an experimental one moving from doing to saying; that is (to put it in more recognizably Cavellian terms) a doing that is at the same time a search for the criteria according to which the process turns into a form of saying, and so becomes meaningful.

Given the way Cavell's description of composition seems to anticipate his later complaint about Dewey's "hundred abstract rejections," we might point to what I take to be another of the affinities between the two philosophers. In *Art As Experience,* Dewey gives an account of the sort of process that would include, as the stages or phases of its activity, both perceptual (causal) and conceptual (discursive, linguistic) moments. Sounding like Cavell in "A matter of meaning it" and "Music discomposed," Dewey writes: "Until the artist is satisfied in perception with what he is doing, he continues shaping and reshaping ... the artist embodies in himself the attitude of the perceiver while he works [and] because the artist operates experimentally [in this way] does he open new fields of experience."[46] Might we see in Dewey's "being in the attitude of the perceiver" a search for criteria as part of the experimental doing of composition? And wouldn't this be one way of understanding what Dewey means by opening "new fields of experience"? This is perhaps what Richard Eldridge means when he writes that in Dewey's aesthetics "significance is a function of the activity with which it is bound up."[47] Instead of language understood as the realm of propositional claims that might be legitimately endorsed or rejected within the community of rational argument, what Dewey describes seems comparable to Cavell's account of the modernist's effort to "discover" the criteria by which a particular work's solving of its problems (the search for the conditions by which "significance" arises from "activity") becomes the *general* search for what is to count as meaning at all. While this form of saying is governed by normative constraint, it is not the sort of norm that would evaluate this or that utterance as either endorsable or rejectable based upon shared rational procedures of reason-giving. Rather, constraints are discovered immanently in composition understood as an experimentation with the "words we are given in common"; a commonness that can be heard in Cavell's description of composition as a "search for an object worthy of *our* attention," and in Dewey's "opening up new fields of experience."

Beautiful Limits (Joyous Science)

Near the middle of the essay "Experience" Emerson moves from the dazed mood within the series where "we find ourselves" to the mood he celebrated in a journal entry made during the composition of "Experience" as being a practitioner of "joyous science."[48] Returning to the way his announced vocation of "being a naturalist" hinges on an idea of experience as method (way or road), Emerson says "everything good is on the highway," which he now calls the "equator of life, of thought, spirit, poetry."[49] Emerson then writes: "How easily, if fate would suffer it, we might keep forever these beautiful limits, and adjust ourselves, once for all, to the perfect calculation of the kingdom of known cause and effect."[50] What Emerson calls the "adjustment" to the "kingdom of cause and effect" might be read as the search within composition for "beautiful limits," finding in what Dewey called the "direction of natural events to meanings" the conditions under which those meanings are had. "Adjusting" to the "kingdom of cause and effect" as a "keeping of

...beautiful limits" is Emerson's effort to remain in the mood of the mid-world, of finding in the practice of joyous science the transfer of nature's serial flow into the flow of the poet's saying.

Such "limits" might then also be read as a concern with the way the meanings that arise from composition are, as Cavell puts it, "had on condition."[51] Again taking the stakes of the Kantian settlement with skepticism as an angle for reflecting on the achievement of Emerson's prose, Cavell writes that it is as if

> [i]n Emerson's writing (not in his alone, but in his first in America) Kant's pride in what he called his Copernican Revolution for philosophy, understanding the behavior of the world by understanding the behavior of our concepts of the world, is to be radicalized, so that not just twelve categories of the understanding are to be deduced, but every word in the language.[52]

To arrive, in one's inheritance of the common stock of linguistic materials, at a deduction of "every word in the language" is, as Cavell puts it, to "turn the [first] *Critique* upon itself."[53] On this account, Emerson's challenge to earlier understandings of experience—say, Kant's project of deducing necessary conditions of possibility in a priori faculties, so that we may have a "theoretical cognition of nature" as he put it—involves rather a "deduction" that would entail the carrying forward of our common implication in the series "where *we* find ourselves" (*our* place in the "kingdom of cause and effect") to an experimentation with "the words we are given in common." If there is in this process a "deduction" it is in the way "every word in the language" carries with it its own "beautiful limit", a deduction that would transpire in the course of "writing out the spirit of your life" so as to arrange it in a "natural order," and by which we find the ways the words we are given in common are conditioned by nature. This naturalist deduction—let's call it Emerson's joyous science— both seems a way of understanding Cavell's claim about Emerson's giving a transcendental deduction for every word in the language and deepens Cavell's earlier account of composition as the discovery of the conditions under which our experiments in language become "common," as the search for the criteria by which they become sharable. We might now then say that Emerson's "challenge to Kant and the classical empiricists," as Cavell puts it, is at work in "Experience" as the agon between two moods that do not believe in one another: the mood of the skeptic, who, in her stupefied, spectatorial bewilderment before the swim and glitter of appearances, discovers what she takes to be a non-tractability between inner and outer matters; and the mood of the naturalist, joyously deducing, in and as composition, the "beautiful limits"—the criteria necessary for meaningfulness—of the series in which we find ourselves.

If Emerson's naturalism is necessarily linked, both to a method of composition and to Dewey's later claim that meanings can be had continuously from out of the "kingdom of cause and effect," then I have found an affinity between Dewey's naturalist construal of Emerson's "Experience" and Cavell's staying (however warily, disappointedly, but always vigilantly) within the mood, or truth, of skepticism. In doing so, I have wanted, first, to de-emphasize one way of understanding how Emerson's "Experience" "explicitly challenges the … idea of experience to be found in Kant and in the classical empiricists" (the way the "nontractability" between inner and outer matters is given over to a logic of moods), which, I have argued, smuggles in skepticism's "self-interpretation" and so returns Emerson's lines to the very epistemological puzzles we are told he elides in favor of a logic of moods. At the same time, I have wanted to find a connection between Dewey and Cavell around the idea of composition as a form of experience that, while not tied to the problem of representation, is nevertheless still "had on condition." If Cavell's point about (specifically "modernist") composition is that it is one defined by its search for criteria, such that particular experiments with the words we are given in common become meaningful and shareable, then, I have claimed, this is precisely what is going on in Dewey's account of the artist's "operating experimentally" in a way that opens "new fields of experience." Accordingly, I have wanted to see *this* version of experience as Emerson's way of "challenging" the philosophical tradition. In both cases the shift in the understanding of experience is in keeping with what Cavell calls Emerson's giving "every word in the language" a transcendental deduction, as if composition were continually arriving at its conditions, continuously finding the criteria by which its specific experiments with words find the "limits" in relation to which its saying becomes intelligible.

If "justification" is the wrong word for the discovery in composition of such conditions (as "knowledge" must also be), let us then at least say that composition is a search for the "limits" operating in a work, in relation to which an individual work's experiments in meaning become commonly accessible. "Limit" in this Emersonian sense is the effect one hears in language not tied to the constraints of representation, nor to those of justification, but to the commitment to make something of "the words we are given in common," through experimentation with a shared linguistic inheritance.

The improvisatory activity of "discovering" meaning through

compositional experiment, might suggest more generally an angle of approach for analyzing literary works critically. A literary criticism worthy of the name ought to be alert to, and vigilant about, exactly this problem. That is, a philosophy of literary (or musical) composition should be the study of the way the work of composition—the whole network of risks, wagers, adjustments, surprises, selections, rejections, and series of decisions by which an incipient object, whether made from tones or paint or words, becomes before us an "object worthy of our attention"—is necessarily at the same time the search for, and establishment or making explicit of, the conditions in relation to which the experiment begins to mean. It is this emergence of meaningfulness—the conditions of possibility for the experience of the work as meaningful—that both Dewey and Cavell find, in their different ways, in Emerson's prose. Emerson's example might thus be extrapolated more generally to the very way we go about studying literature.

Referring to Cavell's own prose, Timothy Gould offers a description of what such experimentation with our common linguistic inheritance entails. For Gould, Cavell's prose (the description is equally applicable to Emerson) "formulates [the way] the precise angle of his thought is to be calibrated and the ear by which his tone is to be apprehended [and so Cavell] wish[es] to intervene directly in the formation of an audience for his words."[54] This process Gould also calls a "working out of art's significance as produced in the realm where the individual's capacity for meaningfulness meets the resources of a given culture."[55] If part of what Cavell means by "discomposed" in his essay on the way "modernist" composition becomes by definition an investigation into what is to count as art, then I have wanted to see this process at work in Emerson's method of nature as a similar investigation into the conditions by which his writing is to count as … well, what? Could we just say "philosophy in America"? Or even just "literature in America"? Is what Emerson called the method of nature—his way of composing up from journal entries, to lectures, addresses and essays (with this last suggesting literally an experimental search; a testing or trying out)—the way philosophy or literature undertakes to discover the criteria by which its own procedures in prose become recognizable under those designations, in New England in the late 1830s and early 1840s? I take it this is in part what Cavell hopes to finds in Emerson: a kind of writing—"not his alone but his first in America"—that amounts to an investigation into the criteria by which a voice might become recognizable as something we could call American literature or philosophy. Such a philosophy or literature (or, more likely, a writing that would not be sortable according to these labels; say a writing like Emerson's or Thoreau's or Cavell's) would not discover its voice in the lining up of reasons as justification for one or another of its sayings, but rather find it in the very doing of composition, sentence by stunning sentence, the making of it happen, the poetry of it.

13   Beside Ourselves

Near, Neighboring, and Next-to in Cavell's *The Senses of Walden* and William Carlos Williams's "Fine Work with Pitch and Copper"

Elisa New

I

Like many whose essays are collected in this volume, I have, for thirty years, been pondering, and endeavoring to understand, a tradition Stanley Cavell first helped me see. In the mid-1990s, while writing *The Line's Eye*, I was reading Cavell's *The Senses of Walden* all the time, for Cavell had language I needed to get at the despair, even "confirmed desperation,"[1] I was reading in poems like William Carlos Williams's "To Elsie" and his long epic, *Paterson*. With chapters called "Words," "Sentences" and "Portions," and with an emphasis on writing as mode of building, Cavell's writings about Thoreau helped me to see why activities of mindful composition functioned in Williams to stanch despair far better than conceptualization or even the most soulful expressiveness. Cavell's work, and especially Cavell's finely nuanced chapters on the two Concord thinkers, Thoreau and Emerson, helped me to describe the way American writers often surrendered eye to line, imperial vision to writing, and selfhood to experience.

It was also around that time, in the 1990s, that I started making mobiles for classes in American poetry. These mobiles were ways of spatializing and rebalancing the relationship of the speaker/artist to the materials, or "content," of his art. Voice was not a medium for expressing content or a device for removed perspective in such works but, ineluctably, part of that content, seen and perceived. I was inspired by Cavell on *Walden* (and also by some wonderful pages in J. Hillis Miller's *Poets of Reality*) to think of a speaker's moods, attitudes, inflections of feeling as objects, now passing in front and now behind phenomena, now breaking into the open and now revolving blindly, desperately, on their own. It also grew increasingly helpful to think, as Williams and his heirs did, about certain compositional devices we all deploy every day (the windshield, rearview and side mirrors of our cars, for instance) and to consider anew those nearer vehicles of apprehension (moveable metatarsals and hip joints, eyeglass hinges and window shades) so crucial to our everyday perspectives and surveyings. Thoreau had been early in considering such factors. He never forgot that houses were made of nails, that sublime views were made of slopes, that no idea can afford to be without its word or its pencil: that as trees emitted sounds on the breeze, so did he. Poetic expressiveness had no special purchase or privileged vantage point above experience. It needed to be included among the other ordinary things of the world—as did, Cavell argued forcefully, the probe of the human voice, that voice whose own weight and history, whose "pitch" had been so long excluded from philosophical discourse.

In more recent years, as I have returned to Williams and other poets writing in Williams's own modernist orbit (Objectivists, Zukovsky and Niedecker in particular) and as my interests have broadened to include various postmodern poets claiming descent from Williams (Creeley especially, but also others, like Susan Howe and Charles Bernstein), I have found myself returning again and again to the last ten pages of *The Senses of Walden*, pages in which Cavell shows how the senses of near, neighboring, and next-to amount in *Walden* to sixth, or maybe seventh— call them the philosophical—senses. With these senses accounted for, something happens: thinking, knowing, reading, speaking (and even perceptions of soul, and even the flexions of reason) are given place in ordinary life, scope for action and time for exercise. "With thinking," Cavell emphasizes, "we may be beside ourselves in a sane sense" (SW 102). His point, deriving from Thoreau's, is that mind merits as much in the way of "elbow room" as material things: that consciousness—no less factual than objects, institutions, physiognomies, or nations—lives with us, whether in the village or "in the woods." The genius of *Walden*, in Cavell's interpretation, is the way it puts thinking, and also technologies of thinking like reading and writing, smack in the middle of any ordinary day, and locates writing in life no less deliberately than one sites a cabin on a hill or by a pond. Cavell shows Thoreau granting a reality, objectivity, to language and thought: "Our imagination, or our capacity for images, and for the meaning or phenomenology of our image—of dawn and day and night, of lower and higher, or straight and curved, hot and cold, freezing and melting and moulting … are as *a priori* as our other forms of knowledge in the world" (p. 103). Further: "Human forms of feeling, objects of human attraction, our reactions constituted in art, are as universal and necessary, as objective, as revelatory of the world, as the forms of the laws of physics" (ibid.). The implications of this are profound. For as Thoreau put books next to sounds, words next to trees, as he accepts visits from a varied host of neighbors (including squirrels and Cellini and Shakespeare, including young hikers but also Aeschylus and Dante, Ben Jonson and Isaac Johnson, his physical and intellectual neighbors from times gone by), he also re-values, rebalances the material and non-material realms. By so doing, he rescues thought not only from its lock-up in heady abstraction but also from its annexation to the figure of the Cartesian subject. Reason, imagination and human forms of feeling are thus demoted *and* liberated by this writer who acknowledges the revelations we do not see or face, the conversations we do not enter, the phenomena we do not address. They exist, as we exist, even in our least conscious states. As Cavell emphasizes by quoting from *Walden*, "*Next* to us the grandest laws are continually being executed. *Next* to us is not the workman whom we have hired, with whom we love so well to talk, but the workman whose work we are" (p. 105).

I shall spend the second half of this essay treating William Carlos Williams's demonstration of a similar nextness, but before arriving there I want first to show some ways in which Cavell's own carefully worded title—*The Senses of Walden*, departing from Thoreau's title—provides its own demonstration of this nextness. Given, as Cavell understands Thoreau's project, that none of the manifold "senses" of "Walden" as word or work or place or book or idea can afford, philosophically speaking, to be left unthought, far less can they be remanded to such categories as "the contents" of the book Henry David Thoreau wrote at Walden. If titles absorb, contain, or possess what follows them, necessarily foreclosing what extravagances of thought may exceed their purview, the "*or*" of *Walden; or, Life in the Woods* renounces title, positing instead a field of possible alternatives. In that spirit, Cavell's own *The Senses of Walden* is not a "title" at all, not a means of holding or keeping, but an experiment in making truly free, a participation, through writing, in that *extra-vagance* Thoreau made watchword.

An incomplete catalogue of the manifold relations that Cavell's title invokes would include:

Senses: suggesting varieties or species, aspects or categories of meaning and, somewhat erosive or in tension with these, senses: suggesting bodily, visceral or perceptual faculties (sight, hearing, smell, taste, touch); and, somewhat in tension with this prior tension: senses, as the plural accommodating those conceptual varieties or aspects that may escape sensuous complication by perceptions, *and* those perceptual faculties that may escape the simplifications of the categorical.

However, even before we arrive at the complications inherent in **Senses**, oughtn't we have acknowledged **The**, an article, capitalized, that not only specifies and delimits a fixed set of senses, but also raises the question of whose "the" anyway? and thence the further question of the authority and power of any **the** to convey a limit and to establish authority? William James's famous reminder in the *Psychology* of these potent little pieces of grammar—so potent that we ought to acknowledge that there is a "feeling of and" and a "feeling of if"—applies just as strongly to this **The**, so that one might need to ponder for some time before determining whether it's the **The** or the **of** of Cavell's title that is noisier, so lively a pair of semaphores are the two.

To wit: **Of**: about, pertaining to or to be found within (a description of place); but, also, derived or descending from, which is to say a part of a history or a temporal line of descent; also, native, or indigenous, or kin to. And (and here is one of its most potent senses) **of**: a preposition of ownership, or possession, of this tied to that. To be "**of**" is to belong to, to be part of, to be subject to some ownership curtailing perfect freedom. How are we to take the orientation of this **of** in *The Senses of Walden*? Does Walden sense, as subjects do, or is it merely sensed, like any other passive object?

Since "Walden" is not apparently human, our first guess might be to call **Walden** an object, a non-human place, part of the empirically observable world out there we use our senses to know. Yet, **Walden**— inhuman, yes—is still so stingingly sensate and alive a place (a great sensorium of organic responsiveness, leaves turning up to sun, frogs tuning up to meet frogs, ice crystals moving vertically, trees fanning oxygen toward our very lungs) that to stipulate that all **The** senses are of and about the object, Walden, none Walden's own, seems stingy and simply inaccurate in treating of an environment so alive, ever pumping and infusing its oxygen-rich life through all manner of beings. Meanwhile, this **Walden** of course also names a "Woods," and also a "Pond" (and also the tract of land including woods and pond), and, since it still exists as a place today, an area of Concord, Massachusetts full of fauna and flora and hunters and hikers and swimmers. To be sure, **Walden** probably was, before it was any of the things just mentioned, the name of some dead man whose name still attaches to the place via conventions of ownership and possession. As it happens, owing to developments in human culture, no one finds it more mystifying than Thoreau himself that certain bizarre conventions of our economic lives will attach a person's name to a woods, as if persons, though dead, remained, via their names, in possession of leaves turning red, of wavelets in the pond, of posterity.

Let us recall, too, that all of the above possibilities exist to be thought about even before we even arrive at *Walden; Or, Life in the Woods*, a work of literature, written by (although, since "it is difficult to begin without borrowing" (p. 355), "by" overstates the case) Henry David Thoreau at (though not really "at" either, if "written at" delimits the place or time too precisely) and about (though, again, not entirely, if "about" implies sticking to the subject of rather than straying into other areas of interest) Walden. We say that *Walden; Or, Life in the Woods* is a work of writing, although just what "writing" is also must also bear thinking about (must one have a pen, pencil or other instrument in hand to write? is vocalization implicit in or constitutive of writing? does the "writing" of a work commence in jottings, drafts, in fair copy? and what of the waking reverie, napping dreams, the after-hours memory through which phrases pass? Ought these latter be grouped with "Life," rather than writing?). Is perhaps writing more *written* when it appears in a book, set in type and purveyed by publishers and booksellers and exchanged for money and displayed on shelves—as it strays further from those events or episodes so mixed up with life? And, if so, does it also grow more a book as **Walden**, whatever manner of place it may be, recedes further and further from *Walden* as *Walden's* relationship to, say, the current **Walden**, a National Park, a daytripper's destination, grows more tenuous. Transformed by its role in the 1960s mythology, in ecological discourse, in high school syllabi, in New England tourism, **Walden** as a word broadcasts connotations of regional cussedness, alternative lifestyle (male, outdoorsy, requiring no social skills, giving vent to lability of mood and feeding on discomforts as much as comfort) that may or may not be compatible with any sense of Walden Thoreau might himself have had.

And to what extent, to return to conundrums of life and *Life*, can one live "life," "in the woods" while reading? Must one *be* in the woods to be in the woods; or will metaphorical versions of the experience count? "Reading" is the very first thing Thoreau tells us he does in the woods after building his cabin, and he finds many ways to represent reading's arduous qualities, many ways to recommend reading as a kind of building and a kind of hiking, a kind of freedom and a kind of work. Skilled reading is, Thoreau shows, the quintessential means of standing beside ourselves, of knowing, if you will, forest from trees. For instance, the conventions of linear reading help us to sweep left to right, top to bottom, page to page, sounding out letters and absorbing aural effects but with the principle in mind that semantic units shall trump aural effects, meanings trump visual interferences, and spaces between words delimit units: thus one makes one's way through the forest: mind swoops over, taking whole phrases, sentences in its beak, as if words had no letters to scan one after another, no sounds to negotiate.

Abstraction enables a certain kind of progress. On the other hand, what depths of understanding may follow the more painstaking experience of re-learning everything! Familiarity, certainty of orientation, can conduce to bad reading, and bad living habits, and so Thoreau recommends getting lost in the woods, going "where there was no cart path, to feel with my feet the faint track which I had worn, or steer by the known relation of particular trees which I felt with my hands" (p. 458). To realize "the infinite extent of his relations" (p. 459) a man does well, Thoreau encourages, "to learn the points of the compass again as often as he awakes, whether from sleep or another abstraction" (ibid.). Thus, the relationships of the visual to aural aspects of reading, become more strange and mysterious as we slow to attend to them. For instance, what makes it possible that when I look at certain typographic marks, those comprising the phrase, **The Senses of Walden**, a soft rustling and buzzing begins as if to rise from print on paper. Where exactly is this domain between the seeing of a word and the saying of a word, this domain in which the curved and brambled typography of "th's" and "v's" and "z's" raise out of a phrase something different from a meaning or a purely retinal apprehension—raise instead a rustling and vibrant hum that is more like the fricative passage of wind through the canopy, or like the drag of a webbed foot across water. Played on the fretwork of four English words, words with dictionary definitions and significances, "The Senses of Walden" is also a study in fricatives, a set piece of lips, tongue, teeth and palate where slight variations in the expelled air past the tongue or teeth drawn from the front to the back of the lips make the difference between "s" and "z," "f" and "v." Presently one may, in repeating the phrase, begin to hear between the words certain mediate non-words—for instance a "zov" between the hard "s" ending Senses and hardened "f" ending "of." One begins to hear, too, the extreme break from the Germanic that the softened pronunciation of the English "W" represents, and so the extreme contingency of orthographic marks as bearers of sound or sense—although, by this time, a reader might also long since have judged these excurses too extravagant, have long since begun to skip ahead in hopes of getting to *the* point, a point more portable than all these multifarious senses displayed without the shorthand of argument. Ought it matter, finally, that the kind of experiment here essayed is the kind in which Thoreau sometimes indulged? Or that, having tried out a philosophical amateur's set of language games, I play them uncredentialed, guessing and hoping but still not certain that the above might be what happens when, following Thoreau's example (and Cavell's), I try to take words and sentences seriously?

To whatever extent the kinds of language games I've played, or attempted to play, above are like those of Cavell—or like those of the ordinary language philosophers, Wittgenstein or Austin, who inspired him—I am fortunate that there are more congenial terms to hand to literary scholars like me and terms still, I trust, conversant with those of the philosophers above. For in taking language to some of its limits, in endeavoring to tease out some of the more radical implications of being "beside ourselves" in language, I operate in a domain that also interested such modernist poets as William Carlos Williams, that interested Niedecker, Zukovsky, and Creeley, and that continues to be of rich and abiding interest to certain poets and critics of the tradition descending from Williams. The same kind of seriousness Cavell demands, and credits Thoreau for putting before us, is abundantly present in the work of certain poets, poet-theorists and theorists of poetry who try to achieve in language what Charles Altieri has called the "new reality" pioneered by Williams. So certainly it's high time for me to acknowledge as interlocutors in this endeavor such critics of twentieth century poetry as Charles Altieri and Charles Bernstein, David Antin, John Hollander, Bob Perelman and Marjorie Perloff, all of whom precede me here in linking Cavell's thought with postmodern poetry and all of whom evince an interest in turning the focus of poetry studies from voice and content, and orienting it more toward writing and composition; away from quests for self-fulfillment, identity, and incarnation, and down by-ways of questioning that turn out to be what philosophy is, and poetry can be. Where thought is not a container or a vector but a turning, or a trope; where language is neither the soul's expression nor a mimetic copy of an outer world but one of the real, ordinary weathers amid which we live—there, we find some twentieth century poets who are Thoreau's neighbors.

Words build; they do not merely address or reflect or make good on the promises or claims of titles. Words generate trails that sprawl and branch; syntaxes budding in new relations, cruxes, conundrums; axes of difficulty arching out over new cliffs of possibility, each turn producing another turn—if, that is, you have time for this kind of thing, for these turns we call thinking. That such exercises of mind, serious and unserious, as that I've ventured above will exclude, or even repel, those too busy for thought is, for Thoreau, precisely what warrants living apart, the turning aside he calls living deliberately. For Thoreau, quality of life is preserved in proportion to scope for deliberation; liberty, a child of de-liberation, is enhanced to the degree to which absorption in busyness, and business, recedes and one takes one's bearings on "essential facts"—beginning with the most proximate, the fact of one's own existence as a thinking being, that species of being (the only one) that can leave a print of its existence in its own particular pitch, in books. Thus the significance of Thoreau's mordant assurance in the opening paragraph of *Walden* that

> in most books, the I or first person is omitted; in this one it will be retained; that, in respect to egotism is the main difference. We commonly do not remember that it is, after all, always the first person that is speaking. I should not talk so much about myself if there were anybody else I knew so well. Moreover, I on my side, require of every writer, first or last, a sincere and simple account of his own life, and not merely what he has heard of other men's lives.

The demand, placed on the author no less than his readers, is highly significant, for it restores to, and exacts of, selves the recognition owed to any palpable fact; it places or stations the self next-to the things of the world, recognized, recognizing, and reporting, but also as part of the world's report. To locate oneself in this way—standing just aside from oneself—is equivalent, for Thoreau, to the highest fulfillment. In this state, as he exults, you "stand right fronting and face to face to a fact, you see the sun glimmering on both its surfaces, as if it were a scimitar, and feel its sweet edge dividing you through the heart and marrow, so you would happily conclude your mortal career" (p. 400). Such is the condition, a double one, to which the writer of *Walden; or Life in the Woods* aspires. It is what Cavell describes when he says that the goal of the writer of Walden is to be "beside" himself "in a sane sense."

Space does not permit a full description of the dire alternatives Thoreau glimpses to such doubleness. Suffice it to say here that without the "broad margin," without the "elbow room" Thoreau would claim for deliberate thought (not excluding thought addressed to the matter of life itself, to facts of Being: that thought we call philosophy), life is not life: "I did not wish to live what was not life; living is so dear" (p. 394). Indeed, the chief reason Thoreau pays so much mind to thought, to the "deliberate" fronting of facts, is that for him the alternative—a quintessentially American, and tragic, alternative to deliberation—is the "desperation" afflicting the purpose-bound, the cause-driven, those without freedom to divide their days. Desperation is the special burden borne by those who cannot apportion their lives or begin to see around the great mass bearing down on them in order to observe the double glimmer on the surface of a fact. Life has no surfaces, and no *"point d'appui,"* for the man who bears a load so expansive, the load of cultural expansionism:

> I see young men, my townsmen, whose misfortune it is to have inherited farms, houses, barns, cattle, and farming tools; for these are more easily acquired than got rid of. Better if they had been born in the open pasture and suckled by a wolf, that they might have seen with clearer eyes what field they were called to labor in. Who made them serfs of the soil? Why should they eat their sixty acres, when man is condemned to eat only his peck of dirt? Why should they begin digging their graves as soon as they are born? They have got to live a man's life, pushing all these things before them, and get on as well as they can. How many a poor immortal soul have I met well-nigh crushed and smothered under its load, creeping down the road of life, pushing before it a barn seventy-five feet by forty, its Augean stables never cleansed, and one hundred acres of land, tillage, mowing, pasture, and woodlot! The portionless, who struggle with no such unnecessary inherited encumbrances, find it labor enough to subdue and cultivate a few cubic feet of flesh.
>
> (p. 326)

Generations of critics have agreed that Thoreau's dystopic reflections above, and the many additional examples he gives in "Economy" on behalf of deliberateness, imply a critique of capitalism and the self-actualizing, and even the liberal, subject. But they are also, as Cavell was so wise to point out, a case and plea for thinking as an *apportioning* activity—an activity preserving the margins and edges, the temporal zones and spatial ranges of a man's experience, and so vouchsafing to the "first person" the full portion of his term on earth. The condition described above, the condition Thoreau means when he uses the word "desperation," has as its most salient feature the loss of the first person in inertial sameness. It will be a few years more before Melville, surveying the postbellum mechanization of his country in the "The utilitarian view of the Monitor's fight," notes the utter foreclosure of human perspective and human scale by the new, modern momentum ("Deadlier, closer, calm 'mid storm;/No passion; all went on by crank/Pivot, and screw/And calculations of caloric"), and it will be some decades more before Henry Adams gives this behemoth drive the name, "Dynamo." Adams's Dynamo will eventually be ramified and magnified, complexified, given megalomaniacal operatives and novelistic sprawl in Thomas Pynchon's post-World War II treatments of "entropy." And runaway intellection—the reasoning self cut loose from space, language, time, and all facts—will find a terrible, poignant updating in Robert Creeley's "I know a Man," a poem that, in effect, turns the Thoreauvian barn into a projectile with an internal combustion engine. But as Cavell was right to argue when he called *Walden* "a book of sufficient scope and consistency to have established or inspired a tradition of thinking" (SW 33), in *Walden* Thoreau anticipates all these episodes. It is Thoreau's unfortunate farmer borne down by his own property, an American buried alive by his very drive, who is the common ancestor—if not neighbor—to Melville's and Adams's, Pynchon's and Creeley's. And why not neighbor? Possession of the self has no neighbors. It is neighborhood—the saving condition of being beside oneself, next to, or near—that the over-portioned man loses. Drive drives him, burns through and gobbles down discrete facts. The credulous faith in identity, cousin to possession, engulfs the self too. For when nothing escapes you, you do not get away either.

So Thoreau sees his neighbor condemned by his own illusions and eating "more than [his] peck of dirt." So, in William Carlos Williams's updating of the same, in "To Elsie," we eat shit:

> as if the earth under our feet
> were
> an excrement of some sky
>
> and we degraded prisoners
> destined
> to hunger until we eat filth
>
> while the imagination strains
> after deer
> going by fields of goldenrod in
>
> the stifling heat of September
> Somehow
> it seems to destroy us[2]

In the second half of this essay I shall show how imagination's succor, the sight of "deer/going by fields of goldenrod" is, in the work of William Carlos Williams, achievable within conditions of modernity. I shall endeavor to demonstrate how those very satisfactions of deliberateness, the fulfillments of "Life" Thoreau finds in the woods, Williams builds in the city. Let me turn at this point, then, to a reading of one of

Williams's breakthrough poems, a work I want to install in that tradition of Thoreauvian adjacency that Cavell first named for me. The poem is "Fine Work with Pitch and Copper," and it takes us to a rooftop construction site at midday.

II

"Fine Work with Pitch and Copper" begins in an instant, in a "Now" as particular and precious as any lunch break on a brilliant day:

> Now they are resting
> in the fleckless light
> separately in unison
>
> like the sacks
> of sifted stone stacked
> regularly by twos
>
> about the flat roof
> ready after lunch
> to be opened and strewn

(p. 405)

The poem goes a long way toward invoking a sort of sublime and unifying timelessness. "Now" is a word for an ephemeral instant, and the present progressive of "they are resting" signals its own impermanence. But what a roundness, what a ringing clarity, this present moment has! Are not afternoons the most ancient of things, this poem conveys; is not light itself, the downbeat of its brilliant baton, agent of some deep and primordial rhythm, five beats each? "Now they are resting/In the fleckless light". The first line begins with a dactyl, the stress leading, DA-da-da and then the second reverses it, cinched in with an anapest, da-da-DA, the lines pleated and folded on an edge as if to exhibit the symmetry of things, this world where pairs in procession, where division by twos lead to order, but where different orders converge: spatial, aural, visual, resting, dynamic, temporal—of yesterday, when the copper was beaten; of tomorrow, when it will oxidize.

As early as Line 3, "unison" confirms a musical coherence that subsequent lines will give a corresponding spatial shapeliness. A few lines on, the phrase "flat roof" crisps the focus like a proscenium, lends ceremony and a sense of occasion by simply naming the space a "roof," while roof itself also suggests a square. By the next stanza, the "t" that organizes the random sacks into stacks of two will order the whole roof: this "t" squares off not only the right angles into which the copper strips have been beaten, but also part of the poem's structure in the form of "foot strips," metrical lengths, some twos, some eights, some fours, that are themselves part of the across of the lines and the up and down of the stanzas. The visual aspects of the poem matter. Run your eye up and down the page, and then across from left to right and back again, and you begin to see angles, as well as the squares that are part of the page's own architecture. Each stanza is three plus or minus words across and three plus or minus lines down, the poem an interlace, a literal building, of blocks and panes, with stanzas propped up on pedestals of white space; or, flecked pedestals of black and white print hoisting the potent, pulsing rests. The rests are as dynamic as the words, for there is a reciprocity of rest and utterance, a reciprocity between poetic speech and silence, that has its counterpart in the world of work and leisure. Recall that Thoreau liked a broad margin to his life, worked in mornings so he could wander afternoons, strove to balance pastime and livelihood, morning and night. Just so, the rests and resting in Williams, which pertain simultaneously to all the makers in and of the poem: construction workers, poets, readers, past and present.

"Fine Work with Pitch and Copper," as many have noticed before me, is of course as much about artists and art as roofers or laborers. Indeed, while it is a modern poem, and bears in it the code of the postmodern, it is a poem whose modernity will not depend on abolishment of tradition. Past craft, inherited tradition, lie ready at hand.

The copper in eight
foot strips has been
beaten lengthwise

down the center at right
angles and lies ready
to edge the coping

Lengths of copper and knowledge of copings are as essential to good roofs as traditions of working them, standards of craft, and the experts and terminologies that refine general specifications into particular instances of fine work. The poem "Fine Work with Pitch and Copper" is no less dependent on prior achievement. From the Hebrew ready-mades (the mannered phrase "two by two" invoking Noah's animals, or the Edenic couple) to the tawny light, cut stone, and primordial geometry of the classical world, the poem gathers in the tools and materials of the primary, ancestral and ancient arts. Male figures, touched beautifully by the fleckless light, seem to sprawl supine in the negative, or "resting," space of the poem, their dynamism latent and waiting to be sprung. This being Williams, the hour is not dawn or an English gloaming but lunchtime, and the setting an American city in New York or New Jersey: to me, these figures are distinctly Whitmanian, tanned, coppery in the light, loafing but also defined by something intelligent, tense, and technical. "One still chewing" will exhibit a casual sapience a few lines later, stepping out from the crowd, and confirm their democratic silhouette: they're built to American specs. This said, however, if one had to choose a most important precursor looming largest in this poem, one might have to choose Wordsworth. The "fleckless" light of this poem is as clear an allusion as we might get to Wordsworth's Westminster Bridge, where a deep draft of "smokeless air" allows the poet an uncanny vision of a city paused.

In Wordsworth, the world is stilled and singularized, as the poet lets himself expand into the same brilliant raiment of the now, he and the city mutually absorbed so that twoness gives way to oneness. And here the differences between the poems are patent, since Williams' poem is all twos, and thinking about and toward the other never ceases. Cavell writes in *Senses of Walden* of a sense of doubleness so important to the writer of Walden, a doubleness of which writing itself is an instance: "We are to reinterpret our sense of doubleness as a relation between ourselves in the aspect of indweller, unconsciously building, and in the aspect of spectator, impartially observing. Unity between these aspects is viewed not as mutual absorption but a perpetual nextness, an act of neighboring or befriending" (SW 108). Wordsworth's "Lines Composed Upon Westminster Bridge" (beautiful and indispensable to all of us, and, I think, to Williams too) epitomize absorptiveness, for they deliver the speaker to an elevation, enroofing him in vision, in transcendent invisibility. They elevate his reason such that his very syntax unrolls, descending, in a straight line of perfect mediation, of sublime apostrophe, in which the bridging mediating function dissolves his location and effaces his objectivity. Here the speaker enjoys, however briefly, the prerogatives of the originator, the first beholder, the consciousness transcending its world. To paraphrase Emerson in a similar mood—and Williams has these moods too, mind you—he is nothing, he sees all.

Not so on this rooftop, which is not only a look-out but is also a looked-at. "Fine Work with Pitch and Copper" is not written "Upon" a place of lofty perspective, and its maker declines to dispatch in advance those harbingers of communicative urgency that would clear away complication and illogic. He even declines, as I'll detail in a moment, to unkink his syntax so as to keep clear the sight lines running from subjects to objects, or to get his words out of the way of his apostrophe. Poetic address, a very high and privileged form of rhetoric, is in fact simply stored or stacked in this poem on the same horizontal plane of adjacencies holding everything else. Williams makes his roof broad and flat for many reasons. A key one is to let the roof be a floor, to give all things their gravity: "Heaven is under our feet as well as over our heads," wrote Thoreau. Another is to recuperate the factuality and shapeliness of words, the way they too, no less than copper or air or a trained pair of hands, exist among the other things of the world.

The reader of the 1936 volume in which "Fine Work with Pitch and Copper" is collected, has in fact already seen various originary and transcendent agents become part of more contingent and piecemeal constructions. The volume in which the poem first appears is *Adam & Eve & the City*. The ampersand is crucial in complex ways, its shape describing a flexible join, a conjunction of the symbolic and the pictorial, a coupling (and decoupling) of syntactic necessity. One thing *Adam & Eve & the City* is not is a traditional title, a conceptual headline. Another thing it doesn't seem to want to be is a sentence headed toward an end, with word order forcing subjects and objects. Not incidentally, the last poem in the volume *Adam & Eve & the City* is called a "Perpetuum Mobile," and this is a good description of what this string of words hooked by ampersands, re-arrangeable and modular, wants to be. Adam and Eve, like all men and women, in fact all words, are part of more compositions than convention (which couples them) likes. Separately in unison, Williams's *Adam & Eve & the City* are assembled in various ways. Here are a few ways they appear in Williams's volume:

ADAM & EVE
& THE CITY
1936

ADAM
& EVE
& THE
CITY

ADAM & EVE & THE CITY 1936

Adam & Eve
& the City

An arrangement or modular composition of resonant, abstractable items—the terms and elements, Adam, Eve, City, moved here and there—leach transcendent, symbolic, and unitary force. Any line that puts Adam and Eve together marshals a massive cultural charge—such a line becomes their garden, their primeval honeymoon suite—while a line that puts Adam, Eve, and the City on separate lines modernizes and demythologizes them, and one that piles Adam on Eve on City turns the city into a walk up for sex. Furthermore, if we look at the first poem in the volume, one tellingly titled "To a Woodthrush" (clearly another Wordsworthian gesture, this time toward the poem "Hark, the Thrush") we see that sublime address in this apostrophe to a "Wood Thrush" (p. 404) is aborted only a few lines on, the reciprocity or mutual absorption of poet and phenomena confuted when the speaker, standing next to the self performing this act, now includes the act, the intention, and the tradition of this intention within the poem's composition. ("First I tried to write/conventionally praising you," he writes, but "found it no more/than my own thoughts/that I was giving.") The distinctly ordinary and unbeautiful sound of these lines' admission—with its flatness, affective awkwardness, and then its reminder of sequence and priority as they gum up all address—present as dense what lyric made transparent: they make objective what would have been invisible. The speaker's effort to communicate congeals halfway across the channel of sequential speech. If the classic romantic address to the "Wood Thrush" nests phenomena in each other, Williams' post-romanticism *nexts* them. His song, which comes "across," "from," "of," "inversely" and "in a lower key" does not obey the reciprocity of subject and object but rather presents itself as more diffusely sourced.

To return to "Fine Work with Pitch and Copper," all phenomena there are diffusely sourced, no special prerogative of a speaker having cleared the way in advance. What, and who—, is this poem about, anyway? "They" might be sacks of stone and they might be workers: Williams lets us encounter how just a word like "they" pairs them, sounds them in unison, and then how just a word separates them, as words themselves are material to the relation between things, up there on the roof with men and stone. Both workers and sacks of stone might rest—but these workers who are resting, are they also ready to be "opened and strewn"? What do we need to say of the bagged stone, "ready" to be opened, and what extra word to bring to the site, or what word to get rid of (to sift out, or repluralize or resingularize or put in the imperfect or subjunctive or make figura)? What word will keep the sifted stone from chewing? So much depends, as Williams later puts it, on how word placement, adjacency, histories and traditions of utterances tell us that here, now, in this case but not in all cases "One-still-chewing" (the words on a line compose a sort of Greek epithet) is not a bag of stone but a guy chewing. Similarly, "fleckless" may be a salute to Wordsworth, the word functioning as an ampersand connecting Wordsworth to Williams in the poetic tradition. But fleckless is part of other paratactic diagrams or twirling mobiles of sense freed from the hypotaxis of reason. If "fleckless" reminds us of how this poem, this construction of poetic thought neighbors Wordsworth's "Lines," it also reminds us that days are different, that this day is a clear day, a windless one, for otherwise the bags of stacked sifted stone would be letting forth flecks, fine particles. The "Now" in which this poem occurs is thus joined to different neighboring days, rather as the "One" who emerges in the poem's last stanza is placed among others, some chewing, some not chewing, some having returned their minds to matters of art and some not:

> One still chewing
> picks up a copper strip
> and runs his eye along it

There is so much to like in these lines: the extra foot that draws our eye along the slightly longer line, a line that is a longer strip. In the end, one feels friendly toward this "One" who can chew and think at the same time, an ordinary possibility very often excluded from poetic expression. For in regarding the "One still chewing" the reader also, of course, regards himself, for he too "runs his eye along" the same, and also a different "it," his eye apprehending the strip in, and also the strip *of*, the poem; his ruminations sweeping back and forth and, in their strokes, not only detecting but buffing, raising the luster, on the warm image of the copper material; not only encountering but building the analogues between copper lengths and line lengths, and between precision work in metal and precision work in words and between works of the hands and the mind to be capable of this doubleness was what Stanley Cavell credited Thoreau with achieving. This is what it is to be beside oneself in a sane sense, as opposed to being beside oneself in an ecstatic, transcendent sense, which Thoreau at Walden and Williams on his rooftop duly regard with neighborly interest.

Reading Thoreau next to Williams makes me wonder—as odd as this will sound to those who think of Thoreau as a man of wild or "natural" environments—if Thoreau wouldn't have liked his "Life in the Woods" just as well in the city where the imitation and conformity are defeated by scale and speed, where individualisms are eroded by repetition, and heights relativized by the jagged scape of rooflines. In William Carlos Williams, city, prospect, far horizon, foreground and background are turned and fractured by the reflection of brick and stone and sky in glass, and the self by the great jigsaw of adjacencies. Who or what is not your neighbor in the city? What aren't you next to? Williams finds in cities a model of consciousness that I think is classically Thoreauvian, based in perceptual nextness, admitting or claiming no sublime prospect, but only freedom to build near and next-to.

14 For All You Know

Andrew H. Miller

I

> The question, "What would have happened if this or that event had not taken place?" is almost unanimously rejected, and yet it is precisely the key question, whereby everything turns ironic.
>
> Friedrich Nietzsche

In the course of concluding a book on the moral perfectionism of nineteenth century Britain—a book in which the pertinence of Stanley Cavell's writing for thinking about the nineteenth century and about Britain and about literature occupied one side of each page; and the pertinence of the nineteenth century and Britain and literature for Cavell's thinking occupied the other—I became aware that this moral perfectionism had been dogged by a separate, companion mode of thinking, a mode I came to call, following Stuart Hampshire, the "optative."[1] Consider, Hampshire writes,

> a type of situation in which judgments of necessity and both theoretical and practical possibility become urgent and important, a type of situation to which poetry and fiction are always recurring: the situation of retrospection and regret. Any person's actual history can be seen in retrospect as a track between two margins. Just over the left margin are all those things that could have or might have happened to him, and that nearly happened to him, stretching back along the margin into the past. On the right-hand side of the track are all those things that he might have done, and that he nearly did, and that were real possibilities or options for him, stretching back into the past.[2]

It is a common enough picture in seeing life as a track (or path, or river), but strange in seeing that track as bounded by ghostly possibilities. We're accustomed (if not always happily accustomed) to thinking of our life as bounded by birth and death, beginning and end. But Hampshire reminds us of other boundaries, to our left and right, as he has it: It is not just that my life will have its end, be limited in the future as it has been

limited in the past, but that it is limited now, and at every moment. I am
this person, and none other. Understanding himself thus, writes Hampshire, a person

> explains himself to himself by his history, but by the history as
> accompanied by unrealised possibilities on both sides of the track
> of actual events. His individual nature, and the quality of his life,
> do not depend only on the bare log-book of events and actions. …
> In self-examination one may press these inquiries into possibilities
> very far, and this pressure upon possibility belongs to the essence
> of moral reflection.
>
> (p. 101)

But how, exactly, do we carry, how do we bear, how do we assess the
thought that other lives might have been ours?

Although this optative mode of contrastive and counterfactual self-
reflection is more complex than Hampshire presents it—we'll see, for
instance, that the distinction between what you have done, perhaps
chosen, and what has befallen you is more unsettled than his schema
suggests—he is right, nonetheless, to associate it so fully with poetry
and fiction. It's most famous expression is no doubt Robert Frost's "The
Road Not Taken" and it is there in Robert Browning's "Cleon," in T. S.
Eliot's "Burnt Norton," in Gwendolyn Brooks' haunted and haunting
"The Mother," in James Schuyler's "Salute," in A. R. Ammons' "Easter
Morning," in George Stanley's vertiginous and determined "Veracruz";
it's there as well in *The Ambassadors* and "The Beast in the Jungle," where
Henry James makes of it a problem of craft and form; it's there in *He
Knew He Was Right*, where Anthony Trollope is shameless in extracting
the pungent emotional rewards to be had in reminding us of all that has
been possible for his characters; it's there at work in *Middlemarch*, which
concludes with a self-justifying appeal to the way things might have
been had those whose tombs we do not visit not faithfully lived their
hidden lives; it's there in Charles Dickens' *David Copperfield*, where the
protagonist remarks, as if in summary, "the things that never happen,
are often as much realities to us, in their effects, as those that are accomplished."[3] The optative is hard at work in later novels like Virginia
Woolf's *Mrs. Dalloway* and Rebecca West's *Return of the Soldier* and is
there in yet more recent books, like Philip Roth's *The Counterlife* and
Marilynne Robinson's *Home*.[4]

Sometimes, the recognition of unrealized selves follows from an
encounter with another person, someone who seems to personify alternative, unlived possibilities; in other cases, these unrealized selves are

more ghostly and abstract, intermittently visible, nagging reminders of limitation. In either case, however, I try to come to terms with who I have become by comparison with whom I have not become. To borrow a distinction from Robert Nozick, in moments of optative reflection we are trying not to *explain* but to *understand* ourselves: "I am tempted to say that explanation locates something in actuality, showing its actual connections with other actual things, while understanding locates it in a network of possibility, showing the connections it would have to ... non-actual things or processes."[5] We understand a life, Nozick would say, by "seeing it in ... its possibility neighborhood" (p. 21).

What preconditions are required for this emotionally saturated self-understanding? At the heart of the optative is the experience of identity as doubled, at once both singular and common. On the one hand, I must experience my life as bounded: for me not to have another life, I must have one life first, only one, this one. In this way, the optative expresses our separateness: in having one life (rather than another) I have one life (apart). And it expresses our singularity: in having one life (rather than another) I have one life only, unlike any other (*this* one). (To the extent that I think of myself as having a fluid, permeable life, not fixed in one identity—or think of myself as having several lives at once—I am unlikely to experience the optative.) The metaphorical language circling this idea of a single life quickly can become that of imprisonment: I am sentenced to this social role, this identity, these habits, this history, this particular body, these thoughts—as if my skin were a boundary, my skull a skeletal cell. It was in jail and looking out at the condemned as they went to the gallows, that John Bradford remarked, "there but for the grace of God go I."

At the same time, while I think of myself as separate and singular, perhaps captive and confined, I must also experience myself as a member of some kind, class, or type—some group with other individuals in it comparable to me, leading lives comparable to mine, that might have been mine. Perhaps we're siblings, or step-siblings; classmates or colleagues; suitors for one person; possible heirs to the same fortune; inhabitants of the same city. Perhaps we've only shared a chance moment, been present at the same opportunity, the same catastrophe, in the past. But in one way or another, I must consider others, as Joe says in *Great Expectations*, as "fellow-creatur[s]"; or, as one of the more obscure philosophers in that novel remarks, "if a man is not his own neighbor, who is?"[6]

The play evinced by my experience of myself as at once unique and common is at the heart of the optative. For when gripped by this mood, I compare myself to another and conceive of myself as exchanging the life in which I am bound with that other life—as if I had traveled down an alternate path or track. "What would it have made of me, what would it have made of me?" Spencer Brydon asks himself in Henry James's "The Jolly Corner," as he reflects on his decision, decades ago, to leave New York. "I see what [staying in the city] has made of dozens of others, those I meet, and it positively aches within me, to the point of exasperation, that it would have made something of me as well."[7] All James' abilities in rendering particularized characters are devoted to making Brydon a unique figure in our minds—and yet there are those dozens of others forming a group of which he is a part, any one of whose path he could have taken and become someone entirely different from who he is. The more distinct my experience, the more contingent it can seem.

Just as the optative individuates persons, segregating them while testing that segregation, so it individuates and segregates—indeed, makes melodramatic—events, identifying *the* event that has led to my becoming this person rather than that, pulling out from the flux of experience one moment and retroactively granting it decisive significance, calling it a crisis. It is important to note that the optative can take as its point of departure the conditions of a life—one's class, or race, one's gender, certainly, but also such things as whether you have siblings. But insofar as it becomes an element within the plot or story, the optative typically takes as its point of departure not such narrative conditions but particular events, what narratologists would call kernels, forking moments that send the plot this way but not that. Perhaps there was a choice to be made and I made it; perhaps I left it unmade and found it made for me; perhaps there was no choice and nothing for me to do, only something for me to suffer—at any rate, there was an event that made all the difference as I became no one other than who I am.

There are endless candidates for such events, but some recur with special force and frequency. Perhaps the most powerful of these are marriage and parenting, because, mythically, they each offer an escape from the doubled structure of subjectivity on which the optative depends. Marriage promises an experience in which our separateness is escaped; it is conventionally (or was conventionally) mythologized as two people living as one. The failure of a marriage, then, can make the experience of one's singularity, one's single life all the more acute. As can, of course, the failure to get married. "If you marry, you will regret it," Kierkegaard drily remarked. But, then, "if you do not marry, you will also regret it; if you marry or if you do not marry, you will regret both; whether you marry or you do not marry, you will regret both."[8] Parenting similarly, perhaps even more powerfully, promises an escape from this separateness: our children are flesh of our flesh, presenting—with whatever truth—the possibility that we might become new people, reborn, and living beyond our death. In defeating this hope, the death of children compels the thought that the past might have been different, that we might be different now—not that we might one day live again but that they might not on one day have died.

There are other, more prosaic occasions which also prompt optative reflection. One we've already seen is moving, as when Spencer Brydon imagines what he would have become if he had not moved from New York. Another is the choice of career, as when William, not Henry, James imagines a young person deciding whether to enter business or the ministry:

> He takes the place offered in the counting-house, and is committed. Little by little, the habits, the knowledges, of the other career, which once lay so near, cease to be reckoned even among his possibilities. At first, he may sometimes doubt whether the self he murdered in that decisive hour might not have been the better of the two; but with the years such questions themselves expire, and the old alternative ego, once so vivid, fades into something less substantial than a dream.[9]

A third is the choice of college, understood as a vast switching yard of possibilities, train cars coupling and decoupling, shunted down these rails rather than those, headed for different destinations. But, as this growing list suggests, the optative need not seize on merely one event; it may isolate a series of them, each one distinct, collectively creating a delta of possibilities that now course around the life you're living. It is a signal accomplishment of Thomas Hardy's writing to have multiplied such events so relentlessly that they form the very texture of his plots, every event—almost it can seem every verb—in his novels harboring possibilities forever unrealized. Indeed, the achievement of his books is to make us see that the things that do happen and those that do not are complementary parts of the narrative machinery, paired cogs with interlocking teeth. The rape of Tess, followed by her non-marriage and marriage, the birth and death of her child, the jobs she takes and leaves, her movements across Wessex: the unrealized alternatives of these events gather and re-gather as we read, so that when we arrive at last to the novel's end and discover Tess asleep on a cold slab at Stonehenge, waiting in the morning mist for the police to arrive, we seem to see, on her left and on her right, all the lives we wished for her, all the lives she has not led.

II

All I could never be,
All, men ignored in me,
This, I was worth to God

Robert Browning

What, then, is the relation between this optative mode of self-understanding and the moral perfectionism out of which my recognition of it emerged? Cavell's writing gives little open guidance. But if we take moral perfectionism to be less a concept than a narrative structure, then its nature may be best identified by the open set of features it typically includes; this is the way that Cavell himself describes it in the opening of his most sustained treatment of perfectionism, *Conditions Handsome and Unhandsome*. Among the features under study there are, prominently, the experience of skepticism (often figured as being lost); a distinctive, turning moment understood to be defining; the relation between one person and an exemplary other; and the ideas of birth and rebirth, of marriage and remarriage, of friendship and education, and of life as a path. If the optative shares these features with moral perfectionism, it also, clearly enough, differs in its treatment of them; we can say it offers an opposing interpretation of them. One way to characterize this difference would be to recall that moral perfectionism, on Cavell's accounting of it, is an expression of youth, and directed towards youth, understood not narrowly as a time of life but as a dimension of it, a stance towards one's experience that, while admitting despondency, counsels hope. It concerns the turns that one's life may yet take. The retrospective contemplation of the optative, by contrast, is an expression of age, again not necessarily understood as a time of life but as a dimension of it, in which one's mortality has come more sharply into view, constraining relations have grown, and alternatives appear to have shrunk—a perspective that can afford relief but that also, as Hampshire notes, readily invites regret. It concerns the turns one's life has not taken.

And that distinctive coloring of regret or disappointment provides a means for further development of the relationship between the optative and perfectionism, one which I'll pursue by considering a poem by the American poet Carl Dennis, titled "The God Who Loves You."[10] The poem, as we'll see, draws on the various motifs I've just catalogued as shared by both modes: friendship, marriage understood as a conversation, the domestic, college and education, and the expression of all these in language. Perhaps most importantly for present purposes, Dennis's poem foregrounds the issue of choice; to anticipate my ending, the acknowledgment of lives unled is understood in the poem as a matter of choice, and of writing as it becomes that choice. The poem opens by evoking a realtor driving home from having sold homes, apparently content in a life platted and subdivided into days and weeks—all the while attended by a hovering, sympathetic god who knows that another life has been possible for him, a life not of dull routine but of passion and creative appreciation. "It must be troubling for the god who loves you," Dennis begins,

> To ponder how much happier you'd be today
> Had you been able to glimpse your many futures.
> It must be painful for him to watch you on Friday evenings
> Driving home from the office, content with your week—
> Three fine houses sold to deserving families—
> Knowing as he does exactly what would have happened
> Had you gone to your second choice for college,
> Knowing the roommate you'd have been allotted
> Whose ardent opinions on painting and music
> Would have kindled in you a lifelong passion.
> A life thirty points above the life you're living
> On any scale of satisfaction. And every point
> A thorn in the side of the god who loves you.

This divine pain—small but sharp—is a projection, I take it, of the realtor's regret, a regret almost inaudible even to himself. To regret can seem a betrayal of who one is, of oneself and those to whom one is bound. Better to silence it within, if only to discover it anew elsewhere. But why, if it is to be projected, should this thorn of regret lodge in the side of a god? Why should regret find that aerial home? When we say, if only I had done this or that, things would have been better for me or for those I care about, we smuggle in, under cover of dark disappointment or darker self-castigation, the assumption that we *could* have known what was best to do. Buyer's remorse, *l'esprit d'escalier*, the familiar feeling you have after the food comes at a restaurant and you consider how you could have ordered better—"I should have had the duck!"— the whole range of second-guessing moves we make as we try to game our ordinary experience: routine self-criticism perversely feeding the thought that perfection is possible, that I could have known what to do. The trouble we cause ourselves with disappointment is in this way merely the price we pay in buying a picture of ourselves as self-loving, all-knowing gods. Such sly flattery is one source of the optative's appeal: it silently transmutes retrospection into omniscience.[11] Better to be a god with a thorn of regret pricking my ribs than to remain within my life, ignorant, unable to see around its edges, merely human.

Siding with the divine, finding the truth of life in that aerial view rather than in any earthbound, human perspective: this is a distinctly skeptical fantasy of the sort Cavell has frequently identified. "Skepticism is a place," he writes,

> perhaps the central secular place, in which the human wish to deny the condition of human existence is expressed; and so long as the denial is essential to what we think of as the human, skepticism cannot, or must not, be denied. This makes skepticism an argument internal to the individual, or separate, human creature, as it were an argument of the self with itself (over its finitude).
>
> (IQO 5)

This recasts our original inquiry as a matter of skepticism. How are we to conduct its argument? In what words are we to express and assess our finitude—our singularity and separateness, the fact that we are living this one life and none other? Not, certainly, in the language of this realtor or his god. "Three fine houses sold to deserving families … A life thirty points above the life you're living": their words are empty. While it is not the task of the speaker of the poem to provide a new language for the realtor—this is something he exactly cannot do—it will be his task, it will be the task of the poem, to point him towards the discovery of such a language. The speaker, as Cavell might put it, is to guide the realtor as he brings his words home—a home, of course, not on the market.

We will see in a moment that the speaker closes his poem by proposing a particular expressive form for the realtor to use. But even before that closing proposal, the speaker silently offers the guiding example of his tone, his modulating attitude towards the reader and the reader's skepticism. The casual diction and gently structured meter, the end-stopped lines and infrequent, stressing caesura that easily accommodate the reader's breath, the free indirect discourse that slides into and out of the perspectives of man and god: all together form the speaker's tone towards his materials:

> You don't want that, a large-souled man like you
> Who tries to withhold from your wife the day's disappointments
> So she can save her empathy for the children.
> And would you want this god to compare your wife
> With the woman you were destined to meet on the other campus?

> It hurts you to think of him ranking the conversation
> You'd have enjoyed over there higher in insight
> Than the conversation you're used to.
> And think how this loving god would feel
> Knowing that the man next in line for your wife
> Would have pleased her more than you ever will
> Even on your best days, when you really try.
> Can you sleep at night believing a god like that
> Is pacing his cloudy bedroom, harassed by alternatives
> You're spared by ignorance?

If in the poem's opening lines the speaker is gently mocking, here his tone glides into something more like paternalism and an insinuating knowingness about the daily efforts of married men, as he attempts to draw the realtor into complicity. Cajoling him, the speaker leverages the realtor's largess—pity this god—to appeal to his unattained but attainable self. This is the poem's gambit: to encourage the addressee, whose choices and efforts seem to have been swamped by chances beyond his control, to conceive of himself as having the power to choose actions of magnanimity and consequence. Choice starts with the attitude he takes on his life; tone, then, is if not everything, at least the first thing.

This is perhaps the place to note that Dennis's critical prose presents poetry as concerned above all with the cultivation and attraction of the reader's sympathetic attention in a relationship akin to that of friendship, theorized in conjunction with the writing of Emerson, especially his idea that the poet must turn from the received languages of his or her culture, thus turning the reader, too, from those languages. It is a view of poetry, realized in "The God Who Loves You," that Dennis presents as being from the start responsive to various forms of skepticism, and one that typically emphasizes the conscious choices made by poets among speech acts.[12] The echoes of Cavell's work are not unfailing, but they are evident enough, and become yet more evident as Dennis's poem draws towards its conclusion:

> The difference between what is
> And what could have been will remain alive for him
> Even after you cease existing, after you catch a chill
> Running out in the snow for the morning paper,
> Losing eleven years that the god who loves you
> Will feel compelled to imagine scene by scene
> Unless you come to the rescue by imagining him
> No wiser than you are, no god at all, only a friend

No closer than the actual friend you made at college,
The one you haven't written in months. Sit down tonight
And write him about the life you can talk about
With a claim to authority, the life you've witnessed,
Which for all you know is the life you've chosen.

No wiser than you are; no closer than a friend: the god who loves you knows too much, is too close to you. This sustains my sense that the poem dramatizes an internal argument. But it also motivates the speaker's final injunction to write: a friend needs our writing as a god does not. For him or for her we must make ourselves public. Against the empty languages of the realtor and the god, then, the speaker proposes the language of the familiar letter, bringing the realtor down from the god's inhuman imaginings and the regret that sustains those imaginings to the life he has authored or will author through this letter in a language which—for all the realtor knows—is the one he has chosen. The poem's last lines recall the realtor to his human ignorance of his choices, hence of himself. It is a picture of the ordinary as an achievement, attained in writing through writing.

It would seem that these last lines enjoin the addressee to leave behind the human argument of the self with itself that the poem itself preserves. (What value lies in any *record* of therapy?) Does Dennis's poem then deny skepticism or acknowledge it? If a reasonable answer is that it does both, then what comes to matter is not the impasse thus represented but, again, the attitude or tone adopted towards that impasse—the speaker's attitude towards his materials, his ambitions for them, for himself. (The poem's achievement lies not only in its tone but in the significance it successfully attributes to tone generally.) And what is most distinctive about that attitude is the assurance it projects; its accomplishment lies in its ease, all awkwardness avoided. Is this to be regretted?

III

And is not this … no less than the very proof of the Cavellian
method: a reading so intense as to internalize the shadow of its own
alternatives?

Garrett Stewart

And so, having spent a couple of years working out the idea of the optative—emerging as it did from a book committed to exploring, whatever else, Cavell's understanding of moral perfectionism—it has been a welcome confirmation to find this idea under more or less continuous study in *Little Did I Know*. The idea enters fairly gently—"It does me some good from time to time," he writes, "to imagine what ordinary thing might have been said or done at a given moment to have changed the drift of the world" (LDIK 176)—but it then becomes more insistent, and we run through the full range of optative thematics that I listed a moment ago. Thus, Cavell writes about being a solitary, siblingless child in a desolating and moving home and about his later travels:

> Travel suggests for me a screen of memories and decisions of its own, oriented around questions of my life marked by the shifts of what I have variously called home, and of course by the inevitable wondering … of what it would have been to have been born just here, where the lives are uncannily similar and different from mine, evidently tied to the familiar wonder of having had different parents, hence the sense of oneself as an unfound foundling.
>
> (LDIK 179)

And thus, too, he speaks about the decisive events in which he discovered a possible career, a vocation, a world, as a musician and then composer, and then relinquished that possibility, murdered it, to discover, slowly, laboriously, another career as a writer. When he later describes his entrance into and exit from a marriage and the entrance into another and the consideration of alternative lives prompted by the women he has met, he speaks of one woman and her daughter in this way: "In another world, they would be the heroines of my account as it seeks out the story of my fate. Which means that they are forever heroines in certain of the worlds among the constellation of worlds of my inner, other, lives—well, of this one life, if you know sufficient ways to read it" (LDIK 398). Subsequently, optative self-reflection is prompted by the fact of his own children, and by comparison of the intellectual luxuries of Harvard students with his own experience as an undergraduate at Berkeley. And, finally, running through all these thoughts, through the book as a whole, is his unending meditation over whether he is odd or not, singular or not, exceptional or representative, a solitary or a member of some as-yet undiscovered group.

By the book's conclusion, such optative considerations form the matter of one of Cavell's most weighty moments of self-reflection as the writing openly draws to its close and he looks to find a way to end:

> I am seeking a way to leave these remarks essentially where they are, so that I have begun looking back at the ground covered. My bargain with myself from the beginning has been to write here of

the past essentially from memory, and to articulate memories, however unpromising in appearance, whenever I could, with some idea of how just these events and images have led to, or shaped, a reasonable life nevertheless also devoted to a certain ambition of philosophical writing, or what is meant as such.

(LDIK 516)

Retrospection doubles, circling us backwards while escorting us on: Cavell reviews the writing that reviews his life, understood as having led to (this) writing, now concluding. Attaining that vantage prompts the lateral glance of the optative, and launches Cavell into a set of counterfactual speculations:

Too obviously these events and images might not have led to this outcome, or rather anything recognizable as an event or image might have been otherwise. If I had not run out into the street that morning and accidentally been knocked unconscious by a car, then what? Since that would probably not have prevented World War II, I would have been drafted into the army when I turned eighteen—unless my sense of physical distortion had been lessened and I had been approachable enough to have been alerted to and to have prepared for the final interview after the physical examination for the navy officers' program a year and a half earlier, and been accepted, hence in either case subject directly to the fortunes of war. If we had not moved from the family house when I turned seven, that would perhaps have meant that there had been no Great Depression, and in that case my father would not have lost that store, or if the Great Miami Hurricane had not hit when and as it did he would not have lost *that* store and in neither case would we have moved to Sacramento, and Mendel would have graduated college and not had to become everybody's father. But then no one would have picked me up on Saturdays from an empty apartment on the north side. But that is absurd, if, as I am imagining, we never moved there. These tiny counterfactual links become impossible before they have hit a stride.

(LDIK 516–17)

Why have these links not hit a stride? They have become impossible we're told—and yet, we've also been told that they are obvious. The experience of the obvious as impossible, the impossible as obvious: these are familiar notes from Cavell's writing, sounding one description of the skepticism that has preoccupied him. Pursuing these links would be no more absurd, no more lunatic, than, say, considering whether the person in front of me, with whom I have been conversing, is in fact a human being or a well-constructed imitation of one. When, then, does Cavell stress their absurdity? I want to say that his imagination of these counterfactuals—his writing of this passage—is not heartfelt; it lacks conviction. (This lack of conviction is the counterpart to Dennis's stylistic ease: both mark the speaker's encampment in the everyday.) Compare, for instance the extended parable of the craftsman in *The Claim of Reason*, where Cavell's conviction in imagining a skeptical scene is exactly at issue; the motivations towards that relentless imagination are under study. But here the imagination finds no footing. Why, then, include these alternatives?

> A human life, a human action, human history, at any moment is underdetermined and overdetermined. If things need not have worked out as they have, they have nevertheless forever so far worked out the way they have, including their immeasurable and specific ignorance of that way. If they are to work out well, I have to choose them. ... For the modern mind this means (mythically) that I am to choose the one body I will ever have. Have I yet begun to choose this one?
>
> (LDIK 517)

For all he knows he has. Writing about the life he can talk about with a claim to authority, the life he's witnessed, Cavell includes its alternatives in order to display in his tone as much as anything else that in choosing the body and life he does have, he has not chosen those he does not, does not now choose them. He doesn't side with them. "I am a being who to exist must say I exist, or must acknowledge my existence—claim it, stake it, enact it" (IQO 109). And, in so doing, stake, claim, enact, choose no other way.

In asking whether he has yet to begin to choose this life, I take Cavell to be asking (asking himself, asking his reader) whether this writing, these diary entries have done so—to be implying that this was one of their tasks, to be both the means and the expression or enactment of that choice. The book was to allow him to incorporate within it and within him what has not happened as a way of choosing, of acknowledging, what has. Having presented his writing in this way, Cavell then reintroduces this idea as a matter of "becoming": "Have I become the one who has done all and only what I have done, accepted that what I have done is no better and no worse than it is?" (LDIK 517). Again, the thought is that this becoming is to have happened, wherever else, in and through the writing of this book. Cavell meditates on a line he takes from Blanchot, where Blanchot speaks of "the awkwardness of death," and then remarks (Cavell remarks), "Telling one's life, the more completely, say incorporating awkwardness, becomes one's life" (LDIK 547). This suggests naturally and familiarly enough that incorporating one's death, incorporating *that* limit, lying ahead, becomes one's life; but it also suggests, now, that incorporating those other limits, to the left and to the right, also becomes one's life—becomes what one's life is, in what it consists. This has been the burden of my comments.[13]

But Cavell's formulation allows us to take one final step here in closing, for the task of writing this book appears to have been not only to have been to come to be the story of all he has done and all he has not done but to render it more attractive, more becoming. As if coming to be something is itself becoming—as if coming into being attracts others, forms an audience. But Cavell goes on: "Telling one's life, the more completely, say incorporating awkwardness, becomes one's life, and becomes a way of leaving it" (LDIK 547). Which presents coming into being as a way of leaving being, an attractive or attracting way—a way of beauty. But what sort of beauty is this?

Beauty seen while drawing away.

15 Empiricism, Exhaustion, and Meaning What We Say

Cavell and Contemporary Fiction

Robert Chodat

Cavell's debts to Emerson, Thoreau, Nietzsche, Heidegger, and Wittgenstein are familiar, not least from Cavell's own writing, yet one overlooked part of his inheritance is how, like them, he has largely ignored the dominant literary form of the last two centuries: the novel. Nietzsche disparaged the genre as an offspring of the Platonic dialogue and celebrated the arts of music and tragic drama. Heidegger's touchstone was typically lyric poetry, and Emerson, in a similar spirit, once dismissed a book by calling it "good for a bookstall, as much worth as a novel,—but no poem."[1] Thoreau preferred Eastern poetry and epics, and Wittgenstein was steeped above all in classical music. In recent decades such philosophical neglect of the novel has receded, thanks to Iris Murdoch, Richard Rorty, and others. Beyond, however, some passing allusions to Austen or Forster or Proust, Cavell has stood to the side in these discussions, concentrating instead on a host of other forms: classical music, modern drama (Ibsen, Beckett), opera, Shakespearean drama, and, of course, Hollywood movies. Given that few philosophers have more insistently considered the role of examples in our thinking, one is entitled to wonder: why this silence?[2]

Answering this requires asking, as *The World Viewed* puts it, what "discoveries of form and genre and type and technique" the novel has historically embodied, what "automatisms" it has "activated" (WV 105–07). At least since Ian Watt's *The Rise of the Novel*, published in 1957—the year, coincidentally, Cavell composed "Must we mean what we say?"—the novel has often been associated with what Watt called "formal realism." Among the things Watt meant by this phrase was that Defoe, Richardson, and Fielding had given new expression to the empiricist spirit reshaping British intellectual life in the eighteenth century. A critical and anti-traditional temperament, a nominalist skepticism toward the general or universal, particularized plots and characters rather than formulaic narratives and types, specified physical settings, a resistance to what Locke called rhetoric's "abuses of language": none of these was exactly new, but as Watt argued, they had never been so comprehensively combined. Northrop Frye, an important figure in Cavell's thinking, sketched a comparable view in *Anatomy of Criticism*, also from 1957. Unlike in the ballad or romance, Frye observed, the supernatural "is difficult to get into a novel," while the novel's social affinities lead it away from heroic characters, whose grandeur makes them "inscrutable," and toward an "objective" or "naturalistic" psychology.[3] Recent histories of the genre have located different sources, but any account that failed to identify the tendencies described by Watt and Frye—and that failed in turn to distinguish novelistic fiction from, say, Homer's epics, Malory's Arthurian tales, or Swift's satires—would be eccentric. Indeed, a deflationary impulse persists in the novel even after, say, Flaubert and James transform it into high art. Though still often contrasted with "realism," Modernist experiments can often be understood as *extending* novelistic realism, make it more exacting and even scientific, in order to better limn modernity's distinctive experiences. Hemingway distrusts anything but the names of villages and roads; the interior monologues of Joyce and Woolf are partly meant to convey the shapelessness of the world and our mental lives.[4]

This literary-historical sketch is schematic, but it is probably enough to convey why the novel, the most modern of literary genres, the genre most intimately bound up with modern disenchantment, may have left Nietzsche, Heidegger, and Wittgenstein indifferent. And though Emerson and Thoreau had less obviously aristocratic sensibilities, it's no accident that, as critics have noted, the Transcendentalist movement never produced a noteworthy novel.[5] In "The Over-Soul" Emerson laments that "the walls of time and space have come to look real and insurmountable" to the modern mind,[6] but to ignore these walls in a novel is usually to invite derision—as suggested by the genre's long history of bumblingly ineffectual clergymen and bookishly distracted philosophers: Fielding's Parson Adams, Austen's Mr. Collins, George Eliot's Casaubon, Woolf's Mr. Ramsey, Bellow's Herzog.

If, then, the novel arises from many of the intellectual dispositions that Cavell's heroes resist, it's unsurprising that he should occasionally allude to the nineteenth-century romance, a form of fiction that from Richard Chase to the New Historicists has seemed foundational to the American canon.[7] What is more surprising, however, is that Cavell has taken so remarkably little interest in the fiction of his close contemporaries. For since World War II, commentaries on the novel have regularly taken the form of caustic diagnoses, with repeated grievances expressed toward what came to be pejoratively called "the classic realist text." Just as Cavell (b. 1926) began publishing, the French novelist Alain Robbe-Grillet (b. 1922) described the novel tradition as a "branch" that was "dead of natural causes, by the simple action of time," its narratives rehearsing "the prefabricated schemas people are used to," imprisoned by the "entire rationalizing and organizing system" of bourgeois life. Ten years after Robbe-Grillet's comments, John Barth (b. 1930) issued a similar complaint in his famous 1967 essay "The literature of exhaustion": "A good many current novelists write turn-of-the-century-type novels, only in more or less mid-twentieth-century language and about contemporary people and topics. ... [It's] dismaying to see so many of our writers following Dostoevsky or Tolstoy or Balzac." Three decades after Barth's manifesto, Don DeLillo (b. 1936) updated these opinions, stating that changes in "our lives and problems and our perceptions" demand a change in our fiction: "I don't know how some contemporary writers can sit down and write what is in effect a 19th century novel."[8]

As quiet as Cavell has been about the traditional realist novel, however, he has been silent about these expressions of dissatisfaction among his fiction-writing contemporaries. Life is, of course, short. But the absence of contemporary American fiction in Cavell's work seems more than just a problem of world enough and time, given that he shares with the authors mentioned here not only a generation but also a clear distaste for the materialist, empiricist strands of the modern intellectual tradition. In what follows I want to focus on Cavell's closest novelistic contemporaries, figures born from the mid-1920s to the mid-1930s and whose writing began, like his, to have an impact in the 1960s. As I'll suggest, investigating such writers can help partially fill out some of the intellectual and cultural setting in which Cavell's work appears, beyond the links sometimes drawn between him and his contemporaries in continental philosophy and literary theory.[9] I do this, however, not in order simply to catalogue a series of as-yet unperceived affinities between Cavell and his novelist peers. There are, I think, reasons Cavell has remained indifferent or unresponsive to the fiction of much of his generation, and the mode here will be contrast as much as comparison. In *Must We Mean What We Say?* Cavell suggestively remarks that "different artistic inventions demand different routes of critical discovery" (MWM 122), and my question will be not just whether certain Cavellian routes of discovery might give access to a set of inventions that Cavell himself has largely ignored, but also how we might measure the distance between these inventions and some of Cavell's most central and original claims.

Talking succinctly about the fiction of an entire generation requires vast oversimplification, and "formal realism" has obviously never entirely vanished, but broadly speaking we can identify two challenges to it in the decades after World War II. The first would include Robbe-Grillet, Barth, and DeLillo, and might be exemplified in a passage such as the following, from Thomas Pynchon's *The Crying of Lot 49*, a book published in 1966, just three years before *Must We Mean What We Say?* The protagonist, a suburban housewife named Oedipa Maas, is in a motel in southern California, where she has met a lawyer named Metzger, who after some drinks proposes a game of "Strip Botticelli." In a half-serious effort to resist his advances, Oedipa goes to the bathroom and dons so many layers of clothes that she can barely walk:

> She made the mistake of looking at herself in the full-length mirror, saw a beach ball with feet, and laughed so violently she fell over, taking a can of hair spray on the sink with her. The can hit the floor, something broke, and with a great outsurge of pressure the stuff commenced atomizing, propelling the can swiftly about the bathroom. ... The can, hissing malignantly, bounced off the toilet and whizzed by Metzger's right ear .... Metzger hit the deck and cowered with Oedipa as the can continued its high-speed caroming .... The can knew where it was going, she sensed, or something fast enough, God or a digital machine, might have computed in advance the complex web of its travel; but she wasn't fast enough, and knew only that it might hit them at any moment, at whatever clip it was doing, maybe a hundred miles an hour. ... The can ... zoomed over to the enclosed shower, where it crashed into and totally destroyed a panel of frosted glass; then around the three tile walls, up to the ceiling, past the light, over the two prostrate bodies .... She could imagine no end to it; yet presently the can did give up in midflight and fall to the floor, about a foot from Oedipa's nose.[10]

Beyond his famously contrived proper names, Pynchon departs here from Defoe and his successors in at least a couple ways. One is how the text plays with readers' dramatic and psychological expectations. We're presented with a seduction scene, the start of an extra-marital affair, but the emotional turmoil typically attending such moments—think of Anna's pained deliberations over Vronsky—is deflated by absurdity: Oedipa's drunken vision of a "beach ball with feet," the frenetic "caroming" of the hair spray can, the comic debasement of the two would-be lovers scrambling to the bathroom floor. Second, and just as strikingly, the intentional states identified in the passage owe more to Looney Toons than to the universe described by Newtonian physics. The can is ascribed a deeply sinister motive, hissing at Oedipa "malignantly," and seems to know "where it was going"—its torture directed all the while by some greater intelligence, "God or a digital machine." Comically suspending our typical beliefs about mass and gravity, the passage works to blur all conventional lines between living "persons" and non-living "things."

This can of hair spray represents a common feature of Pynchon's work: two lifelike automata play supporting roles in his first novel *V.* (1963), a light bulb plots against the international light-bulb cartel in *Gravity's Rainbow* (1973), and the cast of *Mason & Dixon* (1997) includes a mechanical duck that develops into an independent (and sexually aggressive) agent. Such devices represent part of Pynchon's response to what Barth's "Literature of Exhaustion" derisively called the "used-upness" of traditional artistic forms, the sense, in Barth's formulation, that "Beethoven's Sixth Symphony or the Chartres cathedral, if executed today, might be simply embarrassing" (p. 66). Barth wasn't encouraging artistic paralysis; he was asking instead that we "rediscover validly the artifices of language and literature." The goal, he said, was not merely to exemplify "the *fact* of aesthetic ultimacies," but also to use it "to accomplish new human work" (pp. 69–70), and for a precursor he claimed Jorge Luis Borges, an author routinely cited, not accidentally, in discussions of Pynchon as well.

One adjective that came to describe such writing is, of course, "postmodern." In what's still, after a quarter-century, one of the most useful discussions of this contested term, Brian McHale has characterized postmodernism as work that foreground ontological questions, in contrast to the epistemological dilemmas—who knows what, how reliable one's knowledge is, how trustworthy different speakers are—characteristically at play in Modernist works. A text such as, say, *Absalom, Absalom!* is structured like a detective story, unfolding its narrative layers gradually, with different characters offering different pieces of information. Postmodern fiction, says McHale, by contrast turns to problems characteristic not of detective fiction, but of science fiction: not who knows the universe adequately, but what the nature of the universe is; not how we can know the full story, but what things are possible or impossible in the world that the story describes. Thus the proliferation of alternative universes over the last half-century of fiction, what McHale calls (following William S. Burroughs) "zones," the hallucinatory spaces that defy the empirical and historical worlds we ordinarily discuss: apocryphal histories of colonial America (Barth's *Sot Weed Factor*); antebellum Southern plantations with televisions and elevators (Ishmael Reed's *Flight to Canada*); texts in which Israel has jungles and Bobby Kennedy was never shot (Ronald Sukenick's *98.6*);

fantastical worlds where Uncle Sam chats with Richard Nixon about the Rosenbergs (Robert Coover's *The Public Burning*); deranged German towns called Spitzen-on-the-Dien, haunted by dead English soldiers (John Hawkes's *The Cannibal*); fairy tale characters recast as members of a modern commune (Donald Barthelme's *Snow White*); and so on. Such "ontological" inventiveness had appeared in fiction before 1960—think of not only Borges, but Kafka—just as elements of "formal realism" had appeared before Defoe and Richardson. But as McHale makes clear, never before had so many writers so openly rejected the traditional empiricist assumptions of modern fiction, or shucked them off with the same mixture of ferocity and flippancy.[11]

Such fiction shares with Cavell certain anxieties and dissatisfactions while also veering away from his specific response to them. But before suggesting how, I want to look at a second reaction to formal realism that has also pervaded recent fiction. Consider the following paragraph, told from the perspective of an aged Native American named Francisco, who is on his death bed recalling events much earlier in his life:

The drum rolled like thunder in his hand, and he had no memory of setting the deep sound upon it. It had happened …. *He was mindless in the wake of the dancers, riding high like the gourds on the long bright parallels of motion. He had no need of seeing, nor did the dancers dance to the drum. Their feet fell upon the earth and his hand struck thunder to the drum, and it was the same thing, one motion made of sound. … An old man came beside him with another drum* …. *He waited, going on, not counting, having no fear and waiting for the pass, only nodding to the beat. And the moment came in mid-motion, and he crossed the stick to the heated drum and the heavy heated drum was in his hand and the old man turned—and nothing was lost, nothing; there had been nothing of time lost, no miss in the motion or the mind, only the certain strange fall of the pitch* …. *It was perfect. And when it was over, the women of the town came out with baskets of food. They went among the singer and the crowd, throwing out the food in celebration of his perfect act. And from then on he had a voice in the clan, and the next year he healed a child who had been sick from birth.*[12]

This comes at the end of N. Scott Momaday's *House Made of Dawn* (published 1968), which won the Pulitzer Prize the year that *Must We Mean What We Say?* appeared, and which, again, resists formal realism at multiple points—though with different effects than the Pynchon passage. Whereas the traditional novel, says Watt, seeks a plain style, Momaday's prose moves freely into lyricism, employing a wide palate of tropes: simile and metaphor ("riding high like the gourds," "his hand struck thunder to the drum"), zeugma ("He waited, going on, not counting, having no fear and waiting for the pass, only waiting"), repetition ("nothing was lost, nothing; there had been nothing of time lost"), heavy alliteration ("no miss in the motion or the mind"). Whereas the traditional novel, for Watt, attends typically to the particular and the individual, Momaday's passage recounts a moment—heightened by ten full pages of italics—of mystical fusion: the members of the tribe dance in unison, ascending toward a "mindless" state of shared consciousness beyond ordinary perception ("He had no need of seeing"). And whereas Watt identifies the novel with the critical spirit of modern science, Momaday's paragraph concludes with a movement toward the supernatural, evident in the shamanistic powers Francisco gains after participating in the ritual, healing a child "sick from birth."

Momaday's text marks a crucial moment in the history of post-World War II American fiction, articulating the urge for alternatives to "Western culture"—an impulse hardly new to the 1960s, of course, but which had begun by then to have both large-scale socio-political consequences and an increasingly central place among intellectuals. The protagonist, Francisco's grandson Abel, leaves his reservation to fight in World War II, where he confronts the most terrifying products of modern technology, and when he returns to the U.S. a taciturn alcoholic, he struggles to survive amid a group of deracinated Native Americans living in Los Angeles. He finds peace only upon returning home to care for his dying grandfather, a reunion with his tribe symbolized in the concluding pages by his running the traditional race of the dead. Nowhere are readers asked to question the supernatural powers ascribed to Francisco in the passage above, and, similarly, there seems little doubt that Abel's homecoming represents a distinctive moral achievement. "All his being," says the last paragraph, "was concentrated on the sheer motion of running on, and he was past caring about the pain" (p. 185). As with Francisco drumming, this final release from both physical and psychological trauma is never ironized in the text, never set against more prosaic scenes or skeptical voices, and the reader is meant to leave with a sense of how a ruptured modern soul might yet be redeemed.

Momaday wasn't the first writer to present the cultural traditions of a marginalized group as a rejoinder to the classic novel's empiricist temperament. Among twentieth-century Americans one thinks of Bernard Malamud's modern Jewish fables, or Ralph Ellison's use of African-American folklore in *Invisible Man* (1952), or Zora Neale Hurston's similar procedures twenty years earlier. But *House Made of*

Dawn exhibits a greater insistence on cultural identity than these texts, and its success inaugurated what one commentator has called "a phase of radical communitarianism" in fiction,[13] an era when novelists immersed themselves anew in the tales and tropes of a given community. Hence, for instance, the mythologies recovered by such younger Native American writers as Leslie Marmon Silko and Louise Erdrich, the Jewish fabulism of Cynthia Ozick, or the "talk stories" of Maxine Hong Kingston, autobiographies steeped in the traditional magic of Chinese folktales. Such writing has often been marked by individual brilliance, but one of its chief effects is to legitimize a certain conception of social ontology, to suggest that terms like "consciousness" are every bit a property of collective entities (races, language groups, etc.) as they are of individual persons. Perhaps the most vivid précis of such fiction comes from its most ambitious and successful representative, Toni Morrison, who, seven years before her ghost story *Beloved* won her the Nobel Prize, remarked in an interview: "I write what I have recently begun to call village literature, fiction that is really for the village, for the tribe."[14]

If, as I've suggested, the thread common to these fictions—the postmodernism embodied by Pynchon, the village literature embodied by Momaday—is a resistance to the empiricist assumptions of modernity, then it's only appropriate that many of the writers mentioned here have been read as recuperating Romanticism.[15] With Emerson's "Experience" these texts seem to lament "the despair which prejudges the law by a paltry empiricism," and their challenges to the novel's traditional assumptions have sometimes generated among commentators the sort of fractiousness and sense of crisis that Cavell identifies among music theorists in his early essay "Music discomposed." Thus the frequent claim that the fictions of this generation confuse generic boundaries, reweave and subvert traditional tales and fables, indulge in pastiche and prophecy, all to the point that they sometimes seem no longer to be "novels" at all.

As we noted earlier, Cavell has also identified much of his later work with Romanticism, and he has moreover responded with sympathy to much of the continental thought that's often associated with the fiction of his contemporaries. Yet just as Cavell has always qualified his interest in Derrida, Blanchot, and others, so too, I think, his relation to these strands of postwar fiction is fraught with ambivalence. Let's begin with the tradition figured here by Pynchon, whose resistance to empiricism is, as I noted earlier, registered in part by his penchant for describing the non-human world as animated and complexly purposeful. In *In Quest of the Ordinary*, Cavell observes that a wish to animate the things of the world is a consistent impulse running through Romanticism, and some readers might very well be reminded of Pynchon's hair spray when Cavell says: "Against a vision of the death of the world, the romantic calling for poetry ... is to give the world back, to bring it back, as to life. Hence romantics seem to involve themselves in what look to us to be superstitions, discredited mysteries of animism, sometimes in the form of what is called the pathetic fallacy" (IQO 44–45). The hair spray malignantly chasing Oedipa through the bathroom can be read as an updated version of the pathetic fallacy, and thus can seem, like the various "zones" and alternative universes catalogued earlier, consonant with Romanticism's ambitions. As Cavell says of the Romantic interest in the fantastic, such ontological inventions clearly begin "from some adverse relation to the modern scientific sensibility," and clearly evoke a sense of "being on some boundary or threshold, as between the impossible and the possible" (IQO 183).

A clue to Cavell's distance from the postmodern novelist, however, emerges when we hear how these experiments have been artistically and philosophically justified. In, for instance, the same essay where he pronounces the novel "dead of natural causes," Robbe-Grillet claims that the art of the *nouveau romancier* will be "based on no truth that exists before it": he or she, says Robbe-Grillet, "must create a world, but starting from nothing, from the dust." DeLillo uses a comparable vocabulary when he says the task of the fiction writer is "to create a climate, to create an environment, not to react to one," and Barth's "Literature of exhaustion" describes Borgesian writing as a "heroic enterprise," fit not for "the commonality, alas," but only for "the chosen remnant, the virtuoso" (p. 75). In an essay tellingly titled "How to make a universe," Barth makes these claims still more explicit and forceful:

> What [the novelist] offers you is not a *Weltanschauung*, but a *Welt*; not a view of the cosmos, but a cosmos itself. ... My contention ... is that a novel is not a view of this universe ... but a universe itself; that the novelist is not finally a spectator, an imitator, ... but a maker of universes: a demiurge. ... The heavy universe we sit in here ... and the two-pound universe of [a novel] are cousins, because the maker of this one and the maker of that one are siblings.[16]

To be sure, probably not all experimental novelists of the last fifty years have understood their work in these promethean terms,[17] but such remarks capture the type of rupture that the postmodern "zone" often represents. In Cavell's terms, these comments suggest how, for all their brilliance, the novelists remain enmeshed in the Kantian categories that Romanticism sought to overcome. Creating a world from the dust, creating a climate, not a view of the cosmos but a cosmos itself: such phrases betray a readiness to pay what Cavell calls "the price" of Kant's "philosophical settlement"—the belief that skepticism about the external world can be defeated by abandoning any claim to know a thing "in itself," by accepting that what we know is determined by our own cognitive categories. Such an arrangement drifts worryingly close to the claim that our knowledge is simply our own construction, and Romanticism's response, says Cavell, is, "Thanks for nothing (or more strictly, No thanks for everything)" (IQO 53). For Romantics, Kant seems to say that we have made the world in our own image, that we carry "the death of the world in us, in our very requirement of creating it, as if it does not yet exist" (IQO 44). To say that I "construct" or "constitute" the objects of my experience is not to bring the world back to life, but to estrange me further from it, for it implies that things are not merely as lifeless as they sometimes seem, but may also be—still more melancholically—wholly unreal.

Cavell's model of Romantic animism is *Rime of the Ancient Mariner*, a tale whose revivified sailors are meant to suggest that "Kant's lined-off region *can* be experienced and that the region below the line has a definite, call it frozen, structure" (IQO 50). Yet Coleridge's text, as read through Cavell, stands at some remove from Pynchon's motel scene. For one thing, as in many postmodern texts but unlike in Coleridge, the animated hair spray of *Lot 49* gives rise first and foremost to laughter—and not just laughter, but bitingly satirical, absurdist laughter. This bit of modern technology, this can of chemicals produced to sanitize and conceal our aging bodies, has a life of its own, and indeed a far more impassioned one than Oedipa herself, whose life seems to consist mainly of Tupperware parties and suburban despondency. The scene exemplifies Pynchon's habit of giving non-human entities more life than any of his human characters, most of whom seem to step out of *Everyman* or *Pilgrim's Progress*, consumed to caricatural lengths by one or another cultural vice. The hair spray can is not, as it is in Coleridge, animated as a means of reviving the human soul. It is animated *in place of* the human soul.

This depthlessness is what leads commentators to associate such fiction with the philosophical "critique of the subject" that also became prominent around 1960. Yet as the self-descriptions of Barth and the others suggest, and as the loftily inhuman third-person voice of Pynchon's text enacts, one "subject" tends to be exempted from such critique, namely the author himself. The characters in these novels may be one-dimensional, saturated in the hackneyed words of postwar advertising or pop songs or governments, but the authors inventing and orchestrating their stories are decidedly not. Indeed, if the picture of character in these works leans toward anti-humanism, then the fantastic linguistic and imaginative power they embody remind us of Charles Taylor's comments on Jacques Derrida: "Nothing emerges from his flux worth affirming, and so what in fact comes to be celebrated is the deconstructing power itself, the prodigious power of subjectivity to undo all the potential allegiances which might bind it."[18] Against such superhuman undertakings one can juxtapose Cavell's gloss on a favored Emersonian term: "For him genius is … something each person has, not something certain people are" (ETE 217). Cavell's hope, in other words, is not to "make a universe" but to renew the universe we have, which for him means renewing the *words* that we—each of us—already speak. This is, of course, the source of Cavell's lifelong enthusiasm for Austin, whose "linguistic phenomenology" made vivid what Cavell came to refer to as the "world-boundness" of language, its "adequation" to the world (PP 80, 116).[19] This world-boundness, like Taylor's "allegiances," may be "conventional" insofar as it wouldn't exist without the human practices enabling it, the learned habits of knowing what we say when, and the recognition of such conventionality may lead one to seek its continual exposure. Cavell presents no "arguments" "against" the urge to flaunt our existing agreements; doing so represents for him one aspect of our humanness. But our recognition of conventions, he says, can "endanger" as much as "release" the imagination, encouraging us to forget that "ordinary language is natural language," its changes not merely a matter of individual will (MWM 42). To begrudge this "human limitation," he says in the early essay on Wittgenstein, is "to leave us chafed by our own skin, by a sense of powerlessness to penetrate beyond the human conditions of knowledge" (MWM 61). The extreme powerlessness of an Oedipa Maas can engender corresponding fantasies of extreme linguistic and creative power, whereas for Cavell the appeal of ordinary language philosophy lies partly in its ability to "coax the mind down from self-assertion—subjective assertion and private definition—and lead it back, through the community, home" (MWM 43).

These latter terms, "community" and "home," immediately suggest that Cavell's distance from Pynchon reflects a corresponding proximity to the "village fiction" of a writer such as Momaday. Here too, however, we need to qualify this association, and for reasons that bring us into other terrains of Cavell's thinking. Cavell's divergence from *House Made of Dawn*, I would suggest, is crystallized by the fact that the social unit most typically described in his writing is not a culture, nor a village, nor a tribe. It is instead a marriage. This is a theme most explicitly pursued in *Pursuits of Happiness*, which describes the Hollywood remarriage comedy—films whose central drive is not to get two lovers together, but to get them *back* together, to marry even in the full knowledge of past disappointments and potential failure. But the philosophical grounds for this emphasis on marriage are clarified most fully in Cavell's response to Saul Kripke.

What makes us sure that 68 plus 57 equals 125? In Kripke's view, Wittgenstein's discussions of rule-following argue that we're certain on the basis of "our own confident inclination," that we add these numbers "without justification." When someone disagrees with us, when someone refuses to arrive at this sum, then she is not, in Kripke's words, "admitted into the community as an adder," and will be "corrected and told" that she hasn't "grasped the concept of addition." For Cavell, however, such an account underestimates the responsiveness to skepticism that animates Wittgenstein's thinking. Kripke fails, says Cavell (in terms he uses elsewhere for Dewey), to question the "teacher's *confidence*," to put the authority of adult speakers as well as of students into question (CHU 75), thereby missing, as Stephen Mulhall observes, "the moment of hesitation in Wittgenstein's teacher," "considerations of mutual intelligibility and mutual civility."[20] Kripke transforms the scene of instruction into a scene of coercion, and in neglecting the fragility that actually characterizes learning, he winds up reifying what he broadly calls "the community"—the entity "into" which an adder may or may not be "admitted." Communities certainly exist in Cavell's thinking; he's no atomist. But they arise only when the beginner is, in Cavell's term, "initiated" into them successfully, and to talk about "the community" as if it were a stable entity, some ready-made physical space existing apart from the acknowledgment of its members, is to ignore how initiations can always go awry or fail to be renewed. When they are not affirmed and maintained, there is no longer any "we." Agreements about what counts as what, what we say when, are no doubt "intimate and pervasive": such judgments, says Cavell, are not like "arriving at an agreement on a given occasion, but of being in agreement throughout, being in harmony, like pitches or tones, or clocks" (CR 170). Yet these attunements, he also notes, can always erode. Learning the word for *love* is learning what love *is*, but over a lifetime we discover that others understand the concept in different ways, and we ourselves come to hesitate about when to apply it.

Marriage embodies this condition of simultaneous intimacy and fragility, and it's this constant vulnerability—our consent always endangered by separation—that leads Cavell to invoke it as his model for communal life. Seen in this light, what Momaday presents in Francisco's drumming is clearly an "initiation," but one that generates something other than a "marriage." As the ritual begins, the young Francisco stands as an outsider, estranged from others, yet as the moment of initiation develops ("It had happened"), his identity is described as growing seamlessly fused with that of the tribe. The celebrants in the passage come to move with a single body, their dancing and drumming merging into "the same thing, one motion made of sound." In Cavell's terms, the moment too easily overcomes the standing threat of skepticism, too readily ignores the potential for alienation that, for him, is a mark of the human. Whereas Coleridge's Ancient Mariner, in Cavell's reading, can no longer participate in the human world, embodying for us the idea that the "expression of our intimacies now exists only in the *search* for expression, not in assurances of it" (IQO 65), the model of mutuality affirmed in Momaday's text is one in which persons coexist in a settled space beyond negotiation or reflection, living, as the passage figures it, "mindless in the wake of the dancers." Or, to shift the Cavellian point of reference, while *House Made of Dawn* doesn't deny that communities can fracture, they are recuperated not, as in the remarriage comedy, with forgiveness, by overcoming revenge and accepting the repetitive needs of the body and the soul, by the recognition that, for all our natural intimacy, we are also strangers (PH 260–62). They are recovered instead on something like the model assumed by Kripke, by characters submitting themselves, as it were, to coherently integrated traditions, which are themselves transmitted over time, over and above any particular agent.

Indeed, it's telling here that Abel's most important relationship in *House* is not to a spouse but to a grandparent, a blood relation that would persist without or without the awareness of either man. It's similarly telling that the passage I've cited, and indeed most of the novel, is wholly narrative, in what is sometimes called the diegetic mode. Cavell's discussions of remarriage comedies turn repeatedly to the conversations depicted in these films, and the point of emphasizing these dialogues is not merely to laud the ingenuity of Cary Grant or Howard Hawks. It is instead to emphasize that talk—worldly exchanges of ordinary words—is what provides whatever makeshift stability these unions have. Dialogue in these movies displays what Cavell calls the "whirl of organism" on which the speech and sanity of these characters tenuously rest, their shared "routes of interest and feeling, modes of response, senses of humor and of significance and of fulfillment" (MWM 52). By contrast, the passage cited from *House Made of Dawn* includes no dialogue whatsoever, and the actions of the characters seem simply to *happen*: the old man with the drum approaches Francisco, and the women celebrate around him, all apparently without any need for actual communication, as if the ritual were occurring on a plane wholly above our ordinary words. Critics might contend that Cavell's emphasis on "consent" leads him into the pitfalls of all liberal theory, that he ignores the basic or initial forms of sociality that Momaday's novel serves to highlight. But social contracts, though clearly mythical, capture something essential both about our specifically modern self-understanding and about our more general linguistic condition—our words alternately attuned to and estranged from those of others, each of us fated to our particular bodies. As *The Claim of Reason* puts it, sounding almost like a direct rejoinder to Francisco's death-bed memory: "We *are* separate, but not necessarily *separated* (*by* something) ... [W]e are endlessly separate, for *no* reason" (CR 369).

Speaking at Bennington in 1970, a year after *Slaughterhouse-Five* appeared, Kurt Vonnegut declared: "I fully expected that by the time I was twenty-one, some scientist ... would have taken a color photograph of God Almighty and sold it to *Popular Mechanics* magazine. ... What actually happened when I was twenty-one was that we dropped scientific truth on Hiroshima."[21] Vonnegut's acerbic thought, familiar at least since Blake, reminds us that the philosophical and literary issues I've been sketching here are hard to separate from their political dimensions, and that the responses to the novel I've been canvassing here are bound up with questions about modernity, science, democratic politics, and how one understands the concept of "America"—questions that the 1960s, of course, brought starkly to a head. In their different ways, the fictional experiments of Pynchon and Momaday spring from a sense that America warrants our deepest satire and rage, that it personifies modernity's false hopes, violence, vulgarity, and narcissism. And in doing so they anticipate a view often heard in the humanities today, one encapsulated by Simon Critchley's remark, in a discussion of Cavell, that American culture is symbolized by Las Vegas, "a shining beacon of nihilism, a place where European civilization evaporates into a series of casino complexes."[22] Cavell has himself never been immune to such dark judgments, least of all in the years that Pynchon and Momaday were establishing themselves. Writing on *King Lear* at the height of the Vietnam War, for instance, he described the United States as needing love from the world "as proof of its existence," and this need, he continued, was precisely what "makes it so frighteningly destructive, enraged by ingratitude," feeling itself "watched, isolated in its mounting of waters, denying its shame with mechanical lungs of pride, calling its wrath upon the wrong objects" (MWM 345).[23]

Cavell has also, however, expressed uncertainty about such lamentations, confessing in later years that this early essay was "not in control of its asides and orations and love letters of nightmare" (DK x). This kind of doubleness typifies Cavell's distance from the fiction of many of his contemporaries, and epitomizes his effort both to acknowledge "one's sense of being compromised by the persistent failures of democracy" and to remain nonetheless "one who lives in promise" (CHU 125). As Lawrence Rhu has suggested, this capacity to hope against hope may reflect Cavell's status as the successful son of Jewish immigrants,[24] but whatever its source, its aim is not merely to whitewash the horrors of Hiroshima, or the genocide of Native Americans, or the anomie and technological frenzy of postwar consumer culture. Its ambition instead is to help us grasp just how, and in what precise sense, these phenomena represent our distance from mutual understanding and perfect justice. The consent that defines modern society, says Cavell, is always offered "on earth," and this terrestrial condition means it must always be "accompanied by a knowledge of being compromised," made continually in "the knowledge that its object is still in essential part idea, its existence incomplete" (PDAT 108).

Cavell's sense here of incompleteness, of living "on earth," drifting between promise and compromise, reminds one of a well-known remark by the young Georg Lukács, who called the novel the genre of "transcendental homelessness," "the epic of a world that has been abandoned by God."[25] In effect my argument here has been that the postmodernism of Pynchon and the village fiction of Momaday seek to evade this condition—the one hoping to replace God with the author, the other hoping to return us home once and for all. Cavell may, as I noted at the start, struggle against the disenchantments that gave birth to the traditional novel, but his work has enough affinities with Lukács to fight free of such evasions. With more space one could speculate on other authors whose fiction might be seen as embodying something resembling Cavell's vision. Rhu, for instance, has turned to an earlier generation and suggested Bellow, Ellison, and Walker Percy as analogues;[26] and likewise one might consider the more recent generation of writers seeking, in David Foster Wallace's terms, a more riskily "sincere" form of experimental fiction, one that would embrace the human voice and risk "accusations of sentimentality, melodrama," "overcredulity," "softness."[27] Perhaps the deepest measure of Cavell's investment in literature, however, is the sense in his work that exploring the inventions of a Bellow or a Percy or a Wallace need not entail shunning those of a Pynchon or a Momaday; he doesn't ask us simply to choose sides. Every profound philosophical vision, he remarks in his early essay on Beckett, can have the shape of madness, and like the "crazed and paralyzed" states displayed in *Endgame*, the fiction writers of Cavell's generation help envision our minds in what he refers to there as a "characteristic philosophical mood" (MWM 126). As Cavell has frequently claimed, such moods are not things we can eradicate simply by thinking harder or arguing better. The wish to make a cosmos rather than just a view of the cosmos, like the wish to return home and to fuse with others, are temptations to which humans are, in Cavell's understanding, constitutively disposed. It follows, then, that the charge of the critic is not first and foremost to judge whether or not we "agree" or "disagree" with whatever concepts we identify in a given literary text, as if it were an argument we could straightforwardly accept or dispute. Our task is instead to inhabit the words of a text, take them on provisionally, to ask which moods and temptations the work expresses, which genres of interest and feeling it embodies—questions not themselves wholly empirical in nature, but which grant the literary work a distinctive voice in our philosophical labors.

Notes

2 The Adventure of Reading: Literature and Philosophy, Cavell and Beauvoir

1 This essay first appeared as Moi, Toril (June 2011), "The adventure of reading: Literature and philosophy, Cavell and Beauvoir." *Literature and Theology*, 25, (2). Reproduced by permission of Oxford University Press.

2 Calvino, Italo (1986), "Philosophy and literature," in *The Uses of Literature: Essays*. Trans. Patrick Creagh, San Diego, CA: Harcourt Brace Jovanovich, p. 40.

3 This attitude is inspired by Stanley Cavell's reminder: "How we answer the question 'What is X?' will depend, therefore, on the specific case of ignorance and knowledge" (MWM 20).

4 The terms listed here, as well as my general sense of dissatisfaction with this way of setting up the problem of literature and philosophy echo Richard Eldridge's account of the question, in Eldridge, Richard (ed.) (2009), *The Oxford Handbook of Philosophy and Literature*. Oxford: Oxford University Press, pp. 4–6.

5 See PH 9–10.

6 The quotation comes from the preface to the updated, 2002, edition of MWM xxiv–xv.

7 See particularly the discussion of the two "peculiarities" of the judgment of taste in Kant, Immanuel (2000), *Critique of the Power of Judgment.* Ed. Paul Guyer and Eric Matthews, trans. Paul Guyer, Cambridge: Cambridge University Press, pp. 162–66.

8 It doesn't follow that Cavell is uninterested in aesthetic form. One's experience of a work of art is not divorced from the experience of its form. Form can itself be a kind of philosophical reflection. In my own work on Henrik Ibsen, I found his plays to be rich sources of reflections on theater as an artform, both explicitly and implicitly, as an effect of the form. See Moi, Toril (2006), *Henrik Ibsen and the Birth of Modernism: Art, Theater, Philosophy*. Oxford: Oxford University Press.

9 "A matter of meaning it," in MWM 218.

10 Sarah Beckwith's forthcoming book (2011), *Shakespeare and the Grammar of Forgiveness*. Ithaca, NY: Cornell University Press, offers an exciting example of such procedures. In Norway, Christine Hamm explores the

concept of motherhood in Sigrid Undset's work in *Moderne moderskap hos Sigrid Undset* (forthcoming).

11 "[M]y fascination with the *Investigations* had to do with my response to it as a feat of writing. It was some years before I understood it as what I came to think of as a discovery for philosophy of the problem of the other: and further years before these issues looked to me like functions of one another" (CR xvi).

12 [toute parole, toute expression est appel], de Beauvoir, Simone (1944), *Pyrrhus et Cinéas*. Paris: Gallimard, p. 107; trans. by Marybeth Timmermann as "Pyrrhus and Cineas," in *Philosophical Writings*. Ed. Margaret A. Simons, Marybeth Timmermann, and Mary Beth Mader, Urbana, IL: University of Illinois Press, 2005, p. 134.

13 de Beauvoir, Simone (1948), *L'Existentialisme et la sagesse des nations*. Paris: Nagel, p. 12. My translation.

14 de Beauvoir, Simone (1943), *L'Invitée*, Paris: Gallimard (Coll. Folio), trans. by Yvonne Moyse and Roger Senhouse as *She Came to Stay*. London: Fontana, 1984.

15 Originally, this paper contained a substantial reading of Beauvoir's novel, but the analysis started to take on a life of its own, so much so that it no longer fit the frame of this essay. Ashley King Scheu has written a fine essay on philosophy and literature in *L'Invitée*, and Alexander Ruch has shown that Beauvoir genuinely does philosophy in her travel book *America Day by Day*. See King Scheu, Ashley (forthcoming) "The viability of the philosophical novel: The case of Simone de Beauvoir's *She Came to Stay*." *Hypatia: A Journal of Feminist Philosophy*, and Ruch, Alex (2009), "Beauvoir-in-America: Understanding, concrete experience, and Beauvoir's appropriation of Heidegger in *America Day by Day*." *Hypatia: A Journal of Feminist Philosophy*, 24, (4), 104–29.

16 See Merleau-Ponty, Maurice (1964) "Metaphysics and the novel," in *Sense and Non-Sense*. Evanston, IL: Northwestern University Press, pp. 26–40, and de Beauvoir, Simone (1948) "Littérature et métaphysique," in *L'existentialisme et la sagesse des nations*. Paris: Nagel, pp. 103–24; trans. by Véronique Zaytzeff and Frederick M. Morrison as "Literature and metaphysics," in de Beauvoir, Simone (2005) *Philosophical Writings*. Ed. Margaret A. Simons, Marybeth Timmerman, and Mary Beth Mader, Urbana, IL: Univ. of Illinois Press, pp. 269–77. From now on references to "Literature and metaphysics" will be abbreviated to LM. References to the English translation will be marked by an "E", to the French original by an "F". I am grateful to Ann Jefferson for drawing my attention to the importance of the term in France at the time, and to the special issue of the journal *Confluences* dealing with the novel, published during the Occupation. See Prévost, Jean (ed.) (1943), *Problèmes du roman*. Lyon: n.p.

17 [un aspect de l'expérience metaphysique qui ne peut se manifester autrement: son caractère subjectif, singulier, dramatique et aussi son ambiguïté] LM, E275; F119.

18 See LM, E274; F119.

226   Notes

19 [imite l'opacité, l'ambiguïté, l'impartialité de la vie; envoûté par l'histoire qui lui est racontée, le lecteur réagit ici comme devant les événements vécus.] LM, E270; F106. My translation. The published translation has: "imitates life's opacity, ambiguity and impartiality. Bewitched by the tale he is told, the reader here reacts as if he were faced with lived events."

20 [recherche] LM, F109; "Exploration" is my translation; the English translation has "search" (LM, E271). [une authentique aventure spirituelle] LM, E272; F112.

21 [participer sincèrement à l'expérience dans laquelle l'auteur tente de l'entraîner: il ne lit pas comme il réclame qu'on écrive, il craint de prendre des risques, de s'aventurer …] LM, F122–23. My translation. The published translation is: "participate sincerely in the experiment into which the author tries to lead him; he does not read as he demands that one write; he is afraid to take risks, to venture." (LM, E276).

22 [Honnêtement lu, honnêtement écrit, un roman métaphysique apporte un dévoilement de l'existence dont aucun autre mode d'expressions ne saurait fourni l'équivalent], LM E276; F123–24. In 1947, Jean-Paul Sartre further developed the idea that the work of art is an appeal to the reader in his discussion of the "pact of generosity" [pacte de générosité] between reader and writer. See Sartre, Jean-Paul (1988), *What Is Literature? And Other Essays*. Ed. Steven Ungar, trans. Bernard Frechtman, Cambridge, MA: Harvard University Press, p. 61.

23 She uses the word 'take' both in LM and in her contribution to de Beauvoir, Simone, *et al.* (1965), *Que peut la littérature?* Ed. Yves Buin, Paris: Union Générale d'Editions, pp. 73–92. Hereafter references to Beauvoir's contribution to this volume will abbreviated to QP. All translations of QP are mine. For a fuller discussion of QP, see Moi, Toril (2009), "What can literature do? Simone de Beauvoir as a literary theorist." *PMLA*, 124, (1), 189–98.

24 Beauvoir is at pains to stress that she doesn't think that readers ever forget that they are reading fiction: "Only very naïve readers, or children, believe that a book allows them to go straight into reality" [il n'y a guère que les lecteurs très naïfs, ou les enfants, qui croient que par un livre ils entrent de plain-pied dans la réalité] (QP 81). Beauvoir's emphasis on the need be "taken over," to be absorbed by a book, as well as her insistence that this does not make her forget that she is reading fiction would repay further investigation in the light of Michael Fried's understanding of the emergence of modernism. His discussion of Diderot's aesthetics in Fried, Michael (1980), *Absorption and Theatricality: Painting and Beholder in the Age of Diderot*. Chicago, IL: University of Chicago Press, would provide a good point of departure.

25 [Je ne change pas d'univers.] QP 82.

26 Beauvoir's example of a formally innovative essay which nevertheless fails to provide the absorbing experience that literature alone can provide is the anthropologist Oscar Lewis (1961), *The Children of Sánchez:*

The Autobiography of a Mexican Family. New York: Random House. See QP 82.

27 [... Kafka, Balzac, Robbe-Grillet, me sollicitent, me convainquent de m'installer, du moins pour un moment, au coeur d'un autre monde. Et c'est ça le miracle de la littérature et qui la distingue de l'information: c'est qu'une vérité *autre* devient mienne sans cesser d'être autre. J'abdique mon "je" en faveur de celui qui parle; et pourtant je reste moi-même.

C'est une confusion sans cesse ébauchée, sans cesse défaite et c'est la seule forme de communication qui soit capable de me donner l'incommunicable, qui soit capable de me donner le goût d'une autre vie.] QP 82–83.

28 I discuss Beauvoir's notion of identification in "What can literature do?" pp. 193–94.

29 "A travers son héroïne, je m'identifiai à l'auteur: un jour une adolescente, une autre moi-même, tremperait de ses larmes un roman où j'aurais raconté ma propre histoire." De Beauvoir, Simone (1987), *Memoirs of a Dutiful Daughter*. Trans. James Kirkup, Harmondsworth: Penguin, p. 140; trans. amended; de Beauvoir, Simone (1958), *Mémoires d'une jeune fille range*. Paris: Gallimard (Coll. Folio), p. 195.

30 I was happy to write an entry for the term "Ordinary language criticism," for (2010) *A Dictionary of Cultural and Critical Theory*. Ed. Michael Payne and Jessica Rae Butto, Oxford: Wiley Blackwell, pp. 514–16. The very existence of such dictionaries, in fact, is a case for having a relatively specific term.

31 The term "ordinary language criticism" is used in the title of Dauber, Kenneth and Jost, Walter (eds.) (2003), *Ordinary Language Criticism: Literary Thinking after Cavell after Wittgenstein*. Evanston, IL: Northwestern University Press.

32 Quoted by Cora Diamond (1995), "Missing the adventure: Reply to Martha Nussbaum," in *The Realistic Spirit: Wittgenstein, Philosophy, and the Mind*. Cambridge, MA: MIT Press, p. 313. The square brackets are my omissions, the dots are Diamond's. I have corrected a misprint in Diamond's quotation. The original can be found in Robertson, David (1969), *George Mallory*. London: Faber and Faber, p. 217.

33 Diamond, "Missing the adventure," p. 315.

34 Ibid.

35 Cavell writes: "At some point, the critic will have to say: This is what I see." Cavell, "Aesthetic problems" (MWM 93).

36 See MWM 89.

3   "Is 'Us' Me?": Cultural Studies and the Universality of Aesthetic Judgments

1   Portions of this essay originally appeared in Dunn, Allen and Haddox, Thomas F. (eds.) (2011), *The Limits of Literary Historicism*. Knoxville, TN: University of Tennessee Press.
2   Bérubé, Michael (ed.) (2005), *The Aesthetics of Cultural Studies*. Malden, MA: Blackwell, pp. 2–3. Hereafter cited in text as ACS.
3   Frith, Simon (1996), *Performing Rites: On the Value of Popular Music*. Cambridge, MA: Harvard University Press, p. 19. Bérubé discusses Frith (ACS 7–8).
4   Levine, George (ed.) (1994), *Aesthetics and Ideology*. New Brunswick, NJ: Rutgers University Press, p. 9. Both Levine's introduction and Bérubé's review may be found in Richter, David H. (ed.) (2002), *Falling into Theory: Conflicting Views on Reading Literature* (second edn.). Boston, MA: Bedford/St. Martin's, pp. 378–97.
5   In Richter, p. 395.
6   MWM first edition, pp. 188–89.
7   Lacoue-Labarthe, Philippe and Nancy, Jean-Luc (1988), *The Literary Absolute: The Theory of Literature in German Romanticism*. Trans. Philip Barnard and Cheryl Lester, Albany, NY: SUNY Press; original French publication 1978). Hereafter cited in text as LA.
8   Frith's account of the evaluative distinctions "most of us" (p. 51) make is supported by a collection of data on audience responses to films gathered by the British research group Mass-Organization in the 1930s and 1940s (pp. 47–52).
9   Kant, Immanuel (2000), *Critique of the Power of Judgment*. Ed. Paul Guyer, trans. Paul Guyer and Eric Matthews, New York: Cambridge University Press, §8, p. 101. Hereafter cited in text by page and section number as CJ.
10   In *Distinction* Pierre Bourdieu surveys preferences, not aesthetic judgments. This remains true even when the preferences are for particular art works, artists, or styles. See his questionnaire (pp. 512–18).
11   Cavell elaborates this subjectivity as a universal condition of the knowledge of art in MWM 189–93, but he describes its relation to our present historical situation in his essay on Kierkegaard (MWM 163–79), locating its origin as a practical problem for aesthetics in the mid-nineteenth century (p. 176).
12   Wittgenstein, Ludwig (1958), *Philosophical Investigations* (third edn.). Trans. G. E. M. Anscombe, New York: Macmillan. Hereafter cited in text as PI.
13   Victoria, TX: Fiction Collective Two, 2001.
14   Yates, Donald A. and Irby, James E. (eds.) (1964), *Labyrinths: Selected Stories and Other Writings*. New York: New Directions, p. 13.

4   Cavell and Kant: The Work of Criticism and the Work of Art

1   Moore, G. E. (1939), "Proof of an external world." *Proceedings of the British Academy*, XXV, 273–300; also (1925), "A defence of common sense," in *Contemporary British Philosophy* (second series). Ed. J. H. Muirhead, London: G. Allen & Unwin. It is taken up by Wittgenstein, Ludwig (1969), in *On Certainty*. Trans. Denis Paul and G. E. M. Anscombe, New York: Harper and Row, p. 2e.

2   Wittgenstein, Ludwig (1958), *Philosophical Investigations*. Trans. G. E. M. Anscombe, New York: Macmillan, p. 44 (henceforth PI).

3   MWM 98–99, regarding the (poetic, metaphorical) words of Romeo and Juliet in relation to "ordinary language."

4   Mulhall, Stephen (1994), *Stanley Cavell: Philosophy's Recounting of the Ordinary*. Oxford: Clarendon Press.

5   Kant, Immanuel (1986), *Critique of Judgement*. Trans. James Creed Meredith, Oxford: Oxford University Press, here from the "Fourth moment," §19, p. 82 (AK B64) (henceforth CJ: I cite the second part of this work (the ["Critique of teleological judgement"] separately, as CJII).

6   Emerson, he notes, introduces Shakespeare as one of his six "Representative men" by remarking that "representativeness" implies the obverse of originality-implies, that is, exhibiting a quality that each member of the species possesses. Emerson writes, "The Genius of our life is jealous of individuals, and will not have any individual great, except through the general ... Great genial power, one would almost say, consists in not being original at all; in being altogether receptive; in letting the world do all, and suffering the spirit of the hour to pass unobstructed through the mind." In Joel Porte (ed.) (1983), *Emerson: Essays and Lectures*. New York: Library of America, pp. 710–11. See Cavell, PDAT 49. I note here; for further exploration, that the question turns also on what "exhibiting" means, and why we wish to locate it in works of art. Mulhall discusses a related matter in taking up the question of the critic's exemplary individuality, *Stanley Cavell*, pp. 28–33.

7   TOS 9.

8   SW 94.

9   Cavell faithfully records Emerson's echoing of Kant on this point in the chapter of SW entitled "Portions" (SW 94). Richard Eldridge (2001) provides a compelling discussion of the broader set of issues involved here in "Kant, Hölderlin and the experience of longing," in his *The Persistence of Romanticism: Essays in Philosophy and Literature*. Cambridge: Cambridge University Press, pp. 31–51.

10 The question of whether Kant's aesthetics requires a theory of the artwork has been much debated. For cogent arguments see Kemal, Salim (1986), *Kant and Fine Art*. Oxford: Clarendon Press; and Guyer, Paul

(1993), *Kant and the Experience of Freedom.* Cambridge: Cambridge University Press.

11 This question has been much discussed in the secondary literature. Among those with a different emphasis, I mention Paul Guyer's. His position is that Kant's basic theory of our pleasure in the beautiful "is linked to the experience of the attainment of some objective ... but where pleasure is to be especially noticeable it cannot appear to be guaranteed by any concept" (*Kant and the Experience of Freedom* (second edn.). Cambridge: Cambridge University Press, 1996, p. 104). This nonetheless presupposes a framework for distinguishing between aesthetic pleasure and other kinds of pleasures, and likewise risks losing the fundamental sensuousness that is part of all pleasure, including "disinterested" aesthetic pleasure.

12 The matter is first broached in the (second) Introduction to the CJ, though discussion is deferred until the "Critique of teleological judgement." "The principle of the finality of nature is a transcendental principle of judgment" (CJ Introduction, §V, p. 20). This principle is

> "abundantly evident from the maxims of judgment upon which we rely *a priori* in the investigation of nature, and yet which have to do with no more than the possibility of experience ... These maxims crop up frequently enough in the course of this science, only in a scattered way... 'Nature makes the shortest way (*lex parsimoniae*);' yet it makes no leap, either in the sequence of its changes, or in the juxtaposition of specifically different forms (*lex continui in natura*)."
>
> (CJ Introduction, II, §V, p. 21)

13 Heidegger, Martin (1977), "The age of the world view," in *The Question Concerning Technology.* Trans. William Lovitt, New York: Harper and Row, pp. 115–54.

14 IQO 46, citing Coleridge, Samuel Taylor (1975), *Biographia Literaria.* Ed. George Watson, London: Dent, pp. 153–54. For Cavell's discussion see IQO 46.

15 See especially the essay "Kant, Hölderlin and the experience of longing."

16 See Horowitz, Gregg M. (2001), *Sustaining Loss: Art and Mournful Life.* Stanford, CA: Stanford University Press, p. 39.

17 I acknowledge here the fact that artworks within the sphere of modernism began consciously to call this uniqueness into question.

18 These are important concerns of Cavell's in IQO.

19 Kant's specific questions and response are formulated thus:

> What now is the end in man, and the end which, as such, is intended to be promoted by means of his connexion with nature? If this end is something which must be found in man himself, it must either be of such a kind that man himself may be satisfied by

means of nature and its beneficence, or else it is the aptitude and skill for all manner of ends for which he may employ nature both external and internal. The former end of nature would be the *happiness* of man, the latter his *culture*.

(CJII §22, p. 92, original emphasis)

5 Cavell and Wittgenstein on Morality: The Limits of Acknowledgment

1   In his earlier pre-perfectionist writing Cavell at times seems downright Wittgensteinian about the limitations of moral discourse: "We do not have to agree with one another in order to live in the same moral world, but we do have to know and respect one another's differences. And what we can respect, and how far and how deeply, are not matters of what 'feeling' a reason 'causes' in us" (CR 269).

2   Wittgenstein, Ludwig (1961) *Tractatus Logico-Philosophicus*. Trans. D. F. Pears and B. F. McGuinness, London: Routledge & Kegan Paul, henceforth *Tractatus*.

3   The best summary I know of how versions of Wittgensteinian ethics have developed is Alice Crary's "Introduction" and the essays in her edition (2007), *Wittgenstein and the Moral Life: Essays in Honor of Cora Diamond*. Cambridge, MA: MIT Press.

4   I elaborate this distinction in "Exemplification and expression," in Garry L. Hagberg and Walter Jost (eds.) (2010), *A Companion to the Philosophy of Literature*. Malden, MA: Wiley-Blackwell, pp. 491–506. But I do not cite there this powerful Wittgenstein passage from 1946: "Where in such cases [of being withdrawn and mistrustful] is the line between will and ability? Is it that I will not open my heart to anyone any more, or that I cannot. … If people are wary even in ordinary life why shouldn't they—perhaps suddenly—become much more wary? And much more inaccessible?" (from G. H. Von Wright with Heikki Nyman (eds.) (1980) *Culture and Value* [hereafter cited in the text as CV]. Trans. Peter Winch, Chicago, IL: University of Chicago Press).

5   Wittgenstein, Ludwig (1958) *Philosophical Investigations*. Trans. G. E. M. Anscombe, New York: Macmillan. Hereafter PI.

6   Wittgenstein, Ludwig (1969) *On Certainty*. Ed. G. E. M. Anscombe and G. H. Von Wright, Oxford: Basil Blackwell. Hereafter OC.

7   What would "know" mean in such cases, where clearly no picture theory is possibly appropriate? When we cannot resolve questions about sincerity or psychological lucidity it becomes difficult even to talk of either knowing how to respond or knowing quite what is involved in the statement. For we risk treating the avowal as a picture of an inner state that causes the pain or generates the hope.

8   Wittgenstein uses "confession" on only one occasion in the *Philosophical Investigations* (p. 222e) and two crucial times in the remarks collected in

CV pp. 18e and 46e, crucial because the remarks show complete continuity between 1931 and 1945, a period during which Wittgenstein felt the need to reconcile his grammatical approach to philosophy with his concern for the values dealt with by religion. The reference to "confession" in the *Investigations* is interesting because it claims an exposure of the person not claimed at all for "avowals": "The criteria for the truth of the confession that I thought such and such are not the criteria for a true description of a process. ... It resides rather in the special circumstances which can be drawn from a confession whose truth is guaranteed by the special criteria of truthfulness." And then the second passage from *Culture and Value* becomes apposite because it makes clear that the exposure is not part of any human dialogue but a revelation of a painful individuality that bids to be accepted as such, so close and yet so far from Cavell's perfectionist bent:

> The Christian Faith—as I see it—is a man's refuge in this *ultimate* torment.
>
> Anyone in such torment who has the gift of opening his heart, rather than contracting it, accepts the means of salvation in his heart.
>
> Someone who in this way penitently opens his heart to God in confession lays it open for other men too. In doing this he loses the dignity that goes with his personal prestige and becomes like a child. ... A man can bare himself before others only out of a particular kind of love. A love which acknowledges as it were, that we are all wicked children.
>
> We could also say: Hate between men comes from our cutting ourselves off from each other. Because we don't want anyone else to look inside us, since it's not a pretty sight in there.
>
> Of course, you must continue to feel ashamed of what's inside you, but not ashamed of yourself before your fellow men.

9   I think Cavell's early essays on modernist art understood how there had to be all sorts of attunements before explanation could take place at all. But that was before what we could call "his Emersonian turn to perfectionism."

10 "Propositions of the form of empirical propositions, and not only propositions of logic, form the foundation of all operating with thoughts (with language).—This observation is not of the form 'I know ...'. 'I know ...' states what I know, and that is not of logical interest" (OC 401).

11 The role of display in late Wittgenstein extends to the claim that agents cannot be expected to be argued into changing values but have to be led to "look at the world in a different way" (OC 92). Notice too how in 1946 he still echoes the motif that ethics is a matter not of explaining the self

but of making determinations about the possibility of changing one's life to accord with the simple fact that the world exists:

> I believe that one of the things Christianity says is that sound doctrines are all useless. That you have to change your life. (Or the direction of your life.)
>
> It says that wisdom is all cold; and that you can no more use it for setting your life to rights than you can forge iron when it is cold. ...
>
> Wisdom is passionless. But faith by contrast is what Kierkegaard calls a Passion.
>
> (CV 53e).

12 It is important here that one reason Wittgenstein has so little to say about morality is that he is more concerned with being justified before his God than before a community of human beings. My invocation of grace (or luck in relation to the domain of personal relations) allows for this dimension of something close to a misanthropy that by no means has to be confined to theological contexts.

13 I develop this criticism of Cavell in "Wonder in the Winter's Tale," in John Gibson, Wolfgang Huemer, and Luca Pocci (eds.) (2007), *A Sense of the World: Essays on Fiction, Narrative and Knowledge*. London: Routledge, pp. 266–86.

6 The Word Viewed: Skepticism Degree Zero

1 Stewart, Garrett, (forthcoming) "Self-Relayance: Emerson to Poe," in Andrew Taylor (ed.), *Cavell and America*; Stewart, Garrett (2008), "Phonemanography: Romantic to Victorian," in "Soundings of Things Done," special issue, Susan J. Wolfson (ed.), of *Romantic Circles Praxis Series* (electronic edition, April, at www.rc.umd.edu/praxis/soundings/stewart/stewart.html).

2 See Derrida, Jacques (1981) *Dissemination*. Trans. Barbara Johnson, Chicago, IL: University of Chicago Press, p. 221, where the term "syllepsis" is applied very loosely to the undecidability of Mallarmé's phrase "hymen entre": "marriage between" versus the maidenhead between that defers it.

3 WV 72.

4 DK (1987 edition), p. 140.

5 "Being odd, getting even: Descartes, Emerson, Poe" (IQO 124).

6 This is a formula summoned under deflection, in fact, by Hamlet's hinted sense of "speak out" in "For murder, though it hath no tongue,/ Will speak with most miraculous organ" (II.ii.593–94).

7 Edgar Allan Poe, *The Complete Tales and Poems of Edgar Allan Poe* (New

York: Vintage, 1975). Subsequent references to this work will be given by page number in the text, preceded by Poe.

8   Flagged in the subtitle of my most recent book on nineteenth-century writing (2009), *Novel Violence: A Narratography of Victorian Fiction*. Chicago, IL: University of Chicago Press, narratography as a method (or lens) of attention concerns the demonstrable zone of overlap between medium-blind narratology and a linguistic (or cinematic) stylistics. Narratographic reading notes the marked features of textual succession as they mark out in turn a nexus of narrative advance in the microplots of technique (inscription) per se, whether verbal or visual. See also a complementary grain of analysis in my (2007), *Framed Time: Toward a Postfilmic Cinema*. Chicago, IL: University of Chicago Press.

9   Ryle, Gilbert (1949), *The Concept of Mind*. London: Hutchinson and Company, p. 22 (henceforth CM), his example coming from Ch. 39 of *Pickwick Papers*. I've given a somewhat fuller account of the splintered logic of syllepsis in connection with Ryle's critique of Descartes in Stewart, Garrett (2010), "The ethical tempo of narrative syntax: Sylleptic recognitions in *Our Mutual Friend*." *Partial Answers: Journal of Literature and the History of Ideas*, 8, (1), 119–45, with many further examples of the trope from this late work. Unmentioned by Ryle is another sylleptic joke from Dickens's first novel, *Pickwick Papers*, from Ch. 19, where the hero "fell into the barrow, and fast asleep, simultaneously." And in his third novel, Dickens's "Conclusion," in Ch. 65, begins with a tamer version of such splayed grammar when "Madeline gave her hand and fortunes to Nicholas."

10   Agamben, Giorgio (1999), *The End of the Poem: Studies in Poetics*. Trans. Daniel Heller-Roazen, Palo Alto, CA: Stanford University Press. Henceforth EP.

11   Agamben, Giorgio (2008), "Difference and repetition: On Guy Debord's films," in Tanya Leighton (ed.), *Art and the Moving Image: A Critical Reader*. London: Tate, p. 330.

12   Agamben's sense, after Valéry, of sound postponing sense recalls Hartman's definition of a "pun" either as "two meanings competing for the same phonemic space" or as "one sound bringing forth semantic twins" (p. 347). The inevitable deferral of one meaning by the other is only the clearer in the distributed, skewed fusions of syllepsis.

13   In this, I agree with Charles Altieri, (2001), "Taking lyrics literally: Teaching poetry in a prose culture." *New Literary History*, 32, (2), pp. 259–81, that the power of lyric (and, I would add, of a prose equally marked by Altieri's crucial values of "intensity" and "plasticity" (p. 267)), is not epistemic but performative, not a way of knowing but a way of experimental participation in states of feeling that writing draws out in us rather than merely depicts—and so draws us into. In Cavellian terms, literature offers a defeat of skepticism, then, not by proof but not just by suspended disbelief either; rather, by a linguistic experience

keyed to exceed what it names, to enact what waits unsayable—though still formally articulated—in its run of words.

7   A Storied World: On Meeting and Being Met

1   LDIK 6.
2   I also need to acknowledge that I don't know what to make of this fact, not even if it's a fact about what was the case or a fact about what I—did and did not—notice. But I do know that professional philosophy was then, and to a distressing extent, remains today, unwelcoming to those who are not, or are not willing and able to pass as, middle-class heterosexual white men.
3   In my (1993), *Engenderings: Constructions of Knowledge, Authority, and Privilege*. New York: Routledge.
4   Cavell, Stanley (1987), "Freud and philosophy: A fragment." *Critical Inquiry*, 13, (2), 386–93 (389).
5   "We" needn't include the person(s) being addressed and can quite explicitly exclude them, but the uses of "we" that I'm concerned with—and those that raise the problems I'm addressing—are inclusive in this way. Whether or not I mean to include various others, I do mean to include *you*. And just as there is an inclusive and an exclusive *we*, there is the sort of inclusive *you* I have been discussing and a quite different *you* that, as Norton Batkin reminded me, is hardly one of respectful connection. Quite the contrary: the *you* of, for example, "you people" is one of distancing estrangement. As different as this *you* is, it underscores my point that, while the third person can be merely descriptive, the second person is fundamentally relational—in this case, not merely objectifying, but confrontational.
6   In *Engenderings*.
7   In Sluga, Hans and Stern, David (eds.) (1996), *Cambridge Companion to Wittgenstein*. Cambridge: Cambridge University Press. Reprinted in Scheman, Naomi (2011), *Shifting Ground: Knowledge and Reality, Transgression and Trustworthiness*. Oxford: Oxford University Press.
8   The point would be clearer in French or German: it would be about using the familiar *tu* or *du*. Strikingly, in German, *Sie*, the formal "you" is also the third person plural.
9   The situation is, however, changing, going back at least to Baier, Annette (1985), "Cartesian persons", in *Postures of the Mind: Essays on Mind and Morals*. Minneapolis, MN: University of Minnesota Press. Feminist philosophers have taken up a second-person conception of persons: see particularly the work of Lorraine Code, especially (1991), *What Can She Know?: Feminist Theory and the Construction of Knowledge*. Ithaca, NY: Cornell University Press; and (1995), *Rhetorical Spaces: Essays on Gendered Locations*. New York: Routledge. Other notable recent work includes Darwall, Steven (2006), *The Second-Person Standpoint: Morality, Respect,*

and Accountability. Cambridge, MA: Harvard University Press; and Kukla, Rebecca and Lance, Mark (2009), *Yo! and Lo!: The Pragmatic Topography of the Space of Reasons*. Cambridge, MA: Harvard University Press.

10 Lugones, María (1991), "The logic of pluralist feminism", in Claudia Card (ed.), *Feminist Ethics*. Lawrence, KS: University of Kansas Press. Reprinted in Lugones, (2003), *Pilgrimages/Peregrinajes: Theorizing Coalition against Multiple Oppressions*. Lanham, MD: Rowman and Littlefield. See also Ortega, Mariana (2006), "Being lovingly, knowingly ignorant: White feminism and women of color." *Hypatia*, 21, (3), 56–74.

11 Baier, "Cartesian Persons."

12 Althusser, Louis (1971), "Ideology and ideological state apparatuses," in his *Lenin and Philosophy and Other Essays*. New York: Monthly Review Press.

13 Young, Iris Marion (2000), *Inclusion and Democracy*. Oxford: Oxford University Press; Taylor, Charles (1992), "Multiculturalism and the politics of recognition", in Amy Gutmann (ed.), *Multiculturalism*. Princeton, NJ: Princeton University Press.

14 Kukla and Lance, *Yo! and Lo!*

15 Martin Gustafsson supports Cavell against John McDowell on the question of whether Austin's and Wittgenstein's appeals to "what we do" should, if we fully take them in, leave us feeling safe (McDowell) or scared (Cavell). Gustafsson, Martin (2005), "Perfect pitch and Austinian examples: Cavell, McDowell, Wittgenstein, and the philosophical significance of ordinary language." *Inquiry*, 48, (4), 356–89.

16 Frasier, Debra (1991), *On the Day You Were Born*. San Diego, CA: Harcourt Brace Jovanovich.

17 A set of questions I do not have space to address here concern the heterosexuality that is also at the heart of Cavell's thoughts about gender, hence about philosophy: The *we* of Cavell's philosophizing is not only male, but also straight, which is not to say that gay men (or straight women or lesbians) do not "have" philosophical problems, only that to a great extent our having them is bound up with our enmeshment in forms of subjectivity with respect to which we are not paradigm examples and in which we have ambiguous stakes.

18 In addition to "Othello's doubt/Desdemona's death," there was "Though this be method, there is madness in it: Paranoia and liberal epistemology," and "Missing mothers/desiring daughters: Framing the sight of women," all in *Engenderings*.

19 "Texts of recovery," in IQO.

20 Wittgenstein, Ludwig (1958), *Philosophical Investigations*. Trans. G. E. M. Anscombe, New York: Macmillan, Part II, p. 178.

21 Sedgwick, Eve Kosofsky (forthcoming), "The weather in Proust," cited in Josh Wilner, Chapter 11 this volume.

22 Janet Bystrom, personal email correspondence, January 29, 2011.

23 Barker, Francis (1995), *The Tremulous Private Body: Essays on Subjection* (second edn.). Ann Arbor, MI: University of Michigan Press.

24   Adams' argument bears similarities with Cora Diamond's philosoph-
     ically much richer account; the simplicity of Adams is useful here. See
     Adams, Carol (1990), *The Sexual Politics of Meat: A Feminist-Vegetarian
     Critical Theory* (Twentieth Anniversary Edn.). New York: Continuum;
     and Diamond, Cora (1991), "Eating meat and eating people," in her *The
     Realistic Spirit: Wittgenstein, Philosophy, and the Mind*. Cambridge, MA:
     MIT Press.
25   For an examination of the ethics and politics of intelligibility, see
     Hoagland, Sarah Lucia (1988), *Lesbian Ethics: Toward New Value*. Palo
     Alto, CA: Institute of Lesbian Studies.
26   See "Forms of life."
27   On companions (etymologically, those who break bread together: she
     calls them "messmates"), see Haraway, Donna J. (2008), *When Species
     Meet*. Minneapolis, MN: University of Minnesota Press. One of the
     prompts for my framing this paper in terms of meeting was my reading
     this book at the same time as Barad, Karen (2007), *Meeting the Universe
     Halfway: Quantum Physics and the Entanglement of Matter and Meaning*.
     Durham, NC: Duke University Press.
28   Spelman, Elizabeth V. (1988), *Inessential Woman: Problems of Exclusion in
     Feminist Thought*. Boston, MA: Beacon Press, p. 184.

8   Skepticism and the Idea of an Other: Reflections on Cavell and Postcolonialism

1   This would be the sense of otherness that has figured in certain strands
     of the phenomenological tradition, used to designate, for instance, a
     primitive relationship between the self (or ego) and in effect everything
     that is experienced as external to it. This is the sense of the "other" that
     contrasts not with the familiar but with the "same," and indeed the
     same/other pairing is basic to much work in the phenomenological
     tradition.
2   This is a condition—the condition of not seeing a "face" in another—that
     Levinas at times equates with "war." See, for example, Levinas, Em-
     manuel (1998), "Freedom and command" in his *Collected Philosophical
     Papers*. Trans. Alfonso Lingis, Pittsburgh, PA: Dusquene University
     Press, and the various reflections on the face and the experience of the
     Other's humanity in Levinas' (2003), *Humanism of the Other*. Trans. Nidra
     Poller, Urbana, IL: University of Illinois Press. For an excellent general
     discussion of the face and its relevance to both philosophy and litera-
     ture, see Rhie, Bernard (forthcoming), "The philosophy of the face: An
     introductory overview." *Philosophy and Literature*.
3   See especially CR 491–96.
4   IQO 126.
5   See Affeldt, Steven (1998), "The ground of mutuality: Criteria, judg-
     ment, and intelligibility in Stephen Mulhall and Stanley Cavell."

European Journal of Philosophy, 6, (1), 1–31, for an excellent discussion of the role of criteria in Cavell's philosophy.

6 CR 109.
7 MWM 61.
8 Wittgenstein, Ludwig (1969), *On Certainty*. Ed. G. E. M. Anscome and G. H. Von Wright, trans. Denis Paul and G. E. M. Anscombe, Oxford: Basil Blackwell, §379.
9 SW 106–07.
10 As Cavell puts it,

> Acknowledging is not an alternative to knowing but an interpretation of it. Incorporating, or inflecting, the concept of knowledge, the concept of acknowledgment is meant, in my use, to declare that what there is to be known philosophically remains unknown not through ignorance (for we cannot just not know what there is to be known philosophically, for example that there is a world and I and others in it) but through a refusal of knowledge, a denial, or a repression of knowledge, say even a killing of it."
>
> (IQO 51)

11 See the essays collected in DK.
12 For an excellent discussion of Levinas and skepticism, see Morgan, Michael L. (2007), *Discovering Levinas*. Cambridge: Cambridge University Press.
13 See Fanon, Frantz (1967), *Black Skin, White Masks*. New York: Grove Press; and his (1968), *The Wretched of the Earth*. New York: Grove Press.
14 We put "racial" in scare quotes because the very notion is deeply problematic. See Taylor, Paul C. (2005), *Race: A Philosophical Introduction*. Malden, MA: Blackwell.
15 It may be interesting to note that ethnology, the very discipline that studies foreign cultures, often assumes a similar picture of the problem of communication with the other (or what amounts to it), at least if we follow the lesson of Michel Leiris and James Clifford. Their ethnological model emphasizes writing as construction rather than as representation, and it seeks to demonstrate that when one is trying to capture the foreignness of a culture, what one is ultimately just left with is a translation of that foreignness into your own language, your own body, your own resources of tradition and modes of articulation. Leiris's ground-breaking (1934), *L'Afrique fantôme*. Paris: Gallimard, is still essential reading on this topic. See also Clifford, James (1988), *The Predicament of Culture: Twentieth Century Ethnography, Literature, and Art*. Cambridge, MA: Harvard University Press; and his (1997), *Routes: Travel and Translation in the Late Twentieth Century*. Cambridge, MA: Harvard University Press.
16 Brontë, Charlotte (first published 1865), *Jane Eyre*. Ch. 26.
17 Conrad, Joseph (1995), *Heart of Darkness and Other Stories*. Ware: Wordsworth Editions, Ltd., pp. 118–19.

18 All quotations in this paragraph are of Conrad (1995), p. 124.
19 Spivak, Gayatri (1985), "Three women's texts and a critique of imperialism." *Critical Inquiry*, 12, (1), 243–61 (253).
20 Attridge, Derek (2004), *J. M. Coetzee and the Ethics of Reading: Literature in the Event*. Chicago, IL: University of Chicago Press, p. 12.
21 Coetzee, J. M. (1986), *Foe*. London: Secker & Warberg, pp. 121–22.
22 Ibid., p. 115
23 Ibid., p. 157.
24 Ibid.
25 Attridge (2004), p. 82.
26 For his work on moral perfection see SW and "Themes of moral perfectionism in Plato's *Republic*" in CW.

9 William Shakespeare and Stanley Cavell: Acknowledging, Confessing, and Tragedy

1 Jonathan Cullen, during a memorable class we co-taught at Duke University in the Fall of 2010. This hit home not only for its logic and wisdom but also because it helps to explain why the recurrent dream of "not knowing your lines" is such a perennial nightmare and not, I am sure, for myself alone.
2 First published in MWM in 1969, and subsequently included in DK in 1987.
3 LDIK 218. Cavell composed incidental music for several university productions, "the most lasting of which" was writing music for the production of *King Lear* (LDIK 215). Playing music cues for rehearsals, run-throughs and actual performances, he came to know almost every line of *King Lear* and also to realize that he was more interested in the action, words, and ideas on the stage, and what he had to say about them, than the music.
4 Ibid., p. 215.
5 Ibid.
6 Ibid., p. 217.
7 "Criticism is always an affront, and its only justification lies in its usefulness, in making its object available to just response" (MWM 46).
8 Cavell, Stanley (2004), "A reply to four chapters" in Denis McManus (ed.), *Wittgenstein and Skepticism*. London/New York: Routledge, p. 290.
9 LDIK 217.
10 See, for example, Cascardi, Anthony J. (2003), "Cavell on Shakespeare," in Richard Eldridge (ed.), *Stanley Cavell*. Cambridge: Cambridge University Press, pp. 190–205; and James Conant's earlier essay (1990), "On Bruns, on Cavell." *Critical Inquiry*, 17, (3), 616–34. See now Rhu, Larry (2006), *Stanley Cavell's American Dream: Shakespeare, Philosophy, and Hollywood Movies*. New York: Fordham University Press.
11 The terms "fieldwork in philosophy" or "linguistic phenomenology"

are J. L. Austin's from his seminal essay, "A plea for excuses" in J. L. Austin (1979), *Philosophical Papers* (third edn.). Ed. J. O. Urmson and G. J. Warnock, Oxford: Oxford University Press, p. 182:

> When we examine what we should say when, what words we should use in what situations, we are looking again not *merely* at words (or 'meanings', whatever they may be) but also at the realities we use the words to talk about: we are using a sharpened awareness of words to sharpen our perception, though not as a final arbiter of, the phenomena.

See my (2011), *Shakespeare and the Grammar of Forgiveness*. Ithaca, NY: Cornell University Press, for an exploration of forgiveness, and Fleming, Richard (2010), *Evil and Silence*. Boulder, CO: Paradigm Publishers, for an exploration of silence in this idiom.

12 For an excellent exploration of confession and its centrality to "voicing" in Cavell, see Gould, Timothy (1998), *Hearing Things: Voice and Method in the Writing of Stanley Cavell*. Chicago, IL: University of Chicago Press.

13 Wetzel, James (2008), "Wittgenstein's Augustine: The inauguration of the later philosophy." *Polygraph: An International Journal of Culture and Politics*, special issue, "Cities of Men, Cities of God: Augustine and Late Secularism," ed. Russ Leo, 19/20, 129–47

14 "Must we mean what we say?" in MWM 71.

15 Medieval orthodoxy taught that sacramental confession and absolution cancelled the "*culpa*" or guilt of sin, the "*poena*", punishment or penalty incurred by the sin, could be canceled through pardons and indulgences, but of course also by performing the penance set by the priest in confession. Stephen Greenblatt's (2001), *Hamlet in Purgatory*. Princeton, NJ: Princeton University Press, makes a compelling argument about the loss of purgatory and a theater of remembrance haunted by purgatorial spirits who could no longer be helped by the actions of those on earth. In so far as he investigates penance, it is exclusively through the investigation of purgatory, pardons and indulgences. For insightful comments on the exclusion of questions of justice from questions of remembrance in this model see Hutson, Lorna (2007), *The Invention of Suspicion: Law and Mimesis in Shakespeare and Renaissance Drama*. Oxford: Oxford University Press, p. 265.

16 See Steinmetz, David C. (1986), *Luther in Context*. Bloomington, IN: University of Indiana Press.

17 Griffiths, John (ed.) (2006), "An homily of repentance and of true reconciliation unto God," in *The Homilies Appointed to Be Read in Churches*. Revised by Ian Robinson, Bishopstone, Herefordshire: The Brynmill Press, p. 385.

18 "When our Lord and Master Jesus Christ said, 'repent' [Mt. 4.17], he willed the entire life of believers to be one of repentance," in Harold T.

Grimm and Helmut T. Lehmann (eds.) (1957), *Ninety Five Theses or Disputations on the Power and Efficacy of Indulgences*. Luther's Works, 31: The Career of a Reformer, Philadelphia, PA: Muehlenberg and Fortress Press/St. Louis: Concordia.

19 All quotations are taken from G. Blakemore Evans (ed.) (1997), *The Riverside Shakespeare* (second edn.). Boston, MA: Houghton Mifflin.

20 "Performative and passionate utterance" in PDAT 155–91.

21 For a precise rendering of versions of community in the work of Cavell and Wittgenstein, where she distinguishes Cavell's understanding from the one more common in communitarian thought, see Laugier, Sandra (2006), "Wittgenstein and Cavell: Anthropology, skepticism, and politics," in Andrew Norris (ed.) *The Claim to Community: Essays on Stanley Cavell and Political Philosophy*. Stanford, CA: Stanford University Press, pp. 19–37.

22 This is a central dimension of Cavell's unique exploration of Wittgenstein's private language argument in the extraordinary Part 4 of CR, especially pp. 348–70.

23 Arendt, Hannah (1958), *The Human Condition*. Chicago, IL: University of Chicago Press, p. 237.

24 The Forgiveness Project is "a charity which explores forgiveness through the stories of real people." See www.theforgivenessproject.com. The stories cited here were accessed on January 29, 2009. They can be found on the website under "Stories." The centrality of storytelling to reconciliation is explored in Chapter 5.

25 Margalit, Avishai (2002), *The Ethics of Memory*. Cambridge: Cambridge University Press, p. 203.

26 *Summa Theologica* Part 2.2, Q.23 Art.2. Quotations from the *Summa* are from St. Thomas Aquinas (1984), *Summa Theologica* (Complete English Edn.). Trans. and ed. by the English Dominican Province, Notre Dame, IN: Ave Maria Press.

27 *Summa Theologica* Part 3, Q.90 Art 2.

28 Ibid.

29 Institutes 3.4. 2. Calvin, John (1960), *Institutes of the Christian Religion*. Trans. Ford Lewis Battles, ed. John T. McNeill, Notre Dame, IN: Ave Maria Press.

30 Steinmetz, David, (2002) *Luther in Context*. Grand Rapids, MI: Baker Academic, p. 110.

31 Bray, Gerald (ed.) (2004 [1994]), *Documents of the English Reformation 1526–1701*, Cambridge: James Clarke & Co., p. 291. The italics represent the 1571 additions to the 1563 articles, themselves a revision of Edward VI's Forty Two Articles (1553).

32 In Chapter 11, Part 3 of CR, Stanley Cavell takes issue with John Rawls' understanding that a promise is an "institution." I take these issues up again in Chapter 5 on "Confessing in Cymbeline" of my book *Shakespeare and the Grammar of Forgiveness*.

33 For a particularly lucid account of Austin's work in distinguishing illo-cutionary force and perlocutionary effect, see Crary, Alice (2007), *Beyond Moral Judgment*. Cambridge, MA: Harvard University Press, especially p. 65; and Timothy Gould's important essay (1995), "The unhappy per-formative," in Andrew Parker and Eve Kosofsky Sedgwick (eds.), *Performativity and Performance*. New York: Routledge, pp. 19–44. For Cavell's elucidation of the deepest implications of Austin's legacy see "Counter-philosophy and the pawn of voice" in PP; and his foreword to Felman, Shoshana (2003), *The Scandal of the Speaking Body: Don Juan with J. L. Austin or Seduction in Two Languages*. Stanford, CA: Stanford University Press.

34 This analysis is dependent on Stanley Cavell's thought and examples in his essay "Performative and passionate utterance" in PDAT 152–91. The phrase "recovery of speech" is taken from Cavell's responses to the essays collected in Andrew Norris (ed.) (2006), *The Claims to Community: Essays on Stanley Cavell and Political Philosophy*. Stanford, CA: Stanford University Press, p. 269.

35 Austin, J. L. (1962), *How To Do Things With Words*. Ed. J. O. Urmson and Marina Sbisa, Cambridge, MA: Harvard University Press, p. 148.

36 On "sensitivity to occasions" see Crary, *Beyond Moral Judgment*, p. 71. It is the aim of Crary's book to show that and how "learning to speak is inseparable from development of a moral outlook" (p. 43).

37 On problems with functionalism and ritual, see Chapter 2 of my (2001), *Signifying God: Social Act and Symbolic Relation in the York Corpus Christi Play*. Chicago, IL: University of Chicago Press.

38 See Chapter 6 of *Shakespeare and the Grammar of Forgiveness* on *Winter's Tale* and also Cavell, "Counter-philosophy and the pawn of voice" in PP 115.

39 This essay contains excerpts from the introduction, Chapter 2, and Chapter 5 of my book *Shakespeare and the Grammar of Forgiveness*, and I thank Cornell University Press for permission to use these excerpts.

10 Competing for the Soul: Cavell on Shakespeare

1 My thanks to Andrew Cutrofello, David Mikics, Scott Newstok, and Nick Pappas for help with this essay.

2 Mulhall, Stephen (2007), *The Conversation of Humanity*. Charlottesville, VA: University of Virginia Press.

3 Sowards, J. K. (ed.) (1985), *The Collected Works of Erasmus* (vol. 25). Toronto: University of Toronto Press. See also Abraham J. Malherbe (ed.) (1988), *Ancient Epistolary Theorists*. Atlanta, GA: Scholars Press, pp. 19–27; Eden, Kathy (2001), "From the cradle: Erasmus on intimacy in Renaissance letters." *Erasmus Society of Rotterdam Yearbook*, 21, 30–43.

4 "Self-reliance," in Joel Porte (ed.) (1996), *Emerson: Essays and Poems*

(college edn.). New York: Library of America, pp. 259–82 (262). Cavell discusses this passage in ETE 171–82.

5   Mulhall (2003), "Reading, writing, and re-membering: What Cavell and Heidegger call thinking," in Kenneth Dauber and Walter Jost (eds.), *Ordinary Language Criticism*. Evansville, IL: Northwestern University Press, pp. 115–33, esp. 121 and 133 n. 6. Note 6 cites PoP 46, which leads back to Emerson.

6   My own sense of liberation in encountering *Philosophical Investigations* (not at first, when I found it arbitrary, unoriginal, and superficial) was that it freed me to explore whatever experience or text (in whatever medium) genuinely interested me, seemed to call for my attention, a freedom which my participation in the English-speaking institutionalization of philosophy over the past half-century has seemed sometimes (whatever other causes I have for gratitude to it) to wish precisely to forbid me.

(PDAT 211–12)

7   In "Beginning Cavell," in Ted Cohen, Paul Guyer, and Hilary Putnam (eds.) (1993), *Pursuits of Reason: Essays in Honor of Stanley Cavell*. Lubbock, TX: Texas Tech University Press, pp. 230–41 (232), Arnold Davidson calls Cavell a "diagnostician of the spirit in which things are said" and thus makes him sound like an allegorist who hearkens to the spiritual sense of a text.

8   "The American scholar," in *Emerson: Essays and Poems*, p. 67, cf. "Experience," in ibid., 491; and Richard Eldridge (1997), *Leading a Human Life*. Chicago, IL: University of Chicago Press, p. 13.

9   Luther, Martin (1961), "The pagan servitude of the Church," in John Dillenberger (ed.) *Martin Luther: Selections from His Writings*. Garden City, NY: Anchor Books, pp. 249–359 (328).

10 Rhu, Lawrence F. (2001), "An American philosopher at the movies." *DoubleTake*, 7, (2), 115–19 (116).

11 *Emerson: Essays and Poems*, p. 261.

12 Critchley, Simon (2005), "Cavell's 'romanticism' and Cavell's romanticism" in Russell B. Goodman (ed.), *Contending with Cavell*. New York: Oxford University Press, pp. 37–54 (51).

13 Watson, Robert N. (2006), *Back to Nature: The Green and the Real in the Late Renaissance*. Philadelphia, PA: University of Pennsylvania Press, p. 54. Besides writing eloquent, profound Shakespeare criticism, Watson is also a poet. His moving lyric, "Winter in the Summer House" (*The New Yorker*, August 9, 2010), reveals yet another side of his response to themes central to *The Winter's Tale*, as both he and Cavell read it.

14 *Emerson: Essays and Poems*, p. 271.

15 Mainly the latter in this case. Cf. V.iii.237–38: "This judgment of the heavens that makes us tremble,/Touches us not with pity." Petronelli,

Vincent (ed.) (2011), *King Lear: Evans Shakespeare Edition*. Florence, KY: Cengage.

16 *Emerson: Essays and Poems*, p. 485; Rossi, William (ed.) (2008) *Walden* (third edn.). New York: W. W. Norton and Co., p. 94.

17 See Gilbert, Allan H. (1940), *Literary Criticism: Plato to Dryden*. Detroit, MI: Wayne State University Press, pp. 290, 351, 369, 427–28, 468, 523.

18 All references come from Rhu, Lawrence (ed.) (2011), *The Winter's Tale: Evans Shakespeare Edition*, Florence, KY: Cengage.

19 See Paster, Gail Kern (1993), *The Body Embarrassed: Drama and the Disciplines of Shame in Early Modern England*. Ithaca, NY: Cornell University Press, pp. 260–80.

20 "Every European philosopher since Hegel has felt he must inherit this edifice and/or destroy it. No American philosopher has such a relation to the history of philosophy." This "edifice" is characterized in the sentence preceding these as "the complete edifice of philosophy as system and as necessary, unified foundation" (ETE 133).

21 See Descartes, René (1996), *Discourse on Method and Meditations on First Philosophy*. Ed. David Weissman, New Haven, CT: Yale University Press, p. 69.

22 Cf. *Emerson: Essays and Poems*, pp. 68–69: "I ask not for the great, the remote, the romantic ... show me the sublime presence of the highest spiritual cause lurking, as it always does lurk, in these suburbs and extremities of nature."

11 "Communicating with Objects": Romanticism, Skepticism, and "The Specter of Animism" in Cavell and Wordsworth

1 Unpublished manuscript, cited with permission. A published version will be forthcoming with the posthumous publication by Duke University Press of a book of unpublished and uncollected essays by Sedgwick currently in preparation under the editorial supervision of Jonathan Goldberg.

2 Strictly speaking, what Cavell calls material objects skepticism is characterized by "the emergence of the generic object as the focus of investigation" (CR 136). But this "generic object" is in turn characterized by Cavell as standing in for the world, "compressing within itself, for [the epistemologist] material reality as a whole, the entire island of reality" (CR 429–30).

3 This, at least in order of presentation (and, I suspect, of composition), consideration precedes the extended discussion of *Othello* with which *The Claim of Reason* concludes.

4 That Cavell draws this inference from the idea that "Othello's (other-minds) relation to Desdemona" is to be taken as "an allegory ... of material-objects skepticism" may seem puzzling, since one might well take the allegorized—material-objects skepticism—as the more

fundamental, the underlying thing at issue for which the story of Othello and Desdemona serves as a means of representation or dramatization. That Cavell does not see the matter in this way suggests to me an understanding of allegory as inverting its repression. The skeptical recital, as it concerns material objects, would, in the first instance, be constructed over the repression of the drama of relation to the other, but this would also, and perhaps especially, be a submergence of the allegorical character of that drama—in which the status of the other (and hence of the self) as person or thing vacillates.

5   For a different perspective on these matters, I refer the reader to Rei Terada's recent (2009), *Looking Away: Phenomenality and Dissatisfaction, Kant to Adorno*. Cambridge, MA: Harvard University Press, especially the introduction and second chapter. In Terada's view, *The Claim of Reason* argues that "Skeptical scruples about appearance and reality transmit fears and desires about interpersonal relations: *'acceptance in relation to objects'* corresponds to *'acknowledgement in relation to others'* " (p. 2). Similarly, "Cavell's reading of Coleridge in *In Quest of the Ordinary* illustrates his argument … that skeptics displace their legitimate doubts regarding others' thoughts onto objects, and thus animate objects by treating them as though they could sustain doubt" (p. 69)—from which it follows that "Cavell treats animism as a delusion…" (p. 70). While my own path through this material approaches Terada's in places, her claim that for Cavell "skeptics displace their legitimate doubts regarding others' thoughts onto objects" appears to me to involve a misunderstanding of what is at stake in what Cavell calls "the oscillation between sensing an asymmetry under every symmetry [between material-objects and other-minds skepticism], and a symmetry under each asymmetry" (CR 451). Presumably Terada reaches this conclusion in part on the basis of such statements in *The Claim of Reason* as "… with respect to the external world, an initial sanity requires recognizing that I cannot live my skepticism, whereas with respect to others a final sanity requires recognizing that I can. I do" (ibid.). But to *recognize* that I "live my skepticism with respect to others" is not to *legitimate* it, to validate it in principle. As Cavell writes, "I already know everything skepticism concludes … that I cannot close my eyes to my doubts of others and to their doubts and denials of me, that my relations with others are restricted, that I cannot trust them blindly.—You'd be a fool if you did.—Spare me that. That aside, my position here is not one of a generalized *intellectual* shortcoming" (CR 432). That our "doubts regarding others thoughts" are anything but "legitimate" if our putative grounds for them are epistemologically categorical (as Terada's way of framing the difference between the two skepticisms would seem to imply) is central to Cavell's reading of Wittgenstein. Cavell's oft-cited formula for the skeptic's invoking of such grounds is the "conversion of metaphysical finitude into intellectual lack" (CR 493).

6   Terada draws the same line of relation, albeit to argue the contraposi-
    tive: "Cavell treats animism as a delusion with no vivifying affects, but
    if it is a delusion, then he should not figure skepticism as murder" (p.
    70).

7   Reference is to book and lines. Unless otherwise indicated, I cite from
    the version of 1805. "In place of that/Which is divine and true ..."
    revises an early manuscript variant, "For that informed with light and
    life and motion," which then returns with modifications in the "final"
    version published in 1850 following Wordsworth's death: "For that
    which moves with light and life informed,/Actual, divine, and true."

8   Freud, Sigmund (1991), "The 'uncanny'," in *The Standard Edition of the
    Complete Psychological Works of Sigmund Freud, Volume XVII (1917–1919):
    An Infantile Neurosis and Other Works*. London: The Hogarth Press and
    The Institute of Psycho-Analysis.

9   The wording here is already noticeably idiosyncratic, as though combin-
    ing the expressions "off limits to" and "beyond the limits of." Perhaps
    one should hear "off the limits of human knowledge" along the lines of
    "off the coast of ...," in anticipation of Cavell's reading of Kant and Col-
    eridge through each other. In the region of "the thing-in-itself," we are,
    like the Ancient Mariner, at sea.

10 Wordsworth made largely minor revisions to "Tintern Abbey" in the
    course of the many republications he authorized following its initial
    appearance in the 1798 edition of *Lyrical Ballads*. Unless otherwise indi-
    cated, reference is to the 1798 text. Where a later variant is drawn on, the
    original year of publication is given in parentheses.

11 The disavowal is reported in John Veitch's 1869 memoir of Sir William
    Hamilton, the great mathematician and physicist:

    > "Sir William thought he saw traces of an acquaintance with Kant
    > in the magnificent passage of the Wanderer's discourse, begin-
    > ning—'And what are things eternal?' But it would seem that this
    > was a case in which the poet and the philosopher had reached the
    > same great truth independently and by different approaches. 'I
    > asked Wordsworth,' says Captain Hamilton [Sir William's
    > brother], writing from the Lakes, where he resided latterly, 'about
    > that passage in the 'Excursion' which William says contains the
    > doctrine of Kant. Wordsworth says he is utterly ignorant of every-
    > thing connected either with Kant or his philosophy, so that it
    > could not have come from that source, but is a casual
    > coincidence' "
    >
    > (88–89)

    The anecdote is alluded to by Wellek (p. 160). The passage from *The
    Excursion* in which Sir William thought he saw evidence of an acquaint-
    ance with Kant begins as follows:

"… And what are things eternal?--powers depart,"
The grey-haired Wanderer stedfastly replied,
Answering the question which himself had asked,
"Possessions vanish, and opinions change,
And passions hold a fluctuating seat:

But, by the storms of circumstance unshaken,
And subject neither to eclipse nor wane,
Duty exists;--immutably survive,
For our support, the measures and the forms,
Which an abstract intelligence supplies;
Whose kingdom is, where time and space are not."

(IV, 66–76)

12 The 1796 date is not directly given in *The Prelude*, but can be readily inferred from indications in the text and is confirmed by other evidence. (See the editors' note 8, p. 408 of Wordsworth, William (1979), *The Prelude: 1799, 1805, 1850*. Ed. Jonathan Wordsworth, M. H. Abrams, and Stephen Gill, New York: W. W. Norton & Company.)

13 It may be objected that what Wordsworth dramatizes in this passage is a crisis of "moral" rather than "other minds" or "material objects" skepticism. As already indicated, however, the whole trend of Cavell's treatment of skepticism works against such taxonomic containments of its problematic. In the present instance, it is worth noting how the language of Wordsworth's self-description, "now believing,/Now disbelieving, endlessly perplexed/… demanding proof …," recalls Othello's famous speech, "By the world,/I think my wife be honest and think she is not;/I think that thou art just and think thou art not./I'll have some proof" (III. iii.26–29), a speech emblematic for Cavell of "the scene of skepticism" and "the structure of [Othello's] emotion as he is hauled back and forth across the keel of his love" (CR 483–84).

14 The figure of fever subtends Wordsworth's quasi-medical identification of this period as "the crisis of that strong disease" (1850, XI, 306), the "disease" being the self-deluding "philosophy," associated with Godwin's *Enquiry Concerning Political Justice*, "Which makes the human reason's naked self/The object of its fervor" (1805, X, 817–18).

15 That the substitution of "composed" for "written" is meant to finesse questions about "where" the poem was written is suggested as well by the Fenwick Note, where "composed" recurs: "No poem of mine was composed under circumstances more pleasant for me to remember than this. I began it upon leaving Tintern, after crossing the Wye, and concluded it just as I was entering Bristol in the evening, after a ramble of 4 or 5 days, with my sister. Not a line of it was altered, and not any part of it written down till I reached Bristol" (p. 66).

16 This doubleness is encoded emblematically in lines from the

"Immortality Ode" that form part of the final apostrophe on which Cavell comments in "Texts of Recovery" (IQO 71), though he does not cite them specifically:

I only have relinquished one delight
To live beneath your more habitual sway.

The "habitual sway" is of course that of the apostrophized "Fountains, Meadows, Hills, and Groves," but "living beneath your more habitual sway" can also not not involve, in Wordsworth, an invoking of the rhythms of poetic language.

17 "The goldfinch, the material object, is … uninscribed and *mute*: but the man *speaks*," Austin, J. L. (1961), "Other minds," in his *Philosophical Papers*. Oxford: Clarendon Press, p. 113.

18 Where Wordsworth's hesitation comes from, for his scruples may well be religious as much as epistemological, and what beliefs exactly it bears on—That there is a life in things? That we can see into that life? That he owes the gift of the mood that lightens to his communication with "the beauteous forms of nature" (1924)?—are all to some degree uncertain, even if contextual indications ultimately permit one to pin down what "this" refers to in the allowance "If this be put a vain belief." The gesture is sweeping enough, it seems to me, to conjure the specter of skepticism in all its self-isolating and de-realizing scope.

For a more extended consideration of the qualifications that attend Wordsworth's expressions of "metaphysical confidence" throughout the poem, the reader is referred to Richard Eldridge's recent discussion (2008) in *Literature, Life, and Modernity*. New York: Columbia University Press, pp. 85–100, though Eldridge's ultimate interest is in the poem's achievement of "measures of human closure and composure … in time" (p. 85) notwithstanding its uncertainties.

19 "The Reader will find that personifications of abstract ideas rarely occur in these volumes; and are utterly rejected, as an ordinary device to elevate the style, and raise it above prose. My purpose was to imitate, and, as far as possible, to adopt the very language of men; and assuredly such personifications do not make any natural or regular part of that language." ("Preface to *Lyrical Ballads*.")

20 The remark from the preface at issue, taking Wordsworth's defense of having chosen "incidents and situations" from "humble and rustic life" for his subject matter another step, specifies further that: "The language, too, of these men has been adopted (purified indeed from what appear to be its real defects, from all lasting and rational causes of dislike or disgust) because *such men hourly communicate with the best objects from which the best part of language is originally derived* …" in Butler, James and Green, Karen (eds.) (1992), *Lyrical Ballads, and Other Poems*. Ithaca, NY: Cornell University Press, p. 745, my emphasis. For Wordsworth's own gloss on the meaning of this phrase, one might consider his reference in

the "Preface of 1815," *à propos* "There was a boy…," to the "commutation and transfer of internal feelings, co-operating with external accidents, to plant, for Immortality, images of sight and sound in the celestial soil of the Imagination" (*Prose*, III, 35).

21 The quasi-disavowal occurs in a letter of January 1815 to Catherine Clarkson: "I have alluded to the Ladys errors of opinion—she talks of my being a worshipper of Nature—a passionate expression uttered incautiously in the Poem upon the Wye has led her into this mistake, she reading in cold-heartedness and substituting the letter for the spirit" in De Selincourt, Ernest (ed.) (1937), *The Letters of William and Dorothy Wordsworth: The Middle Years.* Oxford: Clarendon Press, p. 188.

22 References are to volume, part, and section.

23 De Man Paul (1984), "Wordsworth and the Victorians," Chapter 5 in his *The Rhetoric of Romanticism.* New York: Columbia University Press.

24 Jonathan Culler discusses the ways in which apostrophe is "systematically repressed or excluded by critics" in his well-known essay on the subject, "Apostrophe," in his (1981) *The Pursuit of Signs*. London: Routledge & Kegan Paul, p. 137. The situation has of course changed somewhat since the time of the essay's first publication in 1977.

25 My thanks to Tim Gould, Carrie Lebigre, Laura Quinney, Zach Samalin, Joe Wilner and Richard Eldridge for their contributions.

12 Emerson Discomposed: Skepticism, Naturalism, and the Search for Criteria in "Experience"

1 SW 33.

2 Cavell, Stanley (2006), "Reflections on Wallace Stevens at Mount Holyoke," in Christopher Benfey (ed.), *Artists, Intellectuals and World War II: 1942–1944*. Amherst, MA: University of Massachusetts Press, p. 76.

3 Emerson, Ralph Waldo (1983), "Experience," in *Essays and Lectures*. New York: Library of America, p. 472.

4 SW 126.

5 Emerson, "Experience," p. 472.

6 Immanuel Kant, *Critique of Pure Reason*, "Second analogy of experience: Principle of temporal sequence according to the law of causality" (B233–40). On Cavell's finding in Emerson's "Experience" an engagement with Kant's Second Analogy, see Cascardi, Anthony (1985), "The logic of moods." *Studies in Romanticism*, 24, (2), 223–37.

7 SW 127, my emphasis. My thanks to Richard Eldridge and William Day for suggesting I pay closer attention to this "non-tractability."

8 William Day, "Response to Grimstad," presented at the conference Stanley Cavell and Literary Studies: Consequences of Skepticism, Harvard University, October 16, 2010.

9 Cavell elsewhere calls this Emerson's "tracing out the source of our

sense of our lives as alien to us," and the "world's withdrawal from us
... its shrinking," see "Emerson, Coleridge, Kant (Terms as Conditions),"
ETE 69.

10 SW 107n.

11 Emerson, "Circles," in *Essays and Lectures*, p. 472.

12 Gould, Timothy (1998), *Hearing Things: Voice and Method in the Writings of Stanley Cavell*. Chicago, IL: Chicago University Press, p. 208.

13 "Emerson, Coleridge, Kant (Terms as Conditions)," ETE, 63.

14 SW 127. Cavell himself says as much in his (25 years belated) response to Richard Rorty's 1980 review of *The Claim of Reason*. See Cavell's "Responses," in Russell Goodman (ed.) (2005), *Contending With Stanley Cavell*. Oxford: Oxford University Press, pp. 158–59.

15 MWM 240.

16 Emerson (2010), *Emerson: Selected Journals 1841–1842*. Ed. Lawrence Rosenwald, New York: Library of America, p. 20

17 Emerson, *Essays, and Lectures*, p. 118.

18 Dewey, John (1958), *Experience and Nature*. Mineola, NY: Dover Publications, p. xiii.

19 Ibid., 235.

20 Ibid., 358.

21 Ibid.

22 Dewey, John (1981) "Ralph Waldo Emerson," in John McDermott (ed.), *The Philosophy of John Dewey*. Chicago, IL: University of Chicago Press, pp. 24–25

23 Ibid., 25.

24 Ibid., 26.

25 Ibid., 27.

26 "Music discomposed," in MWM 197.

27 Ibid., 198.

28 "Experiment" is also a guiding term in Cavell's discussion of Thoreau. See SW 3–25.

29 "Thinking of Emerson," in SW 134.

30 Goodman, Russell (1990), *American Philosophy and the Romantic Tradition*. Cambridge: Cambridge University Press, pp. 33, 52.

31 PDAT (2005 edition), pp. 13–14.

32 "What's the use of calling Emerson a pragmatist?" in ETE.

33 Ibid., 221.

34 ETE 12. Richard Poirier also contrasts the "difficulty" of Emerson's writing and the relative transparency of William James's. Poirier writes of Emerson's prose that is "to be experienced as it is written, and not in any clarifying translation, into some other syntax ... Emerson's syntax approximates that only momentary achievement of a simultaneous fusion among agent, action, and words;" what he also calls, referring both to Emerson's essay "Experience" and Cavell's reading of it, the "actual accomplishment *in* the writing, word by word, of the essay."

Poirier, Richard (1992), *Poetry & Pragmatism*. Cambridge, MA: Harvard University Press, p. 198, n.6.

35 Rorty, Richard (1999), *Philosophy and Social Hope*. New York: Penguin, p. xii.

36 Rorty, Richard (1982), "Dewey's metaphysics," in his *Consequences of Pragmatism*. Minneapolis, MN: University of Minnesota Press, p. 81.

37 Rorty, Richard (1998), "Dewey between Hegel and Darwin," in his *Richard Rorty: Truth and Progress*. Cambridge: Cambridge University Press, p. 295.

38 Ibid., 296.

39 Dewey, *Experience and Nature*. xiii.

40 Sellars, Wilfrid (1997 [1956]), *Empiricism and the Philosophy of Mind*. Cambridge, MA: Harvard University Press, p. 76.

41 "Music discomposed," in MWM 198.

42 Ibid.

43 "A matter of meaning it," in MWM 219. Cavell is writing about painting and sculpture in this passage, but I take it as a matter of course that such descriptions apply to other activities of "composition" (say musical or literary). James Conant takes the passage also to apply to philosophy:

> [For Cavell] the task of the contemporary analytic philosopher is to find out what the practice of philosophy depends upon. It doesn't matter that we haven't a priori criteria for defining what philosophy is; what matters is that we realize that these criteria are something we discover through an examination of both our current practice of philosophy and the historical continuity of the subject.
>
> Conant, James (1990), "Introduction," in Hilary Putnam, *Realism With A Human Face*. Cambridge, MA: Harvard University Press, pp. lvii–lviii.

44 "A matter of meaning it," in MWM 219 [my emphasis]. J. M. Bernstein offers a (rather Kantian) description of Cavell's construal of "modernism" as

> the moment in which we no longer have clear criteria for what constitutes a new work of art: neither tradition nor pure reason can determine what a poem or a painting or a sculpture or a musical composition is. But if these things are not known a priori, before we attend to or produce a work, then we also do not know what art is … A modernist work is [then] one that can claim validity or authenticity for itself if and only if its claim is transcendentally valid, that is, if *its* claim to validity is at the same time the lodging and sanctioning of a claim as to what art it. Modernist

works risk the very idea of being an artwork in order to establish, make possible again, what art is."
Bernstein, J. M. (2003), "Aesthetics, modernism, literature: Cavell's transformations of philosophy," in Richard Eldridge (ed.), *Stanley Cavell*. Contemporary Philosophy in Focus, Cambridge: Cambridge University Press, p. 177.

45 "An Emerson mood," in SW 145–46.
46 Dewey, John (1932), *Art As Experience*. New York: Penguin, p. 50.
47 Eldridge, Richard (2010), "Dewey's aesthetics," in Molly Cochran (ed.), *Cambridge Companion to John Dewey*. Cambridge: Cambridge University Press, p. 254.
48 Emerson, *Journals and Miscellaneous Notebooks*, July 6, 1841 from Plumstead, A.W., Gilman, William H., and Bennett, Ruth H. (eds.) (1969), *Journals and Miscellaneous Notebooks of Ralph Waldo Emerson Volume VII: 1838–1842*. Cambridge, MA: Harvard University Press. In his own *Gay Science*, Friedrich Nietzsche lists Emerson as one of "four very strange and truly poetic human beings in [the nineteenth] century who have attained mastery in prose." Cavell recognizes the affinity (what we might call a science of prose) writing that "Nietzsche was one of Emerson's great readers, or writers, who use [him] most radically, in the nineteenth century at least" (ETE 232).
49 Emerson, *Essays and Lectures*, p. 480.
50 Ibid., p. 482.
51 ETE 70.
52 Ibid.
53 Ibid.
54 Gould, *Hearing Things*: p. 212.
55 Ibid., p. 214.

13 Beside Ourselves: Near, Neighboring, and Next-to in Cavell's *The Senses of Walden* and William Carlos Williams's "Fine Work with Pitch and Copper"

1 Thoreau, Henry David (1985), *A Week on the Concord and Merrimac Rivers, Walden, The Maine Woods, Cape Cod*. New York: The Library of America, p. 329.
2 Williams, William Carlos (1986), *The Collected Poems of William Carlos Williams: 1919–1939*. Ed. Walton Litz and Christopher McGowan, New York: New Directions, p. 217.

14 For All You Know

1 Miller, Andrew H. (2008), *The Burdens of Perfection: On Ethics and Reading in Nineteenth-Century British Literature*. Ithaca, NY: Cornell University

Press. The final chapter of that book, and "Lives unled," an article on which that chapter was based, lay out some of the thoughts taken further in what follows here. Miller, Andrew H. (2007), "Lives unled in realist fiction." *Representations*, 98, 118–34.

2   Hampshire, Stuart (1989), *Innocence and Experience*, Cambridge, MA: Harvard University Press, pp. 100–01.

3   Dickens, Charles (2004), *The Personal History of David Copperfield*. Harmondsworth: Penguin, p. 824.

4   *Why* "poetry and fiction are always recurring" to the optative, and how these two genres (and other genres and media) differently recur to it are obvious questions. In anticipation of any full-scale discussion of them, I'll propose below (note 11) one reason that fiction has an especially intimate relation to this mode.

5   Nozick, Robert (1981), *Philosophical Explanations*. Cambridge, MA: Harvard University Press, p. 12.

6   Dickens, Charles (1998), *Great Expectations*. Ed. Margaret Cardwell, Oxford/New York: Oxford University Press, pp. 39, 79.

7   James, Henry (1996), "The Jolly Corner," *Complete Stories, 1898–1910*. New York: Library of America, pp. 697–731 (706).

8   Kierkegaard, Soren (1992), *Either/Or: A Fragment of Life*. Ed. Victor Eremita, trans. Alastair Hannay, London: Penguin, p. 54

9   James, William (1992), "Great men and their environment," *Writings, 1878–1899* . New York: Library of America, pp. 618–46 (626).

10   Dennis, Carl (2001), "The god who loves you," *Practical Gods*. New York: Penguin Poets, pp. 72–73.

11   That the optative can transmute retrospection into omniscience thus suggests a new reason why the optative may, for all my recurrence here to poetry, have a natural home in fiction, where the conventional past tense of narration is regularly voiced by a narrator understood to know all that there is to know.

12   Among the advantages of this emphasis on choice is that it encourages Dennis, in his analyses of poetic form, to revise poems written by various poets—Jonson, Dickinson, Yeats—thus drawing out the effects of particular choices they made. These poems unwritten illuminate the poems written. Dennis, Carl (2001), *Poetry as Persuasion*. Athens, GA: University of Georgia Press.

13   Cavell's writing in *Little Did I Know* is especially open in its acknowledgement of mortality; this is one source of its pathos. But all of his writing acknowledges the optative; that is one source of *its* pathos. "The point of my presence at these events" Cavell wrote early on about attending a performance of *King Lear*, "is to join in confirming this separateness. Confirming it as neither a blessing nor a curse, but a fact, the fact of having one life—not one rather than two, but this one rather than any other. I cannot confirm it alone" (MWM 338). The fact of human separateness, so massive a concern throughout Cavell's career, is thus

understood as being intrinsically optative, and confirmation of the optative intrinsically social.

15 Empiricism, Exhaustion, and Meaning What We Say: Cavell and Contemporary Fiction

1   Emerson, Ralph Waldo (1969), *Journals and Miscellaneous Notebooks of Ralph Waldo Emerson, Volume VIII: 1838–1842*. Ed. A. W. Plumstead and Harrison Hayford, Cambridge, MA: Belknap Press, p. 306.
2   Nietzsche's remarks appear in Section 14 of *The Birth of Tragedy*; Emerson's remark is recorded in Richardson, Robert D. Jr. (1995), *Emerson: The Mind on Fire*. Berkeley, CA: University of California Press, p. 381. Obviously I shouldn't be taken to mean here that these philosophical figures, Cavell included, never read novels at all, only that novels never became especially central to any of their thinking.
3   Watt, Ian (1957), *The Rise of the Novel: Studies in Defoe, Richardson, and Fielding*. London: Chatto and Windus, Ch. 1; Frye, Northrop (1957), *Anatomy of Criticism*. Princeton, NJ: Princeton University Press, pp. 303–14.
4   On Modernism's realism, see also Toril Moi (2008), *Henrik Ibsen and the Birth of Modernism: Art, Theater, Philosophy*. Oxford: Oxford University Press.
5   Myerson, Joel (2000), *Transcendentalism: A Reader*. Oxford: Oxford University Press. Here, Myerson reports that Sylvester Judd's *Margaret* (1845) is usually considered the only novel by a Transcendentalist (p. xxxvi).
6   Emerson (1983), *Essays and Lectures*. Ed. Joel Porte, New York: Library of America, p. 387.
7   See Burdick, Emily Miller (1994), "Sacvan Bercovitch, Stanley Cavell, and the romance theory of American fiction," in Carol Colatrella and Joseph Alkana (eds.), *Cohesion and Dissent in America*. Albany, NY: State University of New York Press, pp. 48–73.
8   Robbe-Grillet, Alain (1989), *For a New Novel*. Trans. Richard Howard, Evanston, IL: Northwestern University Press, pp. 26–27, 31–32; Barth, John (1984), *The Friday Book: Essays and Other Nonfiction*. New York: Perigree, pp. 66–67 (henceforth cited parenthetically by page number); DeLillo, Don (2005), *Conversations with Don DeLillo*. Thomas DePietro (ed.), Jackson, MS: University Press of Mississippi, p. 189.
9   See, e.g., Stewart, Garrett (2005), "The avoidance of Stanley Cavell," in Russell B. Goodman (ed.), *Contending With Stanley Cavell*. Oxford: Oxford University Press, pp. 140–56.
10   Pynchon, Thomas (1990), *The Crying of Lot 49*. New York: Perennial, pp. 36–37.
11   McHale, Brian (1987), *Postmodernist Fiction*. New York: Routledge.

12 Momaday, N. Scott (2010), *House Made of Dawn*, New York: Perennial, p. 181; henceforth cited parenthetically by page number.

13 Reynolds, Guy (1999), *Twentieth-Century American Women's Fiction: A Critical Introduction*. New York: Macmillan, p. 195.

14 Quoted in Reynolds, p. 120.

15 See, e.g., Alsen, Eberhard (ed.) (2000), *The New Romanticism: A Collection of Critical Essays*. New York: Routledge, which includes non-fiction pieces by both Pynchon and Morrison.

16 Robbe-Grillet, *For a New Novel*, p. 45; *Conversations with Don DeLillo*, p. 158; Barth, *The Friday Book*, pp. 17, 29.

17 Not all, but not none either. See, e.g., Sukenick's narrator at the start of his story "Death of the novel": "The contemporary writer … is forced to start from scratch: Reality doesn't exist, time doesn't exist, personality doesn't exist," in Suckenick, Ronald (2003), *Death of the Novel and Other Stories*. Tallahassee, FL: Fiction Collective Two.

18 Taylor, Charles (1989), *Sources of the Self: The Making of the Modern Identity*. Cambridge, MA: Harvard University Press, p. 489.

19 "Linguistic phenomenology" is Austin's own phrase, though one he admitted he found "rather a mouthful." See Austin, J. L. (1961), *Philosophical Papers*. Oxford: Oxford University Press, p. 182.

20 "Cavell's vision of the normativity of language," in Eldridge, Richard (ed.) (2003), *Stanley Cavell*. Cambridge: Cambridge University Press, p. 101.

21 Vonnegut, Kurt (1974), *Wampeters, Foma, & Granfalloons (Opinions)*. New York: Dell, p. 163.

22 "Cavell's 'romanticism' and Cavell's romanticism," in *Contending With Stanley Cavell*, p. 45.

23 On the 1960s, see also Cavell's "Preface to Jay Cantor's *The Space Between*" (TOS 145–51).

24 Rhu, Lawrence (2006), *Stanley Cavell's American Dream: Shakespeare, Philosophy, and Hollywood Movies*. New York: Fordham University Press.

25 Lukács, Georg (1974), *Theory of the Novel*. Trans. Anna Bostock, Cambridge, MA: MIT Press, p. 88.

26 See Rhu, *Stanley Cavell's American Dream*. Links between Bellow, Ellison, and Cavell also run through my (2008), *Worldly Acts and Sentient Things: The Persistence of Agency From Stein to DeLillo*. Ithaca, NY: Cornell University Press.

27 Wallace, David Foster (1997), *A Supposedly Fun Thing I'll Never Do Again*. Boston, MA: Little Brown, p. 81. Cavell's name appears at various points in this essay collection, and Wallace mentions doing a film seminar with Cavell in Lipsky, David (2010), *Although Of Course You End Up Becoming Yourself*. New York: Random House, p. 236.

Bibliography of Secondary Writings about Cavell

1 Book-Length Studies and Essay Collections about Cavell

Bell, Jr., Roger V. (2004), *Sounding the Abyss: Readings Between Cavell and Derrida*. Lanham, MD: Lexington Books.

Chico, David P. and Moisés Barroso (eds.) (2009), *Encuentros con Stanley Cavell*. Madrid: Plaza y Valdés.

Cohen, Ted, Paul Guyer, and Hilary Putnam (eds.) (1993), *Pursuits of Reason: Essays in Honor of Stanley Cavell*. Lubbock, TX: Texas Tech University Press.

Crary, Alice and Sanford Shieh (eds.) (2006), *Reading Cavell*. London: Routledge.

Dula, Peter (2010), *Cavell, Companionship, and Christian Theology*. Oxford: Oxford University Press.

Eldridge, Richard (ed.) (2003), *Stanley Cavell*. Cambridge: Cambridge University Press.

Fischer, Michael (1989), *Stanley Cavell and Literary Skepticism*. Chicago, IL: University of Chicago Press.

Fleming, Richard (1993), *The State of Philosophy: An Invitation to a Reading in Three Parts of Stanley Cavell's "The Claim of Reason."* Lewisburg, PA: Bucknell University Press.

Fleming, Richard and Michael Payne (eds.) (1989), *The Senses of Stanley Cavell*. Lewisburg, PA: Bucknell University Press.

Goodman, Russell (ed.) (2005), *Contending with Stanley Cavell*. Oxford: Oxford University Press.

Gould, Timothy (1998), *Hearing Things: Voice and Method in the Writing of Stanley Cavell*. Chicago, IL: Chicago University Press.

Hall, Ronald (1999), *The Human Embrace: The Love of Philosophy and the Philosophy of Love—Kierkegaard, Cavell, Nussbaum*. University Park, PA: Penn State Press.

Hammer, Espen (2002), *Stanley Cavell: Skepticism, Subjectivity, and the Ordinary*. Cambridge: Polity, 2002.

Jost, Walter and Kenneth Dauber (2003), *Ordinary Language Criticism: Literary Thinking After Cavell After Wittgenstein*. Evanston, IL: Northwestern University Press.

Mulhall, Stephen (1994), *Stanley Cavell: Philosophy's Recounting of the Ordinary*. Oxford: Oxford University Press.

Norris, Andrew (ed.) (2006), *The Claim to Community: Essays on Stanley Cavell and Political Philosophy*. Stanford, CA: Stanford University Press.

Rhu, Lawrence (2006), *Stanley Cavell's American Dream: Shakespeare, Philosophy, and Hollywood Movies*. New York: Fordham University Press.

Rothman, William, Marian Keane, and Stanley Cavell (2000), *Reading Cavell's The World Viewed: A Philosophical Perspective on Film*. Detroit, MI: Wayne State University Press.

Saito, Naoko and Paul Standish (eds.) (2011), *Stanley Cavell and the Education of Grownups*. New York: Fordham University Press.

Smith, Joseph and William Kerrigan (eds.) (1987), *Images in Our Souls: Cavell, Psychoanalysis, and Cinema*. Baltimore, MD: Johns Hopkins University Press.

Taylor, Andrew and James Loxley (eds.) (forthcoming), *Stanley Cavell and Literary Criticism*. Manchester: Manchester University Press.

2 Other Secondary Works:

Affeldt, Steven (1998), "The ground of mutuality: Criteria, judgment, and intelligibility in Stephen Mulhall and Stanley Cavell." *European Journal of Philosophy*, 6, (1), 1–31.

Altieri, Charles (2007), "Wonder in *The Winter's Tale*: A cautionary account of epistemic criticism," in John Gibson, Wolfgang Huemer, and Luca Pocci (eds.), *A Sense of the World: Essays on Fiction, Narrative, and Knowledge*. London: Routledge, pp. 266–86.

Baz, Avner (2003), "On when words are called for: Cavell, McDowell, and the wording of the world." *Inquiry*, 46, (4), 473–500.

Bearn, Gordon (1998), "Sounding serious: Cavell and Derrida." *Representations*, 64, 65–92.

——(2002), "Staging authenticity: A critique of Cavell's modernism." *Philosophy and Literature*, 24, (2), 294–311.

Bernstein, Charles (1981), "Reading Cavell reading Wittgenstein." *Boundary 2*, 9, (2), 295–306.

Bernstein, J. M. (2006), *Against Voluptuous Bodies: Late Modernism and the Meaning of Painting*. Stanford, CA: Stanford University Press. Includes a chapter on Cavell.

Berry, R. M. (1995), "What is a narrative convention? (Wittgenstein, Stanley Cavell and literary criticism)." *Narrative*, 3, (1), 18–32.

——(2003), "Cavell's meaning 1968." *Symploke*, 11, (1–2), 237–41.

Bruns, Gerald (1990), "Stanley Cavell's Shakespeare." *Critical Inquiry*, 16, (3), 612–32.

——(1991), "Reply to Crewe and Conant." *Critical Inquiry*, 17, (3), 635–638.

——(1999), "The last romantic: Stanley Cavell and the writing of philosophy," in his *Tragic Thoughts at the End of Philosophy: Language, Literature, and Ethical Theory*. Evanston, IL: Northwestern University Press, pp. 199–218.

Budick, Emily Miller (1992), "Sacvan Bercovitch, Stanley Cavell, and the romance theory of American fiction." *PMLA*, 107, (1), 78–91. Reprinted in Carol Colatrella and Joseph Alkan (eds.) (1994), *Cohesion and Dissent in America*. Albany, NY: SUNY Press, pp. 48–73.

Conant, James (1991), "On Bruns, on Cavell." *Critical Inquiry*, 17, (3), 616–34.

Costello, Diarmuid (2008), "On the very idea of a 'specific' medium: Michael Fried and Stanley Cavell on painting and photography as arts." *Critical Inquiry*, 34, (2), 274–312.

Danto, Arthur (1982), "Review: Philosophy and/as film and/as if philosophy." *October*, 23, 4–14. Review of *Pursuits of Happiness*.

Davis, Colin (2010), *Critical Excess: Overreading in Derrida, Deleuze, Levinas, Zizek, and Cavell*. Stanford, CA: Stanford University Press. Includes a chapter on Cavell.

Diamond, Cora (2003), "The difficulty of reality and the difficulty of philosophy." *Partial Answers: Journal of Literature and the History of Ideas*, 1, (2), 1–26. Reprinted in Cary Wolfe (ed.) (2008), *Philosophy and Animal Life*. New York: Columbia University Press.

de Vries, Hent (2007), "From 'ghost in the machine' to 'spiritual automaton': Philosophical meditation in Wittgenstein, Cavell, and Levinas," in E. T. Long (ed.), *Self and Other: Essays in Continental Philosophy of Religion*. Dordrecht: Springer, pp. 77–97.

Eldridge, Richard (1983), "Philosophy and the achievement of community: Rorty, Cavell, and criticism." *Metaphilosophy*, 14, (2), 107–25.

——(1986), "The normal and the normative: Wittgenstein's legacy, Kripke, and Cavell." *Philosophy and Phenomenological Research*, 36, (4), 555–75.

——(1991), "Romantic rebirth in a secular age: Cavell's aversive exertions." *The Journal of Religion*, 71, (3), 410–18. A review of *In Quest of the Ordinary*.

——(2001), *The Persistence of Romanticism*. Cambridge: Cambridge University Press. Includes a chapter on Cavell.

Fischer, Michael (1989), "Stanley Cavell's Wittgenstein," in Reed Way Dasenbrock (ed.), *Redrawing the Lines: Analytic Philosophy, Deconstruction, and Literary Theory*. Minneapolis, MN: University of Minnesota Press, pp. 49–60.

——(2006), "Stanley Cavell and criticizing the university from within." *Philosophy and Literature*, 30, (2), 471–83.

Fleming, Richard (2004), *First Word Philosophy: Wittgenstein-Austin-Cavell, Writings on Ordinary Language Philosophy*. Lewisburg, PA: Bucknell University Press.

Furtak, Rick Anthony (2007), "Skepticism and perceptual faith: Henry David Thoreau and Stanley Cavell on seeing and believing." *Transactions of the Charles S. Peirce Society: A Quarterly Journal in American Philosophy*, 43, (3), 542–61.

Goldblatt, David (2005), "Cavellian conversation and the life of art." *Philosophy and Literature*, 29, (2), 460–76.

Gonya, Adam (2009), "Stanley Cavell and two pictures of the voice." *The European Legacy*, 14, (5), 587–98.

Greenham, David (2007), "The skeptical deduction: Reading Kant and Cavell in Emerson's 'Self-Reliance'." *ESQ: A Journal of the American Renaissance*, 53, (3), 253–81.

Gustafsson, Martin (2005), "Perfect pitch and Austinian examples: Cavell, McDowell, Wittgenstein, and the philosophical significance of ordinary language." *Inquiry*, 48, (5), 356–89.

Hagberg, Garry (2003), "On philosophy as therapy: Wittgenstein, Cavell, and autobiographical writing." *Philosophy and Literature*, 27, (1), 196–210. Reprinted in his *Describing Ourselves: Wittgenteins and Autobiographical Consciousness*. Oxford: Oxford University Press, 2008, pp. 240–58.

Hillman, David (2008), "The worst case of knowing the other? Stanley Cavell and Troilus and Cressida." *Philosophy and Literature*, 32, (1), 74–86.

Hollander, John (1980), "Stanley Cavell and 'The Claim of Reason'." *Critical Inquiry*, 6, (4), 575–88.

Kerr, Fergus (1997), *Immortal Longings: Versions of Transcending Humanity*. London: SPCK. Includes a chapter on Cavell.

Kronick, Joseph (1993), "Telling the difference: Stanley Cavell's resistance to theory." *American Literary History*, 5, (1), 193–200.

Lackey, Douglas (1973), "Reflections on Cavell's ontology of film." *Journal of Aesthetics and Art Criticism*, 32, (2), 271–73.

Lemm, Vanessa (2007), "Is Nietzsche a perfectionist? Rawls, Cavell, and the politics of culture in Nietzsche's 'Schopenhauer as Educator'." *The Journal of Nietzsche Studies*, 34, 5–27.

McDowell, John (2007), "Comment on Stanley Cavell's 'Companionable Thinking'," in Alice Crary (ed.), *Wittgenstein and the Moral Life: Essays in Honor of Cora Diamond*. Cambridge, MA: MIT Press. Also in Cary Wolfe (ed.) (2008), *Philosophy and Animal Life*. New York: Columbia University Press.

Melville, Stephen (1993), "Oblique and ordinary: Stanley Cavell's engagements of Emerson." *American Literary History*, 5, (1), 172–92.

Modleski, Tania (1990), "Editorial notes." *Critical Inquiry*, 17, (1), 237–44. Response to two essays by Cavell: "Postscript (1989): To Whom It May Concern," and "Ugly Duckling, Funny Butterfly: Bette Davis and *Now, Voyager*." Includes a response by Cavell.

Moi, Toril (1999), " 'I am a woman': The personal and the philosophical," in her *What Is A Woman? And Other Essays*. Oxford: Oxford University Press, pp. 121–250, (esp. pp. 207–50).

——(2002), " 'It was as if he meant something different from what he said— all the time': Language, metaphysics, and the everyday in 'The Wild Duck'." *New Literary History*, 33, (4), 655–86.

——(2006), "Becoming modern: Modernity and theater in *Emperor and*

Galilean," in her *Henrik Ibsen and the Birth of Modernism: Art, Theater, Philosophy.* Oxford: Oxford University Press, pp. 188–222.

Mooney, Edward (2003), "Two testimonies in American philosophy: Stanley Cavell, Henry Bugbee." *The Journal of Speculative Philosophy,* 17, (2), 108–21.

——(2009), *Lost Intimacy in American Thought: Recovering Personal Philosophy from Thoreau to Cavell.* New York: Continuum, esp. Chapters 6 and 7.

Mulhall, Stephen (1998), "The givenness of grammar: A reply to Steven Affeldt." *The European Journal of Philosophy,* 6, (1), 32–44.

——(2009), *The Wounded Animal: J. M. Coetzee and the Difficulty of Reality in Literature and Philosophy.* Princeton, NJ: Princeton University Press. Chapter 5 considers Cavell's response to Cora Diamond's "The difficulty of reality and the difficulty of philosophy."

Norris, Andrew (2002), "Political revisions: Stanley Cavell and political philosophy." *Political Theory,* 30, (6), 828–51.

——(2005), "Stanley Cavell and the claim to community." *Theory & Event,* 8, (1).

——(2009), "Thoreau, Cavell, and the foundations of true political expression" in Jack Turner (ed.), *A Political Companion to Henry David Thoreau.* Lexington, KY: University Press of Kentucky, pp. 423–46.

Owen, David (1999), "Cultural diversity and the conversation of justice: Reading Cavell on political voice and the expression of consent." *Political Theory,* 27, (5), 579–96.

Parini, Jay (1985), "The importance of Stanley Cavell." *The Hudson Review,* 38, (1), 115–19.

Perl, Jeffrey (ed.) (1996), "A taste for complexity: Ten nondisciples of Stanley Cavell." *Common Knowledge,* 5, (2), 21–78.

Putnam, Hilary (2001), "Rules, attunements, and 'applying words to the world'," in Ludwig Nagl and Chantal Mouffe (eds.), *The Legacy of Wittgenstein: Pragmatism or Deconstruction.* New York: Peter Lang.

Rhu, Lawrence (2002), "*King Lear* in their time: On Bloom and Cavell on Shakespeare," in Christy Desmet and Robert Sawyer (eds.), *Harold Bloom's Shakespeare.* New York: Palgrave Macmillan, pp. 227–46.

Rodowick, D. N. (2007), "An elegy for theory." *October,* 122, 91–109.

Rorty, Richard (1981), "From epistemology to romance: Cavell on skepticism." *Review of Metaphysics,* 34, (4), 759–74.

Rudrum, David (2009), "From the sublime to the ordinary: Stanley Cavell's Beckett." *Textual Practice,* 23, (4), 543–58.

Saito, Naoko (2007), "Truth is translated: Cavell's Thoreau and the transcendence of America." *The Journal of Speculative Philosophy,* 21, (2), 124–32.

Scheman, Naomi (1998), "Missing mothers/desiring daughters: Framing the sight of women." *Critical Inquiry,* 15, (1), 62–89.

Standish, Paul (2007), "Education for grown-ups, a religion for adults: Scepticism and alterity in Cavell and Levinas." *Ethics and Education,* 2, (1), 73–91.

Turvey, Malcolm, "Is scepticism a 'natural possibility' of language? Reasons to be sceptical of Cavell's Wittgenstein," in Richard Allen and Malcolm

Turvey (eds.), *Wittgenstein, Theory and the Arts*. London: Routledge, pp. 117–36.

Viefhues-Bailey, Ludger (2007), *Beyond the Philosopher's Fear: A Cavellian Reading of Gender, Origin and Religion in Modern Skepticism*. Farnham: Ashgate Publishing.

von Rautenfeld, Hans (2004), "Charitable interpretations: Emerson, Rawls, and Cavell on the use of public reason." *Political Theory*, 32, (1), 61–84.

Wolfe, Cary (1994), "Alone with America: Cavell, Emerson, and the politics of individualism." *New Literary History*, 25, (1), 135–57.

Ziarek, Ewa (1996), *The Rhetoric of Failure: Deconstruction of Skepticism, Reinvention of Modernism*. Albany, NY: SUNY Press. Includes a chapter on Cavell.

Index

Page numbers followed by 'n' refer to Notes

"Experience" (Emerson), 1, 144,
    163–6, 172, 173, 174, 215
experimentation, 168, 169
explanation, vs. display, 64
exposure, mutual, 63

faith, 7, 132
Fanon, Franz, 113
feminism/feminist philosophy,
    22, 93, 96, 98, 99; second-
    wave feminism, 94
Feuerbach, Ludwig, 12
fiction, 30, 44, 252n;
    contemporary, 208–23;
    postmodern, 212; see also
    novels
fieldwork, in philosophy, 239n
films, 11, 49–50, 78–9
"Fine Work with Pitch and
    Copper" (Williams), 187–93
finitude of human life, 1
first person plural/singular, 93
first-person narrative, 80
Foe (Coetzee), 117, 118–19
forgiveness, 125, 126, 131, 132
Forgiveness Project, 130–1, 240n
formal realism, 208, 210
formalism, and art, 51
Foucault, Michel, 2, 18
Frankenstein (Shelley), 107
Frantz, Fanon, 238n
Frasier, Debra, 99, 102, 236n
fraudulence of art, 31–2, 34, 35,
    38, 39, 45
freedom, realm of, 55
Freud, Sigmund, 2, 245n
Freudian slips, 80
Fried, Michael, 226n
friendship, 75, 103; of reader,
    139
Frith, Simon, 31, 33, 34, 37, 228n
Frost, Robert, 195

Frye, Northrop, 148, 209
functionalism, 241n

Galileo, 165
gap, philosophical, 109–10
Garrett, Stewart, 233n
gender, 94, 95, 96, 100, 236n; see
    also feminism
genitives, 86, 88, 90, 144
gerunds, 144
Gilbert, Allan H., 243n
"God Who Loves You, The"
    (Dennis), 199–203
Goodman, Russell, 168, 250n
Gould, Timothy, 165, 175, 239n,
    241n, 249n
grace, 129
grammar/grammatical criteria,
    66, 67, 68, 71, 73, 87
Great Expectations (Dickens), 196
Green, Karen, 248n
Greenblatt, Stephen, 240n
greeting, 98–9
Griffiths, John, 240n
Grimm, Harold T., 240n
Guarini, Giambattista, 147
Gustafsson, Martin, 235n
Guyer, Paul, 229n, 242n

Hacking, Ian, 5
Hagberg, Garry L., 231n
Hamilton, Sir William, 245–6n
Hamlet, 81, 82, 83, 85, 103, 133–4,
    233n
Hamm, Christine, 224n
Hampshire, Stuart, 194–5, 199,
    252n
happiness, 59, 60
Haraway, Donna J., 236n
Hardy, Thomas, 198
Harvard, Cavell's teaching at, 142
Haynes, Elwood, 41